Stories and Social Medi

Routledge Studies in Sociolinguistics

Stories and Social Media

Identities and Interaction

Ruth E. Page

NEW YORK AND LONDON

First published 2012
by Routledge
711 Third Avenue, New York, NY 10017

Simultaneously published in the UK
by Routledge
2 Park Square, Milton Park, Abingdon, Oxon OX14 4RN

*Routledge is an imprint of the Taylor & Francis Group,
an informa business*

First issued in paperback 2013

Typeset in Sabon by IBT Global.

Library of Congress Cataloging-in-Publication Data
Page, Ruth E., 1972–
    Stories and social media : identities and interaction / Ruth E. Page.
        p. cm. — (Routledge studies in sociolinguistics ; 3)
    Includes bibliographical references and index.
    1. Social media.   2. Narration (Rhetoric)—Social aspects.   3. Discourse
analysis, Narrative.   4. Storytelling—Social aspects.   5. Online social
networks.   6. Online authorship.   7. Online identities.   8. Identity
(Psychology)   I. Title.
    P96.N35P34 2012
    302.23'1—dc23
    2011024740

ISBN: 978-0-415-88981-0 (hbk)
ISBN: 978-0-203-14861-7 (ebk)
ISBN: 978-0-415-83702-6 (pbk)

For my family

Contents

Figures

Tables

Permissions

Chapter 3 is a revised version of "Blogging on the Body," which is published in *New Narratives: Stories and Storytelling in the Digital Age*, edited by Ruth Page and Bronwen Thomas (University of Nebraska Press). Reproduced with permission.

Table 6.1 is reproduced with permission from *A Million Penguins Research Report* by Bruce Mason and Sue Thomas (2008).

Figures 7.2 and 7.3 are reproduced with permission by [murmur] from the Leith section of the [murmur] archive.

Preface

There are two reasons to write about the stories that people tell about themselves in social media formats:

1. Stories remain one of the most pervasive genres people use to make sense of themselves and the surrounding world.
2. The development of social media formats in the first decade of the twenty-first century has enabled people to document the stories of their daily experiences in online, public, or semi-public domains in unprecedented measure.

The stories that are told on a day-to-day basis on forums, blogs, and social network sites and archived in community projects are interesting for many reasons. This book focuses on the language that storytellers use in their narrative interactions with other people. Because the main focus of the book is on stories, the introductory chapter provides an overview of the key narrative terms that are used throughout. After that, each chapter concentrates on a different social media genre and a different aspect of storytelling. Stories are taken from sites that developed in the first decade of the twenty-first century, moving from earlier genres like discussion forums to more recent sites like Facebook and Twitter. The URLs for the social media sites referred to in the book are provided in the bibliography. Most (but not all) sites are available at the time of writing, but their longevity cannot be guaranteed.

The following format conventions are used to represent excerpts taken from the stories. *Italics* are used for emphasis and for mentioning rather than using words (*here* means I am talking about that word, not using it to refer to the present location). <u>Underlines</u> are retained in quotations to indicate hyperlinks. **Bold** is used in examples to indicate added emphasis or to highlight a linguistic feature. Unless otherwise indicated, it was not added by the original narrator. ***Bold italics*** indicate that a word has an entry in the Glossary. The quoted excerpts from stories keep the exact spelling and punctuation used by the narrators, not using *sic* to indicate unconventional spelling or usage. Sometimes, although not always, that unconventionality is part of the narrator's style.

In the process of writing this book, I have accrued many debts. My favorite part of the book-writing process is expressing my thanks to the many people who have helped along the way. This book would not exist at all were it not for the storytellers who publish their stories on the Internet. I am grateful to the bloggers and forum posters who gave me permission to reproduce their words, and to the Facebook participants who took part in the study that forms the basis of Chapter 4. Thanks also go to the members of my Facebook Friend list who agreed to be interviewed about the controversial and sometimes painful outcomes of unwanted impersonations in the form of Facebook "rape." Special thanks to Aaron Bourne who drew my attention to the phenomenon of "frape" in the first place and graciously allowed me to reuse the examples collected for his undergraduate research project undertaken in June 2010 at Birmingham City University. The directors of the archives discussed in Chapters 6 and 7, Nick Bouton (Protagonize) and Robin Elliot ([murmur]), took time to answer patiently my questions and provided important perspectives on the projects they have developed.

I began work on this book while I was a member of the School of English at Birmingham City University and completed it as a member of the School of English at the University of Leicester. I have been fortunate to find truly collegial scholars in both places, whom I count as friends, and who have helped my work in numerous ways. Jackie Gay made me think about Facebook as a forum for storytelling; Howard Jackson guided me through the principles of corpus linguistics; Philip Shaw wrote the code I used to "vacuum" data from Twitter. Holly Furneaux, Andrew Kehoe, Robert Lawson, Marie Page, and Paul Reilly all read parts of the manuscript and made useful suggestions of further examples to consider. Extra special thanks to Julie Coleman who read the entire draft of this volume and helped untangle some of my most impenetrable sentences and tables. Earlier versions of some chapters have been presented as work in progress at research seminars and conferences. I am grateful for the comments and questions that helped refine my ideas subsequently, particularly at the Georgetown Round Table on Linguistics in 2008 and in 2011. It goes without saying that the book is better for my colleagues' contributions and any remaining errors are my responsibility alone.

The final words of thanks go to the members of my family, who have put up with this project over the last year, and who enrich the story of my life every day. Toby and Isi—you remind me what is important in life. Thank you for lending me space in your bedroom and a desk chair to sit on! Gavin—thank you for sorting through yet another series of pivot tables, for listening to me read parts of the work in progress, for keeping our home life happy, and for understanding my need to work in peace and quiet. Words will never be enough—but you get the last ones here (for once)—with all my love and thanks.

1 Introduction
Stories and Social Media in Context

This book is about stories that are told in social media contexts. It focuses on stories that are told by everyday tellers about their personal experiences, arguing that these stories are important discursive and social resources that create identities for their tellers and audiences. Storytelling is an interactive process, traces of which can be seen in the conversational formats of social media and are interwoven between online and offline contexts. The range of stories told in social media contexts is wide and diverse. The stories discussed in this book include examples taken from the popular social network site Facebook, and the microblogging site Twitter, alongside stories told in older forms of social media like discussion forums, personal and video-blogs, and stories that are collected in formally curated, community online archives.

Stories are told about many different topics. They include reports of professional activity, like this update on Twitter from the mayor of London, Boris Johnson, who reported on a recent visit to the London Tube renovations,

> Incredible amount of work going into improving the Tube. I went to see what happens when part of a line is closed http://bit.ly/hSvpoB
>
> MayorOfLondon: April 14, 2011

and the updates from the British television presenter Amanda Holden, who documented behind the scenes as she got ready to present the talent show, *Britain's Got Talent*,

> Trying on some of my gorg frocks for BGT live today! Very excited x
>
> Amanda_Holden: May 20, 2011.

Social media is also used to document ongoing stories of personal experience from the narrator's private life, like this Facebook updater who told her Friends that she is contemplating cycling to the gym, doing Bootcamp & cycling back. Then I have the rest of the day to get ready for the Ball tonight (& have a nap, maybe!)

May 21, 2011 at 07:22.

Four hours later she updated again,

Ah well, cycled to the gym, tick, did Bootcamp, tick, had tea and toast and nice chat with friends, tick. The come out having mentally prepared for the cycle home, to find bike has a flat tyre! So currently waiting for my husband to come and get me and bike!!! (No tick!!)

May 21, 2011 at 10:45

Stories published in social media formats can include deeply personal, emotive topics. In the blogosphere, the blogger Minerva's most recent post dates from August 2010, where she describes her anxieties about the future after having survived treatment for cancer. She tells her readers,

Already, I am scared stiff and I am still at the computer writing. But it is worth the time to consider the risks of everyday life, to understand how lucky we are that we are able to plan for next year, or even three years after that without having the shadow of the present fog our future. Enjoy the planning, the goal setting and the dreams, but don't forget to give thanks for our present.

Minerva, August 14, 2010.

As these examples show, stories told in social media can range from seemingly lightweight reports of getting a puncture on a bike, to profoundly significant life events, like the accounts of being diagnosed and treated for terminal illness. Social media cross between private and public contexts, with public documentation of professional activity in Twitter, on the one hand (such as Boris Johnson's and Amanda Holden's daily updates), and the semi-private domains of Facebook, on the other. Stories can use words, images, sound, and audiovisual resources, like the videos published in YouTube and the podcasts available from the archives of the oral history project [murmur]. And these examples only begin to hint at the complex variety of stories that continue to proliferate in every form of social media that has been developed thus far.

Ways of studying narrative phenomena are likewise varied. The approach I take in this book is situated in sociolinguistic and discourse-analytic research traditions, but the discussions also touch on concepts that are more familiar to literary-critical narrative theory. The stories selected for discussion in the following chapters are deliberately varied, but are used to address the following key questions:

1. What kinds of stories do people tell in social media formats? What similarities and differences occur in the narrators' choice of subject matter and storytelling style?
2. How are stories embedded in the multilayered contexts of social media? How do different sites, interactive patterns, offline contexts, and participant groups influence the characteristics of social media stories?
3. What purposes are fulfilled when stories are told in social media? What personal, social, and discourse identities are constructed for narrators and their audiences?

Given the expansive scope entailed by analyzing stories in social media, this introductory chapter defines and provides the context for the key terms and concepts that inform the study as a whole. The chapter begins by setting a sociolinguistic approach to stories in social media against the backdrop of earlier narrative research in digital media. It moves on to consider the storytelling potential of social media in terms of the narrative dimensions set out by Ochs and Capps (2001). Collecting stories in social media presents new challenges and opportunities for narrative analysis, and I review the methods and the data that were used to select the storytelling examples covered in later chapters, ending with an overview of the organization of the book as a whole.

EARLIER WORK ON NARRATIVE IN DIGITAL MEDIA

The need to take account of the everyday storytelling that takes place on the Internet is particularly pressing given the increase in storytelling environments enabled by the advent of social media. The story-like fragments found in social media contexts are often ephemeral, small, located on the margins of other kinds of talk, and fall outside the canon of digital narrative. While they are not necessarily presented as works of fiction, many of the day-to-day accounts of life experience are selective, artistic, reflective, playful, emotive, and sometimes as unreliable as the texts more centrally positioned in digital narratology. Digital narratology examines stories that depend on a computer for their production and display (Harpold 2005). In the early 1990s, critics used the distinctive textual qualities and interactive affordances of hypertext fictions (notably those published by Eastgate, and later archived by the Electronic Literature Organization), interactive fiction, and gaming environments to rework key concepts in narrative theory. The digital narratology of the 1990s was characterized by attempts to document and theorize the then novel artistic forms in terms of their narrative potential. At the same time, it sought to rethink the reader's relationship with the text through metaphors of agency, immersion, and interaction (Ryan 1991, 2004, 2006; Aarseth 1997; Landow 1997; Hayles 2001).

Work in this field has gone on to scrutinize examples of digital fiction in relation to debates about fictional worlds (Bell 2010), literary competence

(Ensslin 2007) and complexity (Ciccoricco 2007), temporality (Montfort 2003), and wider critical practices (Page and Thomas 2011). Digital narratology continues to flourish, but it is limited in three ways. First, it tends to focus on fictional examples of narrative art. Second, interactivity is primarily conceptualized in terms of reader–text relations rather than interaction between human participants. Finally, digital narratology is interested in readings of particular texts, rather than a more fully contextualized approach to narrative production and reception.

Although the more recent examples of narrative criticism found under the umbrella term "digital fiction" (Bell et al. 2010) positions itself against earlier work by applying more systematic models of close reading derived from stylistics and narratology, the legacy of literary-critical narratology remains inherent in the text-immanent focus of the readings typical of the field. Readers are treated as abstract figures mostly projected from the critic's own interpretation of the text, and there is little attempt to contextualize the practices of narrative production and reception from an empirical standpoint (e.g., documenting the demographic characteristics of actual readers or comparing communities of readers and writers). More seriously, digital narratology appears to treat "fiction" as if it were a transparent, unproblematic term that automatically excludes contemporary **genres** like blogs, digital storytelling, and life narratives. The literary-critical emphasis of digital narratology has thus resulted in a narrow corpus of texts from which narrative concepts and frameworks are derived, a too simplistic elision of fiction and narrative in digital media, and the need for a greater attention to the contexts of storytelling.

At the same time that foundational work in digital narratology was emerging, research into the wider domain of computer-mediated communication (henceforth CMC) was also being established as a recognized field of inquiry. Like digital narratology, research in CMC developed as an interdisciplinary enterprise. However, in contrast to the literary-critical work of digital narratology, the disciplines that inform CMC have origins in the social sciences and linguistics, including discourse analysis, pragmatics, ethnography, sociology, conversation analysis, and sociolinguistics. CMC research that takes linguistic analysis as its point of entry is focused on the interpretation of textual features found in digital texts but, unlike the individual narrative artifacts interpreted in digital narratology, tends to focus on larger datasets where attention is given to constructing empirically testable research questions that uncover generic rather than text-specific patterns. Examples include tracing the evolution of **turn-taking** patterns from face-to-face to computer-mediated formats (Harrison 1998), establishing the subcategories of particular genres, like weblogs (Herring and Paolillo 2006), and documenting how norms for online interaction are established (Baym 1995).

Although what Androutsopoulos (2006) describes as the "first wave" of CMC tended to focus on the medium-specific properties of different kinds of CMC (Internet Relay Chat, e-mail, text messages, listserv posts, and "netspeak"), the contextualist principles inherent in the research traditions that inform the study of CMC mean that later work has shifted readily to more user-centered accounts of computer-mediated discourse. This later sociolinguistic work has documented the many and varied ways in which the heterogeneity of discourse found in computer-mediated contexts is not random but may be distributed according to patterns influenced by the constraints of a given genre or the characteristics of the CMC participants (such as their declared age or gender). A user-centered approach to research in CMC has also sought to interpret the pragmatic and social functions of the discourse, for example, in terms of the relational, personal, or group identity work being achieved.

Neither the first nor second wave of research in CMC is limited to the analysis of a particular genre. However, forms of CMC that have come under scrutiny have included examples of personal narratives (McLellan 1997 on illness narratives in discussion forums; Harrison and Barlow 2009 on advice narratives in support groups; Georgakopoulou 2004, 2007 on small stories in e-mail; Eisenlauer and Hoffman 2010 on weblogs). These studies have focused more on the interpretation of the data within the specific online context in question, and less on wider treatments of how narrative genres per se are being reworked in discursive online contexts.[1] As such, the rationale for this book proceeds from two points of impetus: the need (1) to broaden digital narratology to include contextualized analyses of everyday storytelling in social media, and (2) to use the discourse-analytic and sociolinguistic work of contemporary CMC to bring close focus to the ways in which narrative genres, and in particular narratives of personal experience, are being reworked in online contexts at the outset of the twenty-first century.

SOCIAL MEDIA

I use the term *social media* to refer to Internet-based applications that promote social interaction between participants. Examples of social media include (but are not limited to) discussion forums, blogs, wikis, podcasting, social network sites, video sharing, and microblogging. Social media is often distinguished from forms of mass media, where mass media is presented as a one-to-many broadcasting mechanism. In contrast, social media delivers content via a network of participants where the content can be published by anyone but is still distributed across potentially large-scale audiences. Social media often refers to the range of technologies that began to be developed in the latter years of the 1990s and became mainstream Internet activities in the first decade of the twenty-first century. The chronological context of social media genres is set out in the timeline in Figure 1.1.

1978	Bulletin Board System
1980	Usenet
1984	SMS concept developed
1988	Internet Relay Chat
1995	eBay, Ward Cunningham coins the term "wiki" and launches first wiki site
1997	John Barger coins term "web log"
1998	Yahoo groups
1999	Live Journal, Blogger.com
2001	Google groups, Wikipedia, Cyworld
2002	Friendster, Last.fm
2003	MySpace, WordPress, Del.ici.ous, LinkedIn, Second Life, Skype
2004	Flickr, Facebook, Digg, Orkut, Ben Hammersly coins the term "podcasting," Tim O'Reilly coins the term "Web 2.0"
2005	YouTube
2006	Twitter
2007	Justin TV, Tumblr, Gowalla
2009	Foursquare, Google Wave, Chatroulette
2010	Instagram

Figure 1.1   Timeline of web genres and terms.

The timeline in Figure 1.1 tells a certain story about the development of social media, which moves toward increasingly interactive forms of dialogue. The dialogic potential of social media is present in earlier forms of CMC. The e-mail lists, bulletin boards, and text messages of the 1980s might be seen as precursors to the participatory culture (Jenkins 2006) that characterizes twenty-first century Internet behavior. But the mid-1990s saw a decisive shift in the way that social media enabled interaction between participants, and placed that interaction in public rather than private or semi-private contexts. Blogs and wikis extended the range of CMC's interactive possibilities, with blogs allowing individual writers to connect to other bloggers (through blog rolls, links, comments) and wikis fostering collective contributions to a single enterprise (Myers 2010). These became mainstream examples of Internet use when sites like Live Journal, Blogger, and later WordPress made it easier than ever for contributors to publish reports and opinions, and Wikipedia was launched in 2001. The years 2003–2006 saw a rapid expansion of social network sites (LinkedIn, Orkut, MySpace, Flickr, Facebook, YouTube, and Twitter) that reframed the dialogic links between participants as a network, increasing the number, visibility, and reach of an individual's connections with others in online spaces. More recent developments, like the Instagram photo-sharing application for the iPhone, Gowalla, and FourSquare, illustrate the extent to which social media networks have become untethered from static computer terminals. Social media interactions are interwoven increasingly with daily experience, through the use of mobile technologies like *smart phones.*

The scale on which social media has been adopted needs to be understood in the wider history of the Internet. The mid-1990s saw several technological developments that would enable the later social media genres to gain popularity. In 1993, Mosaic was the first popular web browser to make the web available to a wider audience. *MP3 file formats* became publically available from late 1994, Real Player was launched in April 1995, and Macromedia's Flash Software was released as a browser plug-in from 1996. These technological developments facilitated digital animation and audio resources that could be created and shared with relative ease, transforming the Internet from a text-based medium to the richly varied multimodality that is now familiar. By 1997, commercial standards for *wi-fi* had been agreed, and 1996 saw the first smart phone (Nokia 9000 communicator). Access to the Internet was no longer restricted to static computer terminals connected to wired power supplies. With increased possibilities for access, social media could be produced and consumed in a greater range of locations and at any point in time. By 2007, 70 million blogs were indexed by Technorati. Two years later, 13 million articles had been posted on Wikipedia. In 2010, the major social network sites boast millions of members each. There are 145 million registered members on Twitter, 500 million active members on Facebook, and YouTube boasts over 2 billion daily views. That said, sites vary in the kinds of demographic groups that use them regularly and not all sites have maintained the same growth. For example, in the United States, the uptake of blogging has increased for those above thirty-four years of age, but halved for teenagers (Kopytoff 2011), and geographically specific sites like the British social network site Bebo soon gave way to the globalized adoption of Facebook.

Social media is more or less synonymous with what O'Reilly (2005) dubbed *Web 2.0* technologies. Although the descriptor Web 2.0 is still current, social media emphasizes the *social* aspects of the web genres in question, particularly the communicative interaction between participants and the implications this might have for macro-social issues such as personal or group identity. By way of contrast, "Web 2.0" was coined within a specific commercial context (Marwick 2010) and has particular business and technical applications that are less of interest to my concerns (Cormode and Krishnamurthy 2008). O'Reilly's use of the label "Web 2.0" was a key rhetorical strategy in demarcating a new era for online interaction, one that created a clear contrast between old and new web genres, However, the social aspects of Web 2.0 did not suddenly appear in the twenty-first century: they had antecedents in earlier forms of CMC and other offline communicative forms. Thus I prefer the expansive scope of the term "social media," which allows us to trace points of similarity and evolution from earlier discursive forms (like bulletin boards, text messages) into later, hybrid communicative environments that form the basis for analysis and discussion in this book.

While it has antecedents in earlier genres, there are five features that combine to make social media a distinctive category of CMC. Social media formats are collaborative, dialogic, emergent, personalized, and context-rich environments. I will describe each of these features briefly. First, social media is collaborative and emphasizes its capacity for people to participate and connect with each other. Blogs, forums, and social network sites are not understood as isolated, static pages but instead as shared spaces that enable collective contributions in the form of content, comments, and edits. These contributions to social media are both for the benefit of the individual contributor and also the wider community represented by the network. The collaborative nature of social media makes them an idealized environment for dialogue. In social media, the way in which you manage interpersonal interactions is as important as the content that you publish, and the dialogue takes place in novel formats (such as comments, discussion pages, ratings, or tags) that reconfigure the relationship between interactive participants in varying ways.

Social media interactions are emergent, that is to say, they are distributed across textual segments (such as blog posts, comments, forum threads, updates to a social network site) that are created and received asynchronously by participants who are often (although not always) geographically remote from each other. Social interaction appears in an episodic form, as sequences of messages develop over time, and draw attention to the processes of storytelling, rather than focusing on a discrete narrative product. The multiple contributions from many participants can be redistributed so that the process of consuming and producing social media can be personalized rather than homogenized. The ability to recontextualize and tailor the emerging content of social media to individual site members is exploited by sites like Facebook, Twitter, and Amazon, which use the growing archive of information about an individual user and their interactions in order to create unique homepages that are reconfigured each time the participant logs on to his or her account. The personalized individuation of social media is further enabled by the diversity of tools used to access or upload contributions to a site. Mobile devices and wi-fi provision give people increased flexibility over the times and places that become sites of engagement (Jones and Norris 2005) as social media connects participants with each other and with the materials hosted on and beyond their sites.

The collaborative, dialogic, emergent, and personalized characteristics of social media contribute to context-rich environments. The multiple elements of social media contexts are dynamic, layered, and complex—facets that will be discussed in more detail for their impact on narrative and the challenges they pose for sociolinguistic methodologies. For now, I contend that the contexts of social media provide a significant, unprecedented opportunity for narrative researchers to observe patterns of storytelling production and reception in a way that is less tractable for offline examples of face-to-face or written forms of narration. Combined with its rapid uptake and its diverse but distinctive characteristics, social media is a vital stimulus to consider once again the seemingly infinite impulse for humans to tell stories.

STORIES

Although probably more commonly recognized than social media, the term *stories* used in this book's title also requires clarification. Story and narrative are familiar synonyms that have generalized and specific uses. In narrative theory, attempts to pin down definitions for these terms have generated considerable debate. Early, structuralist work set out clear criteria that could be used to distinguish between narratives and other kinds of texts. In sociolinguistic research, Labov's definition has been particularly influential. He defined narrative "as one method of recapitulating past experience by matching a verbal sequence of clauses to the sequence of events which (it is inferred) actually happened" (1972, 359–360). Of course, not all stories are told in the past tense, and the sequence of telling does not have to match the sequence in which actual events occurred. Readers and listeners are remarkably adept in recognizing story-like qualities in texts that do not conform exactly to definitions like Labov's. The elasticity of what counts as a narrative has been documented extensively for the last four decades and continues to be brought into focus by the emergent nature of social media stories that appear to be told in real time, like Facebook updates, tweets, and video-blog entries.

In order to accommodate a more expansive, open-ended approach to characterizing narrative, theorists have adopted the concept of narrativity. Instead of treating narrativity as if it were a binary quality where either a text is deemed to be a narrative or it is not, current approaches describe narrative as a "fuzzy set" (Ryan 2004, 2006, 2007). From this perspective, some narratives are recognized as more prototypical cases than others. The qualities that prompt the recognition of narrativity are variable, and a full review is beyond the scope of this introductory chapter.[2] Within literary narratology, narrativity is often associated with three key properties. First, narrativity is generated by the recognition of reported events, ordered within a temporal framework. Second, the inferred connections between temporally ordered events are attributed with distinctive degrees of narrativity where causal connections are understood as more narrative-like than pure temporality. Finally, narrativity is associated with sequences that signal a teleological focus, an overarching framework of complication and resolution, or a clearly defined point of closure attributed with interpretive significance.

Using these parameters, we might judge the structural narrativity of social media stories to contrast with canonical examples of literary narrative or spoken narratives elicited in interview situations. For example, the episodic, ongoing nature of a sequence of blog entries or an archive of Facebook updates in not organized around a predetermined, single end point. In Chapter 3, the stories that narrators tell about their experiences of illness are not told retrospectively from the point of recovery, but as updates that appear discontinuously as the narrator documents their experiences while diagnosis and treatment unfolds. Sometimes the sequence of blog posts stops altogether without warning, perhaps for the distressing reason that the narrator is too ill to continue to write, or has even died. Within the episodic archives of social media posts, there may be little causal connection between one entry and the next. The sequences of tweets taken from public Twitter accounts and analyzed in Chapter 5 are moment-by-moment accounts that relate to what the narrator is doing "right now" rather than selected as part of a causal sequence of clauses. The following series of updates were reported in the American pop star Lady Gaga's Twitter account.

> In a Pub in England, ruining bar napkins with lyrics and memories. Dreams are never weak like we are, drunk or sober.
> Ladygaga: Wed, 26 May 2010, at 17:33
>
> At 12pm London time I will doing a LIVE interview with the amazing Nick Knight on www.showstudio.com tune in to see me answer your questions
> Ladygaga: 30 May 2010, at 08:06
>
> In exactly one hour and 36 min u can watch me being interviewed live @ http://live.showstudio.com answering all your questions lil monsters!
> Ladygaga: 30 May 2010, at 09:24
>
> Just heard ALEJANDRO on the radio in LONDON, what a marvelous day. Showstudio, the O2 Arena, a peaceful lone car ride to hotel. Supreme.
> Ladygaga: 30 May 2010, at 23:58

These updates follow the trajectory of Lady Gaga's activities, but they do not form a closed, plot-like series of a problem followed by a resolution. There is no indication that the first update about drinking in a British pub has any causal or thematic connection to her next update about an upcoming media interview. Instead, the sequencing appears fragmentary and open-ended. But social media stories contrast with more than the structural facets of a prototypical story's narrativity. Narrativity also applies to the characteristics of storytelling as communicative interaction.

A more contextualized account of narrativity is set out by Ochs and Capps (2001) in their description of the dimensions of narrative. Like literary narratologists, Ochs and Capps reject a binary, scalar model of narrativity on the grounds that this suggests fixed, polar contrasts. Instead, Ochs and Capps argue that narratives may combine different dimensions in more or less canonical patterns. The dimensions of narrative included in Ochs and Capps' outline are summarized in Figure 1.2.

The five dimensions include the structural features of narrative (linearity) but place a clear emphasis on contextual elements (tellership, embeddedness), which also influence the interpretation of moral stance and of the content as tellable. As Ochs and Capps point out, canonical narratives of personal experience in sociolinguistic and discourse analytic traditions have tended to privilege narratives that combine factors from the same end of the continua for each dimension. This resulted in a focus on single teller narratives that relate highly tellable topics (usually dangerous events or conflicts), which are relatively de-contextualized, have a clear moral stance, and a defined macro-level linear structure. It is credit to Ochs and Capps' insights that we now know much more about spoken narratives whose characteristics are quite different from the default, single-teller model. However, I contend that we still do not know enough about the everyday storytelling in online contexts that has thus far fallen outside existing sociolinguistic, conversational, literary, and electronic narrative corpora. The personal narratives found in social media contexts are quite different to the canonical forms elicited in interview (Labov 1972) or life history contexts (Linde 1993), and from the conversational examples from face-to-face contexts discussed in more recent work (Norrick 2005, 2008; Georgakopoulou 2007). Instead, the features of social media stories enable

Dimension	*Possibilities*
Tellership	Whether the story is told by a single teller, or multiple tellers
Tellability	The value of a story as highly worth telling, or seemingly irrelevant
Embeddedness	The extent to which a story can be detached from or embedded in its context
Linearity	The structural qualities of a story as closed, temporal sequence, or open-ended and multilinear
Moral Stance	The narrator's attitude toward reported events, which may be certain or fluctuating

Figure 1.2 Narrative dimensions and possibilities (adapted from Ochs and Capps 2001, 20).

and constrain the narrative dimensions of linearity, tellability, tellership, and embeddedness in innovative ways that have as yet to be explored. To set the analysis found in later chapters in context, I begin with some general observations about how the emergent, collaborative, and context-rich qualities of social media depart from the narrative dimensions associated with the canonical forms of personal narrative.

Linearity

The narrative dimension of linearity refers to the ways in which storytelling material is organized into a cohesive whole. Canonical narratives are said to rely on a single sequence of past-tense events organized along a teleologically focused trajectory toward a definitive conclusion. The polar opposite implies qualities of narrativity associated with open-endedness, a move away from the past tense and toward fragmentation and multilinear structures. The emergent stories of social media are often open-ended, discontinuous, and fluctuating. Stories can be told in their entirety within an individual unit of social media, such as a forum post, blog entry, or status update, but they can also be distributed across multiple units, as episodes that unfold between sequenced posts, or posts and comments. They can draw together material connected by hyperlinks (such as a tweet and a link to an external news report) or connect with material available in the wider archive or web genre in which posts are stored. However, open-endedness is not exclusive to social media. Indeed, these qualities are associated with narratives in new media (Hoffman 2010), and Lunenfeld (2000) argues that the "aesthetic of the unfinish" is a defining quality of digital media more generally. Nor is open-endedness exclusively found in digital media: Ochs and Capps point to the function of inconsistency within everyday conversational stories as a means of questioning the coherence that linear narratives impose on life experiences (2001, 45).

Like conversational stories, the episodic quality of social media stories is due in part to the temporal nature of this kind of narration. Stories like the Facebook status updates and tweets posted by celebrity figures may be reported as they are unfolding, rather than as a distantly retrospective reflection on events now completed. But the temporality of blogs, social network updates, or video posts is reworked distinctively by the affordances and infrastructure of social media sites. Temporal sequence lies at the heart of most accepted definitions of narrative and is regarded as one of the core properties that prompts perceptions of narrativity (Ryan 2007). But while canonical examples of personal narrative have largely examined past tense accounts of events (e.g., retrospective accounts in narrative interviews or life histories), the temporal sequencing associated with social media stories is quite different.[3] Perhaps most strikingly, many social media archives present published posts in reverse chronological order.[4] The effect of this is to reduce the reliance on past-tense reports as typical constructions of narrative time and replace this with an emphasis on events that appear to be happening in near synchronicity to the time of reporting and reception.

The pull of the present is not just found in social media. Georgakopoulou (2007) includes Breaking News and Projections as story genres found typically in conversational data, while Fiske (1987) describes the immediacy projected by the rise of reality television as "nowness." The influence of presentism, or the philosophical belief that only the present moment exists (Bourne 2006), is felt more generally in contemporary accounts of narrative time, which suggest that anticipation, rather than retrospection, may prompt more productive ways of understanding narrative dynamics (Currie 2006). The design of social media is clearly shaped by these wider trends but heightens narrative immediacy further still through the use of provocations to report "what's happening" (as the update template in Twitter prompts) rather than what *has happened*, through the use of timestamps that locate the time of publication relative to the present moment (Facebook), which use reverse chronological archiving (blogs, Facebook, Twitter) and the use of recency to promote site activity.

Tellership

The collaborative nature of social media means that the tellership of social media stories tends to contrast with canonical expectations of a single teller and operate instead with different kinds of multi-party, co-constructed narration. Although social media is collaborative, this does not mean that all discursive contributions are equal and that the burden of storytelling is evenly distributed between multiple participants. Instead, the interactive hierarchies that underpin social media provide new avenues to rework the asymmetries of floor-holding activities. The stories discussed in later chapters provide many examples of interactive hierarchies. Some social media genres allow certain members to retain control over the publication of another participant's contributions. For example, the bloggers whose writing is analyzed in Chapter 3 can choose which comments on their blog are published and whether or not they will be given a response; the discussion forum moderators in the bodybuilding forums examined in Chapter 2 and in the creative writing communities of Chapter 6 may have the right to delete certain posts if they are deemed offensive. In other contexts, narrative practices of co-tellership need to be negotiated "from the ground up." For example, the participants who use wiki technology (like the creative project *A Million Penguins* discussed in Chapter 6) must negotiate the right to contribute to a narrative in an innovative environment that enables radical editing, where the contributions from multiple participants are not separated in distinctive turns (as face-to-face co-construction might) but vie for space within the same wiki page.

The distribution of tellership roles in terms of quality and quantity is not random, but varies according to the textual infrastructure of the social media genre in question and according to the identity of the participants and their relationship to each other. Some variation in tellership practices might reflect locally occasioned roles, such as an Original Poster in a discussion thread, but others also change in line with factors such as the participants' declared age and gender. This leads me to question which narrators interact most frequently with the members of their audience and how this relates to their narrative style. In the chapters that follow, narrators are compared according to their gender (see the discussion of blog writing in Chapter 3 and Facebook updates in Chapter 4), according to whether or not they are inscribed with celebrity status (Chapter 5's analysis of Twitter stories), and in terms of their contribution to a storytelling community (Chapter 6). Plotting the narrative consequences of variation in tellership patterns once again calls for a more contextualized and comparative analyses of the story texts and their tellers than digital narratology has yet provided. This requires us to rethink what context might mean for social media stories.

Embeddedness

The emergent linearity and collaborative tellership of social media stories mean that the narrative qualities of social media stories cannot be assessed without reference to the contexts in which they are embedded. But determining what counts as context is not straightforward. For the last three decades, socially oriented accounts of discourse have recognized that context is not a static, stable entity that discretely frames linguistic interaction (Duranti and Goodwin 1992). If discourse contexts are multilayered, slippery, and interactive in offline environments, computer-mediated discourse multiplies the challenges to assessing context. From the earliest studies in CMC onward, linguistic and sociological analysts alike have repeatedly drawn attention to the contextual factors that might be important when interpreting data (Baym 1995; Herring 2004; Thurlow et al. 2004; Jones and Norris 2005; Bazzanella 2010). But there is no prescriptive consensus about which contextual elements might be most important for the analysis of CMC. Instead, the following factors are important in different ways for the discussion in later chapters.

Participants: the people who take part in the interaction and their relationship to others in the group.

Imagined context: the projected contexts created cognitively by participants on the basis of their world knowledge and cues provided in CMC.

Extrasituational context: the offline social practices in which the participants are involved, which might be shaped by their participation in localized communities of practice and cultural values relating to macro-social factors such as age, gender, ethnic, or national identity.

Behavioral context: the physical situation in which the participants' engagement with social media takes place.

Textual context: the verbal co-text in which stories are positioned, the surrounding discourse (comments, discussion posts, other posts in the archive), the screen layout and resources.

Generic context: the website in which the story is created, including its wider resources, stated purpose, topic, and rules for conduct.

The assessment of these multilayered aspects of context is complicated by the convergent nature of contemporary Internet use. Social media is characterized by complex forms of hybridity and intertextuality, where the boundaries of generic and textual contexts become porous and bleed into other sites through parody, hyperlinks, and quotation. The wider context of the Internet as a networked public (boyd 2008) means that a teller's sense of the audience is quite different from face-to-face interactions.[5] Even where a sense of an audience can be constructed through a visible network like the Followers on a Twitter account, and displayed through comments (such as those on the cancer blogs in Chapter 3 or in the creative writing communities in Chapter 6), at least some part of the audience will only ever lurk and not make themselves known to the narrator. Conventions of online representation can also vary in terms of assumed authenticity, visibility, and degrees of self-disclosure, so that the process of interpreting the identity of the narrative participants can only ever remain partial and subjective. In the stories covered in this book, some tellers use pseudonyms (like the contributors to Protagonize in Chapter 6 and the bodybuilding forums in Chapter 2), while others do not (like the celebrity figures who tell stories in Twitter and the Facebook Friends discussed in Chapter 4). Some tellers take pains to claim their authenticity, while others like the Facebook "rape" narrators in Chapter 8 play with the possibility of impersonating someone else.

Finally, like other forms of CMC, the contexts of social media stories are dynamic. Sites are constantly updated with new content, templates change, and genres evolve, as the longitudinal analysis of Facebook updates in Chapter 4 suggests. One solution is to capture data and archive it in an offline repository, but this cannot capture the full picture of actual interactive practices in social media. Thus the richness of social media offers significant opportunities for a more contextualized approach to narrative analysis, but is also fraught with challenges.

Tellability

A story's tellability is distinguished from the narrativity prompted by structural elements of linearity and tellership (Ryan 2005). Tellability is the quality that makes a story worth telling in the first place. The diversity of social media stories mean their tellability can be highly varied. Unlike stories told in other contexts, they do not depend on the assessment of detached content (such as "trouble" or "conflict") but are judged against locally negotiated demands of relevance (Norrick 2007). The rhetorical effectiveness and interpersonal engagement inherent in successful tellability is closely related to the dialogic and interactive characteristics of social media. The dimension of tellability brings to center stage the question of how tellers orient themselves and the stories they tell to their audiences (even when the audience is indeterminate), and how their audiences respond. Tellability is thus at the heart of the *social* quality of social media and results in varied patterns of interactive engagement.

When the tellability of a social media narrative fails, then the withering response "so what?" predicted by Labov (1972) finds an online correlate where audiences simply refuse to contribute to the story at all, reflected in patterns of diminished page views, comments, ratings, or edits. But tellability is not just signaled through a participant's interaction with the text. It is reflected in and contributes to the social interaction between a teller and their audience. The tellability of social media stories thus concerns the role of storytelling in constructing social relationships. For example, stories can be used to claim group membership or demonstrate alignment with or distance from another, as do the stories told by novice and expert bodybuilders in discussion forums (Chapter 2). Storytelling practices operate within negotiated contracts for the rights to tell a story in the first place, practices that storytellers sometimes misappropriate, as did the fictional narrator of the video-blog Lonelygirl15 whose story is considered in Chapter 8. Like narrative dimension of embeddedness, tellability points to the work which stories accomplish in social media contexts, in shaping narrators' identities and their interactions with others.

IDENTITIES AND INTERACTION

Identities and interaction are concepts that have become central to social science research since the 1990s, influencing key trends in sociolinguistics and discourse-analytic narrative research. The sheer number of recent titles invoking "identity" and "interaction" in conjunction with "narrative" and "discourse" attests to the currency of these interests: *Narrative and Identity* (Brockmeier and Carbaugh 2001), *Narrative Interaction* (Quasthoff and Becker 2005), *Discourse and Identity* (Benwell and Stokoe 2006), *Discourse and Identity* (De Fina, Schiffrin, and Bamberg, 2006), *Selves and Identities in Narrative and Discourse* (Bamberg, Schiffrin, and De Fina, 2007), and *Small Stories, Interaction and Identities* (Georgakopoulou 2007). This work draws attention to the human activity of storytelling as a way of presenting and making sense of ourselves and others (accomplishing identity work), and understands storytelling as situated practice (and hence as interactive), rather than a static text.

The interest in narrative as an interactive site for constructing identities springs from the current view of identity as discursively formed. The discursive view stands in opposition to an essentialist perception of the self as a stable, unified entity and rejects the proposal that collective social categories are natural and homogenized. In this sense, discursive approaches to identity mark a paradigm shift from earlier work in variationist sociolinguistics, where the analyst placed the research participants into preexisting categories (according to their gender, age, ethnicity, class, education) and then interpreted the participants' language choices as a symptom of their identity. Instead, the discursive approach is influenced by poststructuralist tenets that the text is preeminent (in Derrida's [1976] words, "there is nothing but the text"). It is also influenced by concepts of performativity that present language as the means by which identity is brought into being (Butler 1990), and by the dramaturgical metaphors put forward by Goffman (1959) that the self is a "social actor" who alters their behavior and costume in order to manage the impressions given to different audiences in the course of everyday interaction. From a discursive perspective, identities are plural, constantly negotiated, and fluid, manifest and made meaningful through the participants' discourse and enacted in relation to localized contexts of interaction.

Many criticisms have been leveled at this discursive approach to identity, including the relative neglect of embodiment, questioning how agency might be attributed to a subject, and recognizing the ongoing relevance of collective categories in the day-to-day activities of the general public (Benwell and Stokoe 2006, 45–46). Nonetheless, a discursive view is ideally positioned to interpret the identity work that occurs in online contexts. Online interaction primarily takes place by means of discourse: text that is created by its participants, but that is not usually received in face-to-face contexts. The apparently disembodied nature of CMC and its potential for identity play through the use of anonymity, pseudonyms, or inauthentic personae would seem the environment par excellence for the enactment of identities through discourse.

Early CMC theorists presented online identity as a "mask" that was entirely separate from "real life" (Turkle 1995). Later critics have questioned the extent to which identity play takes place in CMC (Roberts and Parks 1999), while others have recognized that offline and online behaviors need not be separate but can overlap (Herring 2003). Ethnographic studies have signaled that forms of CMC still have behavioral contexts: their human participants are not disembodied (Jones 2005), while others have criticized the implication that "real life" identities are somehow more stable than online performances, and pointed out that identity work is carried out both offline and online (Thurlow et al. 2004). As the use of social media becomes more closely interwoven with day-to-day management of social relationships (especially through the use of sites like Facebook and Twitter), some critics have begun to argue that the distinction between online and offline identity work is no longer relevant (Marwick 2010). Although I think it is too strong to abandon online and offline as a point of distinction, it is clear that a contextualized approach to social media stories requires a multidimensional approach to identity online. This approach must go beyond a surface level interpretation of the discursive text alone and, where possible, take into account the ways in which identity work online connects with the identities that are performed in offline extrasituational and behavioral contexts.

Identities: Transportable, Discourse, and Situated

There are a number of ways in which people might construct their identity through discourse. Here I distinguish between the aspects of identity that relate to a person's attributes (performances of who they are) and the role they adopt in a particular interaction with others. This distinction maps on to the categories described by Zimmerman (1998) who contrasts transportable, discourse, and situated aspects of identity work. Transportable identities are attributes or characteristics that a participant carries across multiple discourse situations, while discourse and situated identities are locally occasioned roles adopted in relation to a particular speech situation.

Transportable identities can be inscribed (explicitly stated in the text) or invoked (indexed through stylistic choices). This echoes Goffman's (1959) contrast between the performance that an individual "gives" and the expressions that the individual less concretely "gives off." Participants may choose to make direct reference to their transportable identities in the course of their storytelling. For example, members of the bodybuilding discussion forum (Chapter 2) and the bloggers describing their cancer diagnosis and treatment (Chapter 3) explicitly make reference to their gender. Others, like the oral history narrators (Chapter 7) include details about their age and geographical location. The paratextual profile that the participant chooses to offer about his or her self can include a name or often a nickname and information such as a photograph, along with information about their age, gender, or location.

Participants may also invoke, or "give off," performances of their transportable identity. In Goffman's description, this aspect of identity performance is unintentional and often nonverbal. Transportable identities may be indexed through stylistic choices, where the use or frequency of a particular discourse feature has become associated with a social group over time. Examples include the use of dialect features (lexis, syntax) to reflect geographical or national identities, the use of accent to signal the speaker's class, and the use of emotionally expressive resources to index performances of age and gender. While inscribed, transportable identities result from information given by the narrative participants, invoked identities are often a more subjective matter, attributed by the analyst.

In addition to transportable identities, participants adopt roles in the process of interacting with others. Where these interactive roles are specific to the genre in question, they correspond to what Zimmerman (1998) describes as situated identities. Sometimes these enact well-recognized scenarios from the offline world, such as institutional pairings of doctor and patient. In other contexts, situated identities are attributed by the specific roles in a social media site, as in the case of forum moderator, Facebook Friends, or Twitter Followers. These situated identities are distinguished from the turn-by-turn roles taken up as discourse identities, such as a narrator, the person who asks a question or so on (Zimmerman 1998, 91) and that are so important for a Conversation Analytic approach. In addition to Zimmerman's situated and discourse identities, the frequency with which a person contributes to a dialogue and the kinds of contributions they make might also be used as a basis for inferring their interactive identity. Using discourse-analytic criteria, a person might be classed as a relatively frequent or infrequent user of a site, influencing their identities as core or peripheral members of an online group.

Interpreting the different facets of a participant's identity constructed through online discourse is a challenging and provisional process. Balancing the interpretation of identity made by the analyst against that of the participants is fiercely debated in identities-in-interaction research as led by Antaki and Widdicombe (1998), who claim that if identity is to be analyzed, it must be made relevant by the discourse participants themselves in their interaction. The interpretation of identity in relation to discourse on the part of the analyst might be quite different from that as perceived by the participant his- or herself (Androutsopoulos 2008). There are no guarantees of authenticity for the demographic information offered in profile slots, and these should be treated as performances rather than attributes that map on to "real world" qualities. But this does not mean that the project of interpreting identity should be abandoned or that the analyst's interpretations should be regarded as invalid. Instead, the discussions that I present in the later chapters of this book are preceded by the caveat that they are interpretations of data, and necessarily selective in their emphasis.

DATA AND METHODS

Ethics

The data analyzed in this book come from a variety of Internet sources, including discussion forums, blogs, Facebook profiles, Twitter profiles, curated archives, and YouTube. The extent to which these environments operate as publically available or privately secured varies, and entails different requirements about the collection and representation of data (Markham and Baym 2009). Where sites are understood as private or semi-private, such as Facebook, informant consent was necessary and gained from all the participants. All the other sites made their material publically available. However, informant consent was sought wherever possible. Where sites indicated that personal information should not be disclosed publically in its members' profiles, as in the discussion forum examined in Chapter 2, then like privately available data (Facebook), any quotations are anonymized or use pseudonyms. However, where the published material was "intended as a public act or performance that invites recognition for accomplishment" (Ess 2002, 7), the authors' names have been retained as published on the web page (e.g., as the blogger's screen name, the celebrity Twitter identity).

Online data are ephemeral, and not all the data that were analyzed in later chapters are still available. In the case of the cancer blogs (Chapter 3), this is a sensitive issue as some blogs have been taken down following the death of their author. In these cases, although the blog posts are still included in the quantitative analysis, no quotations are included in the discussions. In order to preserve anonymity, quotations from the data are not presented in their online templates, as these might include names or photographic images. But where appropriate, I have annotated quotations with contextual information like timestamps and included wider information about the layout of web pages in which the stories appeared.

Data-Logs or Ethnographic Study

I have argued that an analysis of stories told in social media needs to be multidimensional, focusing on the language of the stories and their online and offline contexts. This approach is informed by linguistic discussions of CMC, which remain focused on data logs as a source of information (Herring 2010), and sociolinguistic accounts of CMC, which have begun to include a greater use of ethnographic perspectives (Androutsopoulos 2008). The analysis that follows in this book is still largely focused on textual datasets, supplemented by the contextual factors that are observable on the screens of social media. However, where appropriate, I have sought to enhance the textual analysis by gaining participants' perspectives.

Following the blended approach set out by Hine (2000), the discussion of Facebook updates was supplemented by a survey of the participants' beliefs about their online behavior (Chapter 4), and I carried out e-mail interviews with victims of "frape," discussed in Chapter 8. I had e-mail correspondence with the bloggers whose work is analyzed in Chapter 3. In order to gain a fuller understanding of the generic contexts in question, I started a blog in 2006 and opened a Twitter account in 2009. I registered membership on the discussion boards and the collaborative storytelling community, Protagonize. In each case, I chose to lurk and observe the profiles that are analyzed in this study, rather than directly interacting with them. This allowed me to access the sites' contexts as a member would, and to observe the interactional practices and dynamics for longer periods of time than that reflected by the textual extracts I have chosen for analysis. I also interviewed Nick Bouton (who created Protagonize) and Robin Elliot, (executive director of [murmur]) both of whom were able to provide perspectives on the sites that were impossible to judge from observing the content of screens alone.

Multimodality

The multimodal nature of CMC is often cited as a further challenge to the text-immanent and quantitative paradigms used in variationist sociolinguistics (Androutsopoulos 2011). Without doubt, the stories told in social media are communicated in multimodal ensembles. But multimodality is not exclusive to CMC. Analysts of multimodality recognize that monomodality is a myth and that all communication (including print) uses more than one *semiotic* resource to convey meaning (Kress and van Leeuwen 2001). Conversely, Herring maintains that most CMC still takes the form of written text (2010). From a narrative perspective, while transmedial and intermedial approaches recognize the contributions of sound, space, visual, and kinesthetic resources (Ryan 2004; Page 2010a; Grisakova and Ryan 2010), it is verbal resources that are narrative's "native tongue" (Ryan 2004, 11).

Given the ongoing significance of verbal resources in CMC and narrative, the analyses that follow in later chapters are focused on linguistic matters. But this does not mean that I adopt a media-blind perspective. In particular, the role of image, sound, and gesture are included in the discussion of podcasts and video-blogs, and the analysis of affective discourse in Chapter 4 includes nonverbal forms like emoticons. The main focus on verbal resources is further narrowed to English-language texts. This is regrettable, and is far from representative of the multilingual state of the Internet, reflecting instead the limitations of my own interests and expertise. In the conclusion (Chapter 9), I point to the multicultural and multilingual opportunities for further research that are already being taken up by others (Androutsopoulos 2010; Abdul Mageed et al. 2011; Sebba et al. forthcoming).

ABOUT THIS BOOK: AN OVERVIEW

Although necessarily limited, the data and the narrative analyses discussed in the later chapters of this book signal the heterogeneity of the stories told in social media. Each chapter focuses on a different web genre. The stories I analyze are told about different topics and for a range of purposes. Thus the narrators and their audiences also vary from chapter to chapter, and enact identities that vary from the public performances of celebrity to peer friendship in Facebook. This diversity reflects the theoretical emphasis of the book on exploring the various manifestations of storytelling, as opposed to an ethnographic study of a single community or set of participants. Nor do I seek to uncover a universal pattern that accounts for all and only the stories that emerge from social media. Given the rapid change and expansion of online contexts, this would be an untenable project. Instead, the discussion in the chapters that follow show that there are a number of factors that contribute to the form and function of stories that are found in these contexts, and while there are common threads, there is no isomorphic relationship between a narrative's interactive qualities and the social accomplishments of identity work.

Several threads run throughout this book, which reflect its central concerns with narrative, interaction, and identity. Each chapter contains analysis of the participation patterns that surround the storytelling situation in question. This might be an account of the frequency of posting or commenting interaction (Chapters 3, 4, 5, and 6), analysis of the links between the story text and other sites (Chapters 4 and 5), or the different modalities brought to bear when a story is experienced through a mobile device rather than at a static computer terminal (Chapter 7). The relationship between turn-taking and storytelling is also important for the discussion of forum posts, which appears in Chapter 2 and 6.

Each chapter also interprets the linguistic features found in the stories as strategies that are used to forge connections between tellers and their audiences, including the use of recognized phenomenon such as *politeness* (Chapters 2, 6, and 8), evaluation (Chapters 3, 4, and 5), person *deictics* (Chapter 7), or reference to time (Chapter 5). Lastly, each chapter discusses how these interactive and linguistic factors can also be interpreted in the light of their extra-situational contexts and the identities that are constructed in the process.

The chapters begin with the earlier forms of social media and move toward later genres and phenomenon. There is also a move from everyday topics toward more consciously literary or edited storytelling activities. Chapter 1 examines the sequences of stories that emerge in the threads of a discussion forum used to seek and give advice for bodybuilders. I extend Sacks' notion of Second Stories (1995) to account for how participants negotiate solidarity and distance between changing novice and expert membership of the group. In Chapter 2, I examine a selection of personal blogs as sites that rework narratives of illness for people being diagnosed and treated for cancer. The reflective and connective capacities of blogging are exploited by writers to create a new story genre of the Reflective Anecdote. In both chapters, gender is an important factor in the identities that are enacted and influences the expectations of interactive styles. Female bodybuilders have to negotiate their place in a predominantly masculine environment, leading to conflicting discourse strategies of assertion and support. For the bloggers, the trauma caused by critical illness can cause them to reflect on the biological and social bases used to gender their identity.

Chapters 3 and 4 turn to the international social network site Facebook and microblogging site Twitter. Both chapters examine the updates that members can publish as short accounts of their daily activity. The Facebook data provides a longitudinal analysis that traces the evolution of an affective style used in Breaking News Stories (Georgakopoulou 2007). The analysis of Twitter compares the behavior of celebrity tweeters with everyday tweet streams, finding the broadcast of "super fresh" news typical of Twitter is an ideal mechanism for amplifying celebrity status. In both chapters, the importance of the stories as a means of attracting interaction between the tellers and their audiences is interpreted as a strategy to gain visibility. In the case of Facebook updates, interaction is desired as a signal of social capital, while in Twitter, celebrity practice is used to increase audience engagement with their mainstream performance and products.

Chapter 6 compares two collaborative creative writing projects: the wikinovel *A Million Penguins* and the ongoing community Protagonize. These projects demonstrate the need to create some kind of social contract between participants in order to negotiate storytelling practices. Chapter 7 moves to a community archive of stories about particular places, curated as the international [murmur] project. Here interaction is less focused on human–human exchanges and on the multimodal realization of storyworlds enabled by on-site reception via mobile devices. Finally, Chapter 8 returns to the question of tellership and the right to tell a story, examining two cases of inauthentic narratorial identities. The process of detecting inauthenticity is used to establish in-group and out-group membership for the narrative audiences of the fictional video-blogger Lonelygirl15 and for the audience of Facebook "raped" updates. All the chapters suggest that the narrative context is important, but the multimodal nature of on-site storytelling and the multiple interpretations of inauthentic narratorial identity emphasize the necessity that researchers move beyond a surface interpretation of the text alone.

The final chapter draws together the findings of earlier chapters and suggests how these help us evaluate the narrative dimensions of social media stories as familiar, reconfigured, and emergent. I reflect on how narrative analysis helps us to critique stories that are told about social media. Initial descriptions of social media presented it as an innovative break with the past, but as time has gone, social media turns out to be rather less radical than it first appeared and may reinforce rather than move beyond familiar social hierarchies. The conclusion ends by setting out a series of questions to stimulate future work on narrative in social media and beyond, for I recognize that although this book is in many respects already overfull, there is so much that I could have covered but did not. It is my hope that this book will prompt you to join future researchers in charting the course that stories in social media will take, and reflect on how these stories relate to the changing contexts we live in.

2   Second Stories Told in Discussion Forums

Discussion forums are one of the longer established social media genres. This chapter examines the ways in which the collaborative potential of the genre reshapes the narrative dimensions of tellership, with a particular focus on the sequenced storytelling that emerges through dialogue between forum members. The sequenced stories told by multiple tellers are also important for drawing attention to the narrative dimension of embeddedness that allows us to distinguish between stories that are pragmatically interdependent and those that can be detached from their surrounding context with relative ease. The chapter begins by reviewing the generic characteristics of discussion forums and then introduces the concepts of face and relational work that will be important in this and several later chapters. The main part of the chapter then identifies different types of sequenced stories and relational work found in a particular bodybuilding discussion forum: Bodybuilding.com.

THE COMMUNICATIVE CONTEXTS
CREATED IN DISCUSSION FORUMS

Discussion forums, also known as Internet forums or discussion boards, are one of the many online environments that enable participants to communicate with one another by exchanging information or opinions.[1] Forums are hybrid environments developed from earlier types of CMC, including private e-mail messaging, publically posted messages on bulletin boards, and the semi-public distribution of information on discussion lists. As in earlier models of CMC, participants contribute to a forum by writing messages to each other (known as posts), and the style of writing is rarely formal, containing structural and pragmatic characteristics also associated with spoken discourse (Harrison 1998). However, talking with others on a forum is distinct from offline, face-to-face talk in a number of ways. Forum communication is usually asynchronous, which means that messages must be archived so that participants who access the site at a later point in time can view or respond to previous material. In order to enable other members to keep track of responses to particular messages, forums usually archive these posts in a hierarchical structure organized by topic, and large forums may designate subforums for specialist areas of interest. Within a forum, conversations are structured into threads: a sequence of posts made in response to an initiating message (sometimes called a *seed message*).

Discussion forums typically have a defined purpose based on a shared topic of interest. Interests can range from serious to lighthearted subject matter, but popular topics include entertainment (Baym 1995), gaming (Steinkuehler and Duncan 2008), health (McLellan 1997; Harrison and Barlow 2009), religion (Graham 2007), finance (Herrmann 2007), politics (Papacharissi 2004), and sport (Peuronen 2011). As even this small sample suggests, forums are by no means a homogenous web genre, and the choice of subject matter can influence the kinds of interactions that might take place between members. Rhetorical diversity is also found within any given forum, for its members may well have differing opinions and different styles of expressing those opinions. Although the infrastructure of forum posting would seem to promote a democratic environment (for any member of the forum can start or contribute to a thread), not all contributions are valued equally.[2] Instead, differences may emerge which challenge the social order created within the forum.

RULES AND ROLES WITHIN A DISCUSSION FORUM

Social order is critical to communicative co-operation within a forum. This is not to say that all forums necessarily aim to promote consensus, or that conflict will not occur. There are many examples of forums where freedom of expression and the need to debate opposing viewpoints are valued highly. But in order to maintain civil communication and to prevent a forum collapsing under the pressure of disputes or impolite behavior, most forums lay out rules with which members must comply. The rules may well be site-specific, as part of a forum's generic context, and often contain guidance regarding the kinds of content that are considered unacceptable breaches of *netiquette*. Typical examples include prohibition of illegal activity (such as distributing pornography), false misrepresentation of another person's identity, flaming, or using insulting or defamatory language.

In order to create and maintain the social order set out by a forum's generic context, participants adopt and adapt particular discourse identities in relation to each other and their interactions. Some forum identities are categories attributed in a "top-down" process. These are roles that are named by the site owners and assigned by them to members of the forum on the basis of individual behavior. Situated identities such as administrators, moderators, and members reinforce a hierarchical model of influence, based on the control that a particular person might exercise over the publication of forum posts. Members may contribute but do not have authority to edit or delete the contributions made by others. Moderators may edit or delete posts, while administrators have overall responsibility for the forum's site design and hold final authority for allowing or disallowing membership of the site. These identities are recognized categories referred to by members of forums and reinforce social ranking based on expertise and co-operation. New moderators are appointed as a reward for a being "particularly helpful and knowledgeable" about a given topic.

Social hierarchies based on interactional behavior are also implied by the discourse identities that the members of the forum self-select for each other. Members invoke these categories by naming themselves or others, including identifiers such as a "newbie" (a new member of the forum), the "OP" (original poster), or "troll" (a deliberately disruptive contributor). The identities associated with these categories have recognizable characteristics that are constituted (and sometimes challenged or reworked) by interactive styles and behavior. For example, the newbie typically asserts self-deprecating deference to more established members of the forum. The OP identity is designated by the act of posting a seed message, but the OP is also expected to produce follow-up posts (thanks, clarification, or evaluation) in response to the developing messages in the thread that they started, while trolls might violate topic coherence or norms of politeness.

Research literature on forums has noted the underlying status as novice or expert that contributors must negotiate as they join and maintain their interactions with others (Benwell and Stokoe 2006; Harrison and Barlow 2009). The basis for claiming either novice or expert identity can rest on the individual's position within the online community of the forum or their relative experience and knowledge of a topic as evidenced by their offline, "real world" activities. This leads Graham (2007, 746) to posit two facets of forum identity: the List Member (who is experienced in the norms and practices of a specific forum) and the Topic Enthusiast (who has detailed knowledge of the topic and communities associated with the subject focus of a given forum). Although members do not explicitly label themselves as experts or novices, List Members or Topic Enthusiasts, the relative contrast in status between the expert and novice identities underpins most of the social structures found in many forums, including those examined in this chapter.

Data Sample: BodyBuilding.com

In recent decades, the pursuit of fitness activities and aspirations have become a significant cultural trend in Western societies, where physical self-improvement (increased fitness, enhanced aesthetic appearance) is related to the construction of an individual's "inner body" or selfhood (Featherstone 1982). The stories that people tell about themselves in the context of their fitness aspirations function to represent and regulate the external and internal aspects of their identities. Bodybuilding.com is the largest English-speaking, fitness-related discussion board (http://rankings. big-boards.com/), with nearly 3 million members, most of whom are based in North America.

The web pages for the community create a generic context that exhibits the convergent, participatory, and multimodal characteristic of social media. The site includes areas for blogs, photo sharing, members' profiles, and an online store where members can buy and review products, along with a range of forums to facilitate topic-led discussion. The forums are divided into twenty-five subforums for particular topics or categories of members (including forums for teens, over thirty-fives, females, personal trainers). At the time of writing, they contained nearly 3.5 million threads and over 62 million posts. The web pages, including the forums, are publically available, but members may also communicate with each other by using an optional private messaging system. Members are encouraged to use pseudonyms for their usernames and not to disclose personal information that might put them at risk. Nonetheless, many members do make reference to aspects of their identity that are relevant to their offline world experiences. These include attributes of their transportable identities, such as their age, gender, nationality, sexual orientation, religious beliefs, education, occupations, and, most importantly, their experiences of bodybuilding.

Bodybuilding has been characterized as an individualistic, rather than communal endeavor, where displays of power and posturing are considered "natural" behavior (Andrews et al. 2005). The hierarchical infrastructure of the bodybuilding community is realized through physique and strength (where increased muscularity and strength are equated with increased power) and through commitment to the regime of activities required to produce physical strength, including training. Within this system, recreational bodybuilders are outranked by serious trainers who eschew sociality and focus on training alone. The importance of the body as a site for performative identity work brings the bodybuilders' gendered identity to center stage. The hypermuscularity emulated by bodybuilding is sometimes conceptualized as deviant, pushing ideal gender boundaries to their limits and resulting in hypermasculine men and de-feminized women (Obel 1996). Indeed, the identity work that women bodybuilders must negotiate has been scrutinized for its feminist potential (Boyle 2005), juxtaposed with an ongoing dependence on strategies of spectatorship. It is untenable to suggest that there is a single discourse style that is used by all bodybuilders, and there are many contradictory facets of bodybuilding identity for women and men (Wiegers 1998). Nonetheless, language is part of the symbolic repertoire that bodybuilders might use to signal their membership within this social category and to position themselves within the Bodybuilding.com forums as expert or novice Topic Enthusiasts. In particular, the identity work accomplished through narrative interaction may be one means by which participants can demonstrate their position within the social hierarchies of the bodybuilding community.

Face, Politeness, and Relational Work

The notion that identity is achieved through interaction with others within a social hierarchy is central to Goffman's concept of face. He defines face as

> [t]he positive social value a person effectively claims for himself by the line others assume he has taken during a particular contact. Face is an image of self delineated in terms of approved social attributes— albeit an image that others may share, as when a person makes a good showing for his profession or religion by making a good showing for himself. (1959, 5)

Face, or the "image of self" projected by the individual, is not a once and for all construct. Rather, face may be adapted according to the speech situation, the "particular contact" in which the person finds his- or herself at that point in time. As these situations change, different "images of self" might become more or less prominent, and the means by which face is articulated will always be under negotiation and vulnerable to disruption in the process of communication. The strategies by which face is maintained or put at risk has been discussed at length, but perhaps focused most sharply in Brown and Levinson's (1987) work on politeness.

Brown and Levinson argue that we have positive and negative aspects of face. *Positive face* refers to the desire to be approved of or liked by others, while *negative face* relates to a person's need to carry out their actions without being hindered, or their right to independence and autonomy. Our daily interactions with others present a constant threat to both aspects of face, where face-threatening acts (FTAs) can be initiated by either the speaker or by their audience. Examples of acts that threaten positive face might include criticism, insults, or implications that one speaker is more powerful than another. Threats to negative face include requests, invitations, or instructions. When a person admits or implies that they are at fault or in the debt of another, for example, by apologizing or expressing thanks, then they too can threaten their own face. Interaction is thus a continuous process of balancing our own face needs with the face needs of others.

Brown and Levinson's work on the strategies which we might use to carry out FTAs with more or less degrees of mitigation is only one of many attempts to explain the complex workings involved in "doing politeness." However, the seminal nature of Brown and Levinson's model is attested by work that has refined their categories through application to discourse found in other contexts, cultures, and modes (including CMC) and the criticisms that have resulted in new approaches to relational work (Locher 2004, 2006; Locher and Watts 2005) and impoliteness (Culpeper 1996; Culpeper et al. 2003; Bousfield 2007b; Bousfield and Locher 2008). Current approaches to relational work recognize that the resources that people use for signaling politeness are not universal but context sensitive. It is not that politeness inherently resides in particular linguistic forms (such as the use of *hedges*, *modality*, etc.), but rather that the resources used to signal politeness or impoliteness must be recognized as such by the participants in the interaction.

Locher's (2004, 2006) model usefully points out that politeness is only one dimension of the facework (which she calls "relational work") carried out in communication. Politeness is part of a broader spectrum that also includes unmarked appropriate and inappropriate forms, along with impoliteness. Locher rejects Brown and Levinson's somewhat ambiguous terminology of positive and negative types of politeness strategies, but makes a general distinction between the activities that generate involvement and solidarity between participants and those that relate to the speaker's independence and relative status within the group. Based on the contrast between involvement and independence, she sets out three broad categories of relational work (2004, 114).

> *Face enhancing work* which aims to increase the involvement between participants, or their self image.

> *Face threatening work* which disrupts the co-operative communication or social order between participants.

> *Face saving work* which might mitigate the effects of an FTA.

All three types of relational work are crucial to the interactions on discussion forums, which shape the members' identities within the social hierarchies of the group.

The transactional and interpersonal purposes of Bodybuilding.com, like many other forums, present challenging territory against which to meet the demands of relational work. The forum is characterized as a center for shared interests, implying at least some measure of involvement and solidarity between its members and so requiring face-enhancing work. The homepage for Bodybuilding.com headlines the forums as a place to "interact with other fitness-minded people." From another perspective, forums are typically presented as venues to seek or offer information. Bodybuilding.com is no exception, and the homepage describes the site as a place to "learn from others who share your goals" where the forums can help members "get questions answered within minutes." Requesting and offering information or advice are inherently face-threatening kinds of relational work, for they imply a difference in the relative power between the person seeking and offering the information—a difference that might be further exacerbated by the relative positioning of a member as newbie or expert bodybuilder, member or moderator. The rest of this chapter examines the ways in which the competing needs of face-enhancing and face-threatening work place demands on the identities adopted by members of Bodybuilding.com, focusing in particular on the relational work accomplished through storytelling.

TELLERSHIP AND THE RELATIONAL WORK OF STORIES

As social practice, the interactive potential of stories in talk has attracted considerable attention as a way of conceptualizing narrative tellership away from a model of a single, active, narratorial figure toward a model of multiple tellers who co-construct the story that gets told (Ochs and Capps 2001; Norrick 2005; Georgakopoulou 2007). As Ochs and Capps point out, multiple tellership operates along a spectrum from low to high involvement. Low involvement might be realized in contexts where a single teller prevails, but shapes the narrative to the anticipated demands of their audience since "even the quietest of conversational partners can be active co-authors" (Ochs and Capps 2001, 24). From this perspective, even an isolated message posted to a forum will still be influenced by the member's sense of their intended audience: the other members of the forum. In conversational settings, the audience's role can increase by contributing questions and assessments that shape the ongoing story content. The same can be said in online forums, where requests for clarification can prompt further story episodes to be posted in subsequent messages.

Moving beyond the low involvement of the audience in tellership activities, we find that stories can be told in a sequence, where later stories or story episodes are told in response to an initial story. These parallel stories are not so closely intertwined that the tellers construct interlaced stories (Norrick 2005) or offer contributions to a coherent, overarching single story. Instead, the responses are what Sacks (1995) describes as Second Stories. Second Stories are stories or story episodes that follow a narrative that has been told either immediately before, or in close proximity to, the turns that have preceded it. Second Stories establish clear parallels with the first story, usually by matching the role taken by the tellers in the two cases. For example, if the first story concerned the teller's experience of witnessing a road traffic accident, the teller of the second story might tell a similar story where they too had witnessed a dangerous or difficult scenario. According to Sacks, the impulse of telling Second Stories is prompted by the desire to establish shared experience or common ground between the first and second tellers (1995, 771). The Second Story might then function as a way of showing that the second teller had paid attention to the first teller's utterance, and was confirming the first teller's actions as appropriate and relevant to the current discourse. Telling a Second Story thus seems to be fulfilling a face-enhancing function of generating involvement and social solidarity.

Further analysis of Second Stories has been found in offline storytelling of support groups (Arminen 2004) and in comparable online support groups (Harrison and Barlow 2009; Veen et al. 2010). These studies show that Second Stories fulfill an important range of relational work. Arminen's (2004) study of an Alcoholics Anonymous group suggests that for the most part, the Second Stories function in a face-enhancing manner similar to that proposed by Sacks, where the Second Stories recontextualize and reinforce the core values of the group. Harrison and Barlow (2009) examine an online peer support group for arthritis sufferers. In this context, the Second Stories often co-occurred with the speaker offering advice in response to a request from the OP. Once again, the Second Stories are face enhancing in that they project a shared experience between first and second teller, but the stories are also face saving in that they legitimize the advice given in the same message. Veen and his colleagues (2010) observed another online support community for those with ill health: in this case, Celiac disease. Like the Second Stories told in the arthritis workshop, these Second Stories had a face-saving character, in that the stories were used as an indirect means of offering advice, rather than giving direct instruction to the OP. However, Veen's study also established that Second Stories do not always support the stance taken by the OP, but rather carry out the face-threatening work to "correct a deviant case" (2010, 36). This suggests that Second Stories may not always carry out face-enhancing relational work but can serve other social purposes too.

The stories told in the Bodybuilding.com forums offer examples that compliment and extend the analysis of relational work achieved by the co-constructed nature of Second Stories. Although the focus of the forum is still on health matters and is constructed as an environment in which support is to be offered, the communities of bodybuilders using this site differ from the earlier studies in important ways. First, in the examples analyzed in this chapter, bodybuilding is a self-initiated, leisure-based occupation, not a matter of recovery from a disease that is imposed on the participants.[3] Second, although the forum characterizes itself as a supportive context, there are many elements of competitive behavior between the members (such as building reputation, displaying posed photographs, comparison of training schedules and outcomes of public competitions).[4] Finally, the gendered characteristics of bodybuilding as a predominantly masculine activity and, where femininity is constructed as a contradictory tension between athleticism and softness, brings gender aspects of identity as a relevant concern to the stories that get told. In the analysis that follows I will consider three contrasting sets of story sequences taken from different subforums within Bodybuilding.com. These stories demonstrate the range of relational work that Second Stories might achieve, including cases where the stories become the basis of face-threatening work such as criticism and disagreement.

Embeddedness and Story Sequences: Stories Told by Newcomers

Stories are told in many threads and for many purposes within Bodybuilding.com. However, when a new member first joins the forum, the identity work achieved through storytelling becomes particularly salient. In part, this is because of the member's novice status within the online group. As Vasquez (2007) points out, novices are by very definition in a state of transition. Stories told by newcomers then become a crucial means to negotiate the new member's relative inexperience while simultaneously enabling them to express enough experience to legitimate their membership and later acceptance within the group. Although the stories told by newbies can occur in any part of Bodybuilding.com, some threads are designated as contexts where newcomers should first make themselves known, or in Benwell and Stokoe's terms, "de-lurk" or "come out" (2006, 268). One such thread occurred in the Over 35 folder, titled "Are you New Here?" The thread was started on 10 February 2006 by a long-serving, male member of the Bodybuilding.com community. At the time of writing, the thread consisted of 1,967 messages and was still active, posted prominently in the Over 35 folder.[5] The seed message sets out the context for the thread, and for the forum more generally. It begins with a clear greeting, "Welcome to the Over 35 Forum!" and is addressed to newcomers, "If you're new to Bodybuilding.com." The seed message goes on to describe the range of bodybuilders who contribute, but unifies the group as having "one thing in common: an interest in working out with weights."

The seed message is followed by a series of short posts from fellow forum members who praise the OP for their contribution and repeat the welcome to new members. Twelve posts further into the thread, a newbie contributes with what will become the first in a series of hundreds of stories told by newcomers beginning to participate in the forum. These stories fulfill an important socialization function, providing a template that scaffolds the member's introduction to the group. Much like an orientation element in narratives of personal experience, these stories provide background context setting out identity attributes such as the member's physical measurements, where they come from and what their interests are. Typically, the stories include the following elements:

Self description: descriptive details such as the member's age, weight and height, nationality, or occupation.

I'm a 39y/o caucasian male from South Africa, Johannesburg.

I'm 42 years old and 5' 8" 280 I was 340 pounds and have lost 60 pounds so far.

I'm 36, full time nursing student, and look forward to joining the US Navy's Nursing Corps.

Experience of exercise: how long the member has been active in bodybuilding, what levels of fitness the member has exhibited in the past and at present.

Used to be very fit but played far too much rugby and didn't know when to stop, wrecked my body, now just trying to keep it working.

I began like 10 days ago, working 4 days a week at home. I'm using low weights in the beginning and i'll increase 2 kilos per week.

Relationship to the forum: how long the member has been part of the forum before posting.

I have been reading the forum for awhile and just joined.

I've been reading BB's forums for a while now and finally signed up.

Goals for the future: what the member seeks from the forum, or hopes to change about their fitness.

My goal is to compete by the time I'm 40. My wife and trainer tell me it will happen . . . but I'm suspecting it's all just talk.

I turn 38 next month and hope to surprise everyone when I get home. Hope you won't mind me asking questions and seeking guidance along the way.

These statements of identity are the means by which new members provide evidence that they share similar interests and attributes with others in the group. In the case of the Over 35 forum, age is a defining characteristic that sets the subforum apart from other areas of the site, thus prompting the members to declare their age when identifying his or herself. Likewise, the members narrate their past and current fitness activities as a means of showing themselves to be fellow Topic Enthusiasts, albeit with varying levels of expertise. Both elements project the member's status as eligible to join the group and reinforce the grounds used to assert commonality with others. Not all four elements appear in every newbie's story, and some members provide much more detail about their past experiences than others do. However, in most cases, the members combine these different story elements in a complementary fashion to meet the needs for face-enhancing relational work of becoming a member of the forum.

When a newbie "comes out," here as in other contexts, it is also common practice for them to express their novice status. They may also imply deference toward established, expert members of the group. This strategy reinforces the hierarchical position between novice and expert, by using the polarity implied by Leech's (1983, 132) Approbation and Modesty Maxims: to Minimize praise of self and Maximize praise of other. Lack of experience might be implied by the stories the members tell as Topic Enthusiasts, as does the following participant who self-deprecatingly refers to himself as a "couch potato," "junk-food junkie" with a "stagnant" routine:

I have been a couch potato most of my life. I joined a gym back in my mid-twenties just for the fun of it and for some reason . . . it *clicked*.

I have been working out regularly since then. I am now 36 but for the past few years I have let my routine stagnant. I will also concede I am a junk-food junkie . . . I have never learned how to cook and quite honestly, I am afraid of being in the kitchen. This may sound funny but that's the truth.

Even when new members have more successful stories of their fitness endeavors, their relative inexperience as List Members is used to mitigate any potential threat of self-aggrandizement (avoiding "praise of self") and to enhance the face of other group members as sources of information or expertise (maximizing "praise of others").

Just found this place today and came in to ask a question

Looking forward to learning from the best! I'll try to post more and not lurk so much . . . *this* forum seems promising

I'm really new to this—first forum ever—not even sure what to do but here goes

I hope you guys can help me out too cause i'm the real bodybuilding noob . . . lol.

Given that there are strong similarities in the content of the newbie stories of introduction, and that these parallels rest on the narrators matching their stories on the basis of an assumed similarity in the role they adopt (i.e., they are all newcomers to the forum), we might anticipate that the stories in the "Are you New Here?" thread count as Second Stories. However, there are significant differences between the newbie stories in this thread and Second Stories as described by Sacks.

Sacks' description implies that there are three elements that characterize a paired relationship between a first and second story:

1. Adjacency in a sequence of turns, where a Second Story follows a first
2. Parallels in story content, specifically where the second speaker will adopt a similar role in the narrative to that taken by the first speaker
3. Pragmatic interrelationship between the stories, where the second is used as an analysis of the first.

The newbie stories in the "Are you New Here?" thread conform to the first two parameters: they appear as a textual sequence and there are clear parallels in the story content. But most of the stories do not make reference to any of the introductory stories that have gone before. Sacks' description of Second Stories implies that they are intertextually embedded in their discourse context: that is, that they must be understood in relation to the preceding story. The newbie stories of introduction are not embedded in the discourse context in this way. Although the newbie stories are second parts of an *adjacency pair* (they respond to the seed message welcoming them to the forum), they are not second parts to the other preceding introductory stories. Thus the latter introductory stories do not contain pragmatic signals of alignment or addressivity that might refer the audience back to a story told by another member. Nor do the introductory stories seem to prompt dyadic responses from other members of the forum. Rather, most of the newbie stories stand as self-contained units in the thread, which can be fully understood without reference to any of the other speakers' stories. In other words, the newbie stories of introduction are too detached intertextually from the other narratives in the discourse sequence to count as Second Stories.

This suggests that the characteristics of a Second Story as identified by Sacks exist within a hierarchy where pragmatic interrelationship between stories is a core property and textual adjacency is only a preferred condition. The examples from the "Are you New Here?" thread demonstrate that adjacency alone is not enough to warrant analyzing all sequentially ordered stories as First and Second Stories, for it is quite possible that textually adjacent stories might not be parallel in content. Conversely, parallel stories need not be placed immediately next to each other, especially in asynchronous, multiparty discourse such as that typically found on forums. Instead, it is the conversational embeddedness created by interpersonal alignment that is the most significant element that characterizes Second Stories. This is true not just for the stories that are found in the Bodybuilding.com forums, but for our understanding of Second Stories in other contexts too.

The embeddedness created through interpersonal alignment is significant because it influences the narrative dimension of tellership. Signals of interpersonal alignment, such as quotation, comparing events in the first story directly with those in the second, and referring back to a previous member's contribution all mean that in some measure, the Second Story is not being told (and should not be interpreted) as an isolated unit. Instead, the Second Story is intertextually and pragmatically dependent on narrative material that has been created by a teller other than its own narrator. It is this interpersonal orientation that destabilizes the single tellership of a Second Story and in the work of Sacks (1995) was the basis for establishing common ground between tellers. The co-tellership thus achieves face-enhancing work that benefits the relationship between individual tellers and the wider group by promoting a context of shared experience and support. However, the connections that a Second Story might make with its predecessor need not always emphasize similarity or support. This means that we can extend Sacks' description of Second Stories to include those that are used to carry out face-threatening relational work of criticizing or disagreeing with the first teller. Let us turn now to another story told by a newbie on Bodybuilding.com and examine the range of Second Stories that were produced in the thread that followed.

RELATIONAL WORK AND SECOND STORIES: "GUYS STARING AT THE GYM"

New members of a forum do not just tell stories of introduction. They also tell stories as a basis for seeking advice from others. An example of this occurred in a thread titled, "Guys Staring at the Gym." The thread was posted in the General Chat area of the Female Bodybuilders' subforum. It was started by a female member on October 4, 2010 and was active for the following twelve days, gaining 258 responses to the seed message. In the seed message, the OP tells a story of a problematic experience she encountered at the gym, and asks members of the female subforum for their advice. In the posts that followed, 189 contained a Second Story, half of which were posted by women and half by men. A third of the responses supported the OP and gave advice on how the problem might be resolved. However, many of the responses contained stories where the later tellers distanced themselves from the OP, and criticized or insulted her while still ostensibly offering advice. The thread drifted off topic, degenerated into flaming, and was eventually closed by the OP. Narrative plays a crucial role in the relational work that takes place in this thread, beginning with the story told by the OP in the seed message.

SEEKING ADVICE: NARRATING A PROBLEM

The seed message that initiates "Guys Staring at the Gym" shares some similarities with the stories of introduction found in the "Are you New Here?" thread. The OP begins by describing herself as a newcomer to the forum, and establishing her credentials as someone who pursues fitness activities.

> Okay, this is my first post on here, I have definitely been lurking for a while.
> I have a set nutrition plan and workout routine that has been reviewed by a personal trainer who also competes. So, I know what direction I'm going in, etc.

Immediately afterward, she sets out a multifaceted problem: she is the only woman who uses the weights section of the gym and that she does not like or understand the behavior of men in the weights section who look at her.

> Here's the thing, it feels like NONE of the women at my gym do ANY-THING but CARDIO!!!! The cardio machines are constantly full and

I am the ONLY chick even going NEAR the weights . . . Which is fine for them I guess, However the guys just stare at me, talk amongst themselves, it drives me NUTS.

The OP goes on to narrate a specific episode that exemplifies the problem.

I went to the gym tonight, walked in and saw there wasn't ONE girl in the whole gym . . . I LEFT. . . . that's right, didn't even complete a workout. I feel like crap about this, but honestly, its really awkward.

She closes the post by requesting advice from other members of the forum.

Have any of you ladies encountered this problem and what do you do about it??

The narrative performs significant identity work for the OP. First, it emphasizes and displays her novice status, by stating "this is my first post on here" and placing her in a self-deprecating position in comparison to the expert bodybuilders as an advice seeker. More specifically, her interpretation of "staring" as problematic suggests here her status as a novice bodybuilder as she misunderstands the nature of the gaze within bodybuilding practices. In bodybuilding practice, spectatorship is a significant practice whereby the bodybuilder might display their identity through posture, muscularity, and so on. Looking is also embedded in training regimes through "spotting" for a partner to improve their technique. In this environment, spectatorship does not always carry the sexualized meanings that the OP assumes, and which gives rise to her insecurity and advice seeking. Second, if her goal is to complete her fitness training, then she is inhibited by the men staring, absence of other women weight lifters and her own lack of expertise. This narrative schema places her in opposition to the two groups she might be affiliated with: other women and other weightlifters. In terms of a social identity, her group membership is not yet established and is vulnerable to threat from others.

Giving Advice and Telling Stories

The OP's seed message is constructed as the first part of two adjacency pairs (a question and a request for advice), and therefore generates the expectation of a response, all the more so because her narrative only poses a problem and does not provide a solution (Hoey 2001). However, the manner in which the anticipated response might be given can accomplish very different kinds of relational work. In Western cultures, advice giving is often understood as a face-threatening activity, for it creates a difference between the status of the lesser knowledge of the advice seeker and the greater knowledge of the advice giver. As advice is intended to influence the future actions of the addressee, it also threatens their independence. Because of its face-threatening potential, research on advice giving has pointed out that one option is for speakers to use mitigating strategies (Locher 2006; Harrison and Barlow 2009). Mitigation might be realized through syntactic choices (*declarative* rather than *imperative* constructions), use of face-mitigating forms (hedges, modality, *conditionals*) or the inclusion of involvement strategies (humor, praise, empathy).

One involvement strategy is to accompany the advice with a short narrative (Morrow 2006; Harrison and Barlow 2009). Typically, these are personal narratives that establish a warrant for the respondent to give advice (Galegher et al. 1998). In contrast to citing external sources as a means of authorizing advice, personal narratives are inherently subjective but increase the likelihood that their audience will be able to identify with the experience being narrated: they have the face-enhancing potential to establish common ground. However, existing work suggests that these personal narratives are rarely just expressions of empathy but also function as indirect advice, and therefore can also be regarded as face mitigating in nature. By offering a solution to the OP's problem, the respondent becomes a co-teller in the overarching plot of advice seeking and giving. The OP poses the problem and exemplifies this with a narrative of her own experience, while the respondent provides a solution to the problem, exemplifying this with a parallel narrative of their own. As this description implies, the kinds of parallel stories used for this purpose are fittingly described by Sacks' model of the Second Story.

FACE-ENHANCING SECOND STORIES

The first responses that immediately followed the OP's seed message in the thread "Guys Staring at the Gym" are explained neatly as face-enhancing and face-mitigating work that shows involvement between the members through the use of Second Stories. Typically, these initial responses began with a signal of empathy or alignment with the OP:

> i know how you feel.
>
> I know what you mean.
>
> I was also feeling a bit self-conscious at first
>
> This exactly
>
> I know exactly what you're talking about.

The respondents who aligned themselves with the OP typically went on to offer advice, often accompanied by a Second Story. The Second Stories in this part of the thread are classic examples of personal experience stories where the respondent matches their role with that of the OP, for example, as a bodybuilder who was once new to a gym. The following example, reproduced in full from the thread, illustrates the interpersonal alignment characteristic of Second Stories.

> Agree with above post^
>
> It was a little awkward for me too when I first started. I'm only one of a few ladies who uses the free weights, usually it's just me. I'm so focused on my workout I don't even notice the guys any more! Earphones and music and I'm in my own zone.
>
> Eventually, when they see you're committed and working hard, they'll come to respect you! Hell, my form is better than most of them anyways!
>
> Take a deep breathe and concentrate on what you're doing . . . not on whats happening around you. You've as much right to be there as them! Good luck. . . .

In contrast to the detached stories found in the "Are you New Here?" thread, the Second Stories are embedded in their conversational context through face-enhancing indications of alignment that might foster solidarity. Linguistically, the interpersonal involvement is realized through the use of reference to earlier posts ("Agree with the above post"), formulae for well-wishing ("Good luck"), and comparative statements ("it was a little awkward for me too"). Crucially, the stories do not just narrate parallel situations to that given in the seed message, but also provide additional contexts from which to interpret the OP's problem and provide her with suggested solutions. The respondent casts herself in a parallel role to the OP, by recalling a point when she was also new to the gym, and identifies herself as the only woman working out with weights. The respondent's own experiences are used as the basis to project a positive outcome for the OP's problem ("they'll come to respect you") and to offer advice. The Second Stories construct the OP's experience as an anxious newcomer as normal. This affirmation alleviates her outsider status and places her experience as one that has been shared by other experts in the weightlifting community, summed up in the respondent's declaration, "you've as much right to be there as them!"

FACE-THREATENING SECOND STORIES

Most research on Second Stories has examined contexts in which the purpose of the group has been supportive and the projection of shared experience between members has fostered solidarity. As we have seen, the Bodybuilding.com forums demonstrate similarly supportive characteristics in some measure. But not all responses to the OP's seed message that offered advice were conciliatory in nature. Other respondents chose to dissociate from the OP's stance. The act of dissociation or denying common ground has been interpreted as a form of impoliteness (Culpeper et al. 2003; Bousfield and Locher 2008). Indeed, dissociation would seem to be the converse social behavior to the positive politeness described by Locher (2004, 2006) as face-enhancing involvement, for dissociation threatens a member's status within a group, or what Spencer-Oatey (2002) describes as their social identity. Specifically, it threatens the aspects of relational work covered by "association rights" (Spencer-Oatey 2002, 10), that is, the extent to which we share interests or feelings with another.

Given that dissociation usually implies a difference between the speakers involved, it is remarkable that in the context of "Guys Staring at the Gym," the dissociating respondents still demonstrated the impulse to tell Second Stories. I class these dissociating narratives as a specific subtype of Second Stories, because they remain pragmatically and intertextually embedded in relation to the story in the OP's seed message and provide an analysis of it (albeit somewhat different in stance from the supportive Second Stories). However, they contrast with supportive Second Stories identified by Sacks because the respondent no longer enforces a similarity between their role in the Second Story and that taken by the teller in the first.

The face-threatening Second Stories are similar to the face-enhancing Second Stories in that both are used as a basis to establish the member's authority to offer advice. Whether you agree or disagree with a previous speaker, it is still necessary to provide evidence to support your opinion. But because the dissociating respondent is no longer adopting the same role as the first teller, the ways in which the initial and subsequent stories fit together alters. Instead of matching the OP's role, the tellers of face-threatening Second Stories in this data sample employed four strategies in order to connect their responses to the seed story:

1. Assume the same role as the first teller, but set out a contrasting stance.
2. Adopt an opposing role from that of the teller in the first narrative.
3. Refer to a generalized scenario.
4. Cite a parallel story where an external figure matches the first teller's role.

Each strategy is illustrated with examples from the forum thread.

1   Assume the Same Role, but Set Out a Contrasting Stance

In some cases, the respondents assumed the same role as the teller in the seed story but distanced themselves from the actions and evaluations made by the first teller.

> I was a newbie once too and still am I guess but when I went to the gym I didn't give a rats ass if anyone was looking at me. And now I

just set up my own home gym because I just want to train and not go somewhere for a social experience.

In this example, the respondent begins by aligning with the newcomer role adopted by the OP ("I was a newbie once too"). Unlike the supportive comparisons of shared experience, the respondent uses the adversative conjunction "but" to signal that her attitude is different. The dissociation is emphasized by the respondent's use of impoliteness. Although the use of taboo language is in keeping with the wider discourse norms of the Bodybuilding.com forums, the unmodified expletive "rat's ass" enforces the critical tone that this female respondent takes to the OP's stated anxiety. Not only does the respondent avoid creating common ground of shared experience; she explicitly contrasts her actions with that of the OP ("I just want to train and not go somewhere for a social experience"). In so doing, the respondent positions herself as a serious weightlifter and implicitly criticizes the apparently trivial, social concerns of the OP's inhibitions as a newcomer.

2   Adopt an Opposing Role

Sacks' description of Second Stories places great significance on the matched roles between first and second tellers, proposing a social prohibition on telling a story in which the respondent chooses a role of an opponent from the first tale: "You don't tell [a story] in which the hearer could expectably be the opposite number" (1995, 770). Of course, it is possible for a respondent to contravene Sacks' instructions and tell a story in which they take a role that might be quite different, if not opposite to that of the first teller. In the case of "Guys Staring at the Gym," the opposite role to the OP is that of the male weightlifters who look at her. Despite being posted in the Female Bodybuilding subforum, over half the members who responded to the seed message were men. Unsurprisingly, not all of them identified with the OP. Instead, they posted stories in which they matched their personal experience with the male bodybuilders that the OP describes. Here is one example:

I go to multiple gyms where both men and women workout in the same spots, both cardio and weights and honestly this whole subject is never an issue. It seems an underlying understanding that we're all there to workout regardless of who we are and there's not really an issue. As for myself, yeah, I see 'pretty' girls at the gym all the time, but so what? I'm at a gym and not a night club. [. . .] Finally, going to workout looking 'hawt' or wearing attention grabbing outfits and **expecting** guys not to look is like taking a shower and complaining you got wet. (emphasis in the original)

This post demonstrates the disruptive potential of not matching the roles between first and second teller. If constructing a matched role between members implies understanding of the first teller's situation and affirmation of their status as normative, the failure to match seems to achieve the opposite effect: the first teller could be misunderstood and their non-normativity reinforced. As with other dissociating second stories, this example uses many forms that could be considered impolite. The respondent begins by denying common ground between their situation and that described in the seed story ("this whole subject is never an issue"), emphasizing this stance by repeating it a more concessionary manner two lines later: "there's not really an issue." The "problem" of "Guys Staring" is dismissed by the respondent's experience as someone who looks at women but considers this irrelevant to the gym context ("but so what?"), demonstrating a lack of sympathy for the first teller's concerns. Finally, responsibility for the OP's problem is shifted away from men's behavior and reattributed to the dress code adopted by women, implicitly criticizing the OP's behavior without evidence and abrogating the speaker's potential responsibility for wrongdoing.

3 Refer to a Generalized Narrative

Appealing to a narrative of generalized experience is another strategy that respondents use to distance themselves from the OP's seed story.

> I am SICK and TIRED of these women posting in here to bitch about being stared at in the gym. If you don't like it THEN DON'T GO!!!! Gyms are public places, people are going to be looking at you! And just because a guy looks at you *omg* or talks to you *gasp* doesn't mean he is hitting on you or wants to pursue you!

In the example given here, the respondent dissociates from the OP and all other women who post about "being stared at" by complaining that they are "SICK and TIRED" of such stories, using recognized impoliteness such as shouting (shown by block capitals) which exaggerates the dissociation (Culpeper et al. 2003) along with sarcasm which dismisses the anxiety of the OP (over-exaggerated shock as in "*omg*" and "*gasp*"). The generic statements, such as "Gyms are public places" and generalized figures of "people" and "a guy" construct a universalized experience that does not allow space for the concerns of the OP. This is an extreme form of dissociation. Generalizing experience denies the common ground between individual members (the first teller and respondent's perspectives) and also extends the denial of commonality between the first teller and all other members of the fitness community. In sharp contrast to the face-enhancing Second Stories that constructed the first teller's experience as normal, offered a resolution and inclusion within the bodybuilding community, appealing to a generalized experience excludes the OP, suggesting that "If you don't like it, then don't go."

4   Citing the Story of an Exemplary Figure

If a respondent does not have access to a Second Story based on their own experience, a further alternative is to cite a parallel story experienced by a third party: an exemplary figure. The choice of exemplary figure is crucial in determining the sequenced stories as interpersonally aligned or distanced, but in either case, referring to a well-known figure acts as an external source of authority to reinforce the second teller's stance. In the case of the Bodybuilding.com thread, the exemplary figures are professional body-builders who have achieved high profile celebrity careers (such as Arnold Schwarzenegger and Jamie Eason). Retelling the success stories of such figures reinforces the values of the bodybuilding community by appealing to shared knowledge. Specifically, the hierarchy of expertise based on physical achievement and training is exaggerated by using "super" experts as a point of comparison with lay members of the bodybuilding community. The following example is taken from another post where the respondent criticizes the OP's behavior.

> An ego never hurt anyone. If we didn't have some type of ego we probably wouldn't get very far in the bodybuilding world. Arnold had the biggest of ego of anyone and look how far he got in his career and life.

In the example given here, the respondent defends assertive bodybuild-ing attitudes as the need for "an ego," which is generically constructed as unproblematic ("never hurt anybody") and necessary for bodybuilding success. The aggrandizement of the exemplary figure's success thus con-trasts with the self-deprecation displayed in the OP's seed story, which is implicitly criticized as an inadequate bodybuilding attribute. Once again, the dissociating Second Story is face-threatening and positions the newbie's identity as peripheral, if not outside the wider bodybuilding community.

SECOND STORIES: INTERACTION AND IDENTITY

The Second Stories in the "Guys Staring at the Gym" thread offer members of the forum the opportunity to position themselves as more or less aligned with the attitude and actions exemplified by the OP in her seed narrative. The examples suggest that there is a general distinction between Second Stories that use shared experience to foster the face-enhancing work of building solidarity between first and second tellers and face-threatening Second Stories that deny common ground and inhibit the social cohesion between members of the group. Current work on (im)politeness suggests that relational work does not exist in isolated linguistic units (i.e., just within the story alone), but is embedded across and within interactional exchanges. Similarly, the relational work of Second Stories is an interactive accomplishment that has repercussions that are realized by turn-taking sequences that extend beyond the initial story pair. The later developments in "Guys Staring at the Gym" suggest that the face-enhancing and face-threatening nature of the Second Story can lead to rather different kinds of interactional sequences with contrasting narrative outcomes.

Face-Enhancing Sequences: Completing the Plot

The face-enhancing Second Stories are integrated within a longer, co-constructed narrative trajectory that moves toward a point of narrative resolution. The problematic situation (told by the OP) prompts the need for advice (given by the respondents) where the proposed solution is carried out, and then reported back by the first teller (the OP). Of course, not all recipients produce follow up turns that indicate whether the advice was taken or not (Morrow 2006; Harrison and Barlow 2009). But the later messages from the OP in the "Guys Staring" thread have the potential to complete the narrative sequence in a way that supports the face-enhancing work of involving the members in co-constructing the completion of a goal-achievement pattern (Hoey 2001). In line with this, the OP's later messages include an update that indicates she intends to follow the advice given in the face-enhancing Second Stories.

> Today was the first day i attempted to go at Night and there was TONS of people there. I think the best thing for me at this point is to just go in the early AM when it is more dead. And maybe you guys are right, it may be easiest for me to just ask someone how to do something.

Although this later narrative episode does not report a *definitive* resolution to the original tri-partite problem (men staring, no other women doing weights, feeling inhibited as a newcomer), the OP acknowledges and affirms the expert opinion of the respondent members, saying "maybe you guys are right" and projecting the advice as a course of action which could be taken. The co-tellership of the face-enhancing second stories works to promote solidarity between the OP and later narrators by stressing their shared interests and experience. This constructs an idealized social identity where the tellers associate with each other in a homogenized group of body-builders. The successful co-construction of advice giving and taking promotes the association rights of the group (Spencer-Oatey 2002) where the OP's expectation of appropriate interaction (receiving advice) and affective connection (shared support and interests) is met, enabling the newbie to negotiate membership of the bodybuilding community.

Face-Threatening Sequences: Disrupting the Plot

Second Stories that display dissociation between first and second teller are a trigger for further face-threatening behavior that disrupts the narrative interaction. Rather than supporting a narrative trajectory that moves toward a resolution, the face-threatening stories generate a series of interpersonal conflicts between the members of the group. The macro-level narrative structures of advice seeking, giving, and taking cannot be completed in this case. Instead, escalation of dissociation caused by face-threatening Second Stories halted the narrative sequence before it could reach its final point of resolution.

The responses to dissociating Second Stories indicate that both the OP and other members of the forum recognize the rejection of shared experience as a form of impoliteness. The OP responded, by saying,

> its really ****ty that you can't even attempt to put yourselves in my shoes. you are so off base in your judgments that you can't even attempt to care about others feelings.

Her opinion was echoed by other members of the forum:

> The op is not alone in her experience and I think that is more important to address rather than to keep harping on anything else. I think her questions/concerns have been addressed and to keep harping on negative issues is cruel and uncalled for.

As Culpeper et al. (2003) argue, a recipient of impoliteness can choose whether or not to respond to a face-aggravating act. If a response is made, then the hearer can either accept responsibility or counter the attack. In Culpeper's system, counterattacks are of two kinds: Offensive, where one face threatening act is answered by another, or Defensive, where the face threatening act is deflected by subsequent denial of some kind (2003, 1563). In "Guys Staring at the Gym," the OP and other members of the forum respond to the dissociating Second Stories with both strategies. Some members attempted to reduce the aggressiveness of the dialogue through defensive responses. For example, this member ended a long message in defense of the OP by addressing the forum in general,

> The OP has just actually expressed her apprehension in a public forum, don't get all superior and pretend you lot never felt it or were instantly welcomed with open arms by every gym member.

However, other responses escalated the conflict with counterattacks of criticism and insult. For example, the OP replied to one dissociated Second Story with the following message:

> I can tell you don't give a **** what anyone else thinks, we all get it, but the clear fact is you're a pretty mean girl and your comments aren't helpful OR needed.
>   [. . .]

> Also while we are giving advice. . . . I think that's great that you
> have chosen to isolate yourself in a home gym, its probably best you
> stay at home since you obviously have problems relating to others.

The OP's response employs multiple impoliteness strategies, including
insults ("you're a pretty mean girl") and sarcasm ("great that you have
chosen to isolate yourself in a home gym"), all of which increase the social
distance between the members concerned. Perhaps unsurprisingly, the teller
of the Second Story in question responded with a further Offensive turn
containing criticism and sarcasm directed at the OP, ultimately refusing to
take part in the discussion.

> I'm not going to waste my time trying to help you. [. . .] Period. Done.
> End of conversation.

The dissociation initiated by the face-threatening Second Stories escalated
so that affective association (the extent to which we share feelings with
others) and the interactional association (our appropriate expectation of
conversational interaction) between participants broke down completely,
summed up in the line "End of conversation."

The disruption of interactional and affective association is interwoven
in this thread and works to define the social identity of the group by dif-
ferentiating between the expert members and outsiders, like the newbie.
The OP's expectations of the forum appear in keeping with the generic
context of the Bodybuilding.com web pages, which offered the opportunity
for members to "interact with other fitness-minded people." However, her
expectations of interaction and affective association also seem to be shaped
by gender-specific schema that equated femininity with support and empathy. She wrote,

> I can tell you that I thought this was a FEMALE forum where I could
> maybe get a sympathetic ear and some VALID suggestions about how
> to deal and just push through these workouts until I am a little more
> confident in my form, etc. But what I got was a headache.

These expectations were at odds with the dissociating Second Stories that
were interpreted as impolite, and the opposite to a "sympathetic" display of
support. The explanation that other forum members offered for the break-
down of affective and interactional association was based on an assumption of gender difference: men would not have the same experience as new
female bodybuilders, and therefore were incapable of offering support. For
example, one female forum member responded by saying,

> What does a 25-year-old white male at 511" tall and normal build
> know about being intimidated as in this instance?

However, using gender as an explanation for the ability to share experience with the OP is clearly an over-generalized assumption, for there were men who told face-enhancing Second Stories that aligned with the OP's seed narrative and women who told face-threatening Second Stories of dissociation. Clearly, there is no single factor that might explain the propensity for disagreement in this particular forum thread. Instead, I suggest that the expert members' dissociation from the OP serves to underline her position as an outsider from the group, not in essentialist terms as a woman (indeed, half the respondents who told face-threatening Second Stories chose to represent as women), but as a novice who has misinterpreted the norms for serious bodybuilding practice. In particular, the tellers of dissociating Second Stories took issue with the newbie's expectations of sociality and her interpretation of looking as an intimidating and solely sexualized practice.

SUMMARY

The analysis of the stories told in discussion forum threads has important implications for the narrative dimension of tellership. In particular, close scrutiny of the stories has been used to reconsider the narrative co-construction described by Sacks (1995) as Second Stories. Like Second Stories told in offline contexts, the co-construction of Second Stories in discussion forums takes place when multiple tellers narrate stories contained in separate but sequenced turns. However, in multiparty, asynchronous social media interactions like those found in a discussion forum, the sequencing of the narratives can be disrupted so that textual adjacency is no longer maintained in all cases. The potential for narrative interaction to be non-adjacent is a critical factor in reconsidering the character of Second Stories, for the narrative dimension of tellership is inextricably linked with the narrative dimension of embeddedness.

In the case of the stories told in discussion forums, embeddedness relates to how far a story told in a particular post can be interpreted as a self-contained unit or is pragmatically and intertextually interdependent on a story told in a previous post. When a story is highly embedded in its discourse context through intertextual and pragmatic referencing, it can no longer be interpreted as told by a single teller: it is constructed by material authored by more than one person. The importance of intertextual and pragmatic interdependence in establishing multiple tellership refines the criteria used to identify Second Stories, not just in this data sample but also for sequences of stories more widely. Adjacency in a sequence of turns is relegated to a preferred but nonobligatory condition for Second Stories, while pragmatic interrelationship is of paramount importance.

In addition, the kinds of pragmatic interrelationship between stories need not always emphasize face-enhancing solidarity between the multiple narrators. Instead, Second Stories can also be used to create face-threatening dissociation between one narrator and another. The co-tellership of face-enhancing and face-threatening Second Stories extends beyond the dyadic pairings documented in earlier studies of Second Stories to longer, interactional sequences that accomplish different kinds of identity work for the tellers involved. Face-enhancing Second Stories are used to generate macro-level goal-achievement patterns of advice seeking, giving, and taking, which support the sociality rights of the tellers and promote an idealized social identity of the group. In contrast, face-threatening Second Stories disrupt and do not complete the goal-achievement patterns of advice seeking and taking. The dissociation between tellers erodes the affective rights of the participants and is used to assert boundaries that exclude outsiders from membership of an established group. In the stories discussed in this chapter, the social identities negotiated by the Second Stories include membership of the bodybuilding community as an expert or a novice, woman or man. The meanings associated with gender are particular shaped by the practices and values created within these communities. In the following chapter, gender remains an important focus in the stories told by a very different set of speakers. These are narrators who have been diagnosed and treated for critical illness: cancer.

3 Narratives of Illness and Personal Blogs

ILLNESS, NARRATIVE, AND IDENTITY

In recent years, research in sociology and sociolinguistics has recognized the importance for patients of creating a narrative in response to their experience of the trauma caused by critical illness. Narrative's potential for constructing patterns of coherence through linearity and causality offers a privileged mode for carrying out identity work by selecting and ordering experience in a way that presents the narrating self as similarly ordered and coherent (Bamberg, Schiffrin, and de Fina 2007). The role of narrative as a sense-making resource is felt keenly when illness ruptures the speaker's illusion of continuity in life experience, for example, through the impact of illness on a narrator's body, the ability to perform particular social roles (especially within the family or the workplace), or more general identification as a "healthy" person. The apparent coherence offered by narrative schemata is often viewed as a therapeutic means of healing the discontinuity between the person's sense of his- or herself and the disrupted life experiences (Cheshire and Ziebland 2005) and has been shown to benefit the narrator's physical and mental well-being (Pennebaker 2000). However, the means by which narrative coherence is expressed can vary considerably and has focused primarily on stories told in offline contexts.

The tension between coherence and chaos underpins Frank's (1994, 1995) influential distinction between the voices of illness narratives. Frank contrasts the unified coherence of the restitution narrative (where health is restored) with the fragmentation of chaotic stories (where untellable pain is manifest as narrative silence) and quest narratives (where the narrator works through the processes of change brought about by illness). Robinson (1990) similarly presents a model of progressive, stability, and regressive narratives in order to contrast the ways that narrators attribute value to their experiences with reference to a teleological framework of coherence. This emphasis on coherence is perhaps a product of the corpus of illness narratives from which these models emerged. Much work on illness narratives has taken data from life stories elicited in narrative interviews (Cheshire and Ziebland 2005; Hyden and Brockmeier 2008) or from published autobiography (Rimmon-Kenan 2002; Bingley et al. 2006), including mainstream media (Dubrinwy 2009). These text types tend to privilege retrospective accounts of illness. The demands of the publishing industry, like the mainstream media, emphasize coherent narratives with a positive outcome, hence favoring restitution and progressive narratives (Rimmon-Kenan 2002). As C. Ryan (2004) and Dubrinwy (2009) point out, this leaves little space for the expression of pain and dissent, and for the fragmentation associated with chaotic illness narratives.

CMC AND E-HEALTH

At the same time, developments in e-health and the increased visibility of certain illnesses (such as breast cancer and prostate cancer) have led people to turn to the Internet as a source of information, support, and self-expression. The benefits gained through participating in health support groups (Lepore et al. 2003) and through expressive writing (Stanton et al. 2002) have also been found in Internet-based support groups managed through discussion boards or e-mail lists. Particular interest has focused on cancer support groups and their online equivalents. This has included the study of single cancers, such as breast cancer (Orgad 2005, 2006; Balka et al. 2010; Wen et al. 2011) and comparisons of different groups, such as those diagnosed with breast cancer and prostate cancer (Klemm et al. 1999; Owen et al. 2004; Charteris-Black et al. 2006). Over the last decade, the comparative analysis of online talk about prostate and breast cancer in early forms of CMC have documented consistent and striking patterns of discourse. Put baldly, these findings characterize women's behavior in online breast cancer support groups as showing more frequent interactions with the forum, emphasizing emotional expression, and using the forums to seek and provide social support with others in a similar situation. In comparison, men's behavior in online prostate cancer support groups focuses on finding and discussing information about treatments and is less likely to contain examples of personal disclosure.

The gendered patterns of discourse behavior in online groups have been interpreted in relation to studies of offline cancer support groups, where breast cancer groups are better established and where participation in prostate groups is generally lower (Gray et al. 2000). In particular, men's reticence to participate and self-disclose personal information is seen to be influenced by gendered stereotypes of masculine behavior, such as being stoic, strong, and silent (Kiss and Meryn 2001), scripts that do not sit easily with strategies of emotional expression expected to bring benefits to health and well-being (Burns and Mahalik 2008). However, these trends are not to be interpreted as reinforcing universalized and binary stereotypes between emotionally expressive women and emotionally inexpressive men. Instead, the men's emphasis on information is associated with the specific issues and stigma related to prostate cancer and the greater complexity and uncertainty surrounding treatment options (Owen et al. 2004), and the different coping strategies used to manage anxiety (Gray et al. 2000). These studies clearly state the limitations of their data on the ways in which gendered behavior might be enacted, for example, constrained by a national bias toward North American participants (Orgad 2006), and that might vary according to sexuality (Wen et al. 2011), class (Seale and Charteris-Black 2008), and ethnicity (Rivera Ramos and Buki 2011).

The studies of e-health practices have only focused on early forms of CMC. The development of social media, and in particular blogs, offer an opportunity to review how illness narratives might be reworked in online contexts. Blogs (also known as web logs) are web pages in which dated entries appear in reverse chronological order, so that the reader views the most recently written entries first. Blogs emerged as a web genre in the late 1990s, and since then blogging activity has increased exponentially. It is perhaps unsurprising that the term "blog" masks considerable variation, for blogs may be written about diverse subjects and for many different purposes. Herring, Scheidt, Bonus, and Wright (2004) put forward the most important categorization, resulting in a three-way division of Filter, Knowledge-Logs, and Personal Journals. Herring and colleagues note that by far the most common (but frequently overlooked) subcategory is that of personal journals (2004, 6). In turn, personal blogs are best characterized as a highly varied and hybrid genre, influenced by online forms of communication such as e-mail and personal web pages, along with offline genres, particularly diary writing and autobiography.

The hybrid nature of personal blogs makes them an interesting environment in which to trace the evolution of illness narratives. Blogs enable the three communicative practices that emerged from the survey of online cancer support groups, namely, information sharing, personal reflection, and interaction with others. Unlike discussion forums or e-mail lists, blogs are not necessarily connected to a contextual frame of an organization's home page that sets out the expectations for interaction, or might bias an emphasis on information or personal disclosure through site design (Seale et al. 2006). Instead, blogs are more personalized spaces that may challenge the mainstream media's depiction of cancer survivorship as a uniform narrative of restitution. Given that blogs are less retrospective than narrative interviews and autobiography, and are usually written in discontinuous, episodic posts, it is possible that blogs might offer those diagnosed with and being treated for cancer an alternative context in which to express the fluctuating and fragmented voice of the chaos illness narrative. In the discussion that follows, I examine the interactive practices that contextualize a sample of twenty cancer blogs, and go on to explore the identity and interpersonal work that is accomplished through the language of the stories that are told about illness.

DATA SAMPLE

The primary data sample consists of slightly more than two hundred blog posts, taken from twenty-one cancer blogs. Ten blogs were authored by women, eleven by men. Seventeen of the cancer blog authors were North American, two were British, one was Canadian, and one was Spanish (but wrote in English). All the women wrote about their experience of breast cancer, whereas the men's blogs covered a range of cancers, but half were prostate cancer. A smaller sample of travel blog entries was examined as a secondary point of comparison. The second sample contains thirty travel blog entries, authored in equal proportions by women and men.

As with other online contexts, the gender of the author is inferred from the information given on the blogs. Even where e-mail correspondence with the blogger has taken place, there is no requirement that the authors say who they are. As such, the blogger's self-representation is taken as an enactment of their gender identities, even though there is little evidence from the blogs that the authors were engaging in postmodern identity play. Gender is an important aspect of transportable identity for these writers. Bloggers make references to their gender as they describe their identities on their blog homepages:

> I am an ordinary 36 year old Canadian woman. (Sylvie, homepage)

> I live in London, a mother, a teacher, a daughter and a sister. (Minerva, homepage)

The bloggers also make reference to their gender in relation to their experiences of illness. Studies in e-health have pointed to the symbolic gendered meanings that are disrupted by surgical treatments of a woman's breast (Dubrinwy 2009) and the erectile dysfunction that may result from treatment of prostate cancer (Kiss and Merwyn 2001). The secondary side effects of cancer treatment also affect physical appearance, such as hair loss. For some women at least, such effects are felt keenly as a disorienting experience that influences their sense of identity (Bingley et al. 2006). For the blog writers in this sample too, the bodily disruptions of cancer and its treatment led them to question and in some cases rework the biological and social bases for their gender identity. In the two excerpts that follow, the narrators reflect on how the physical changes wrought by cancer treatment cause them to question how gendered identities are produced.[1]

> What is an outwardly physical sign that I am a woman? Is it my breasts? My softly curled flowing locks of hair? Is it my soft skin and nicely shaped fingernails? If my breasts are damaged, my hair erased, my nails and skin dry and flaking, am I still a woman?
> (Jeanette, 14 November 2006)

> Surgery + radiotherapy equals sexual potency vanished for ever. Add to this adjuvant hormone treatment and the magic mirror will say that you are perfect angel. Why an Angel? someone may ask: well, angels are said not to have sexual desire, and you don't have it either;

further, Angels are perceived by many people as having no sexual differentiation, and you sometimes feel the same: your testicles may have shrunk, your penis may have almost disappeared and your sexual life is just history. . . .

(Manuel, 12 and 25 December 2005)

Gender is also enacted through the stylistic resources that the narrators employ, where an emphasis on emotional self-disclosure is taken as an index of hegemonic femininity. Although I recognize the limitations of comparing the blog posts on the basis of their author's stated gender, I use this information as one way of distinguishing between the narratives told on these cancer blogs.

INTERACTIVE CONTEXT

Post Length

The illness narratives are embedded in a wider discursive context that can be described in terms of the length of the blog posts. A summary of the posts in the data sample is given in Table 3.1. A first glance at the size of the data sample suggests variation in the length of blog post that correlates with both the blogger's stated gender and the blog topic. Within this sample, men wrote markedly longer travel blog posts than did the women. Conversely, the women's posts about experiences with cancer were twice as long as the men's. The variation in the length of the men's posts in particular is worth reflection. While this could be skewed by the size of the data sample, it would seem that men write much more on personal blogs when the topic is externally focused and stereotypically masculine (Coates 2003). There is much less variation in the length of the women's posts, but the smaller difference suggests the opposite to be true: women write more on personal blogs when the topic is personally centered on the self rather than on external events or objects.

Table 3.1   Data Sample of Blog Posts in Detail

Topic	Author	No. of Blogs	No. of Posts	No. of Words	Average Words / Post
Cancer	Women	10	100	54,155	541.6
	Men	11	97	23,411	241.4
Travel	Women	15	15	7,050	470
	Men	15	15	30,037	2,002
Total		51	227	114,653	

Comments

Unlike the private world of offline diaries or autobiography, blogging is not a solitary occupation, but takes place within a community of web users. It is the interactive potential of the blog that distinguishes it above all from its offline counterpart of diary writing (Sorapure 2003, 5) and, in the case of illness narratives, marks it as distinct from the kinds of interactions enabled in narrative interviews; as McLellan puts it, "[T]he most remarkable feature of the electronic narrative is its connection with an audience" (1997, 99). The importance of audience is signaled clearly by nearly all the authors of the cancer blogs. Regardless of their gender, they tell their stories explicitly with the purpose of connecting with a community of users:

> I decided to deliver my story in real time, as it happens, in this journal. This is my therapy, and my way of sharing the story in its raw, unedited form. It is my hope that other people who encounter difficulties can read this and gain strength from knowing that they are not alone.
> (Sylvie, August 8, 2006)

> Here are my random thoughts as I get a grip on having cancer at 42 (now 44) years old. I would like to inspire hope in all of you and in myself as well as to provide a place for you to keep track of me through this ordeal.
> (David E., homepage)

The blogger's awareness of his or her audience is evident throughout the writing, and shapes the blog posts in various ways. Many bloggers directly invite comments, encouraging members of the audience to make their identities known:

> If you have comments please leave them because they do help us. Please add yourself to our Frappr map as we would love to know where our readers are from.
> (Dan, Homepage)

The quotation from Dan's homepage suggests the dialogic relationship between audience and blogger. Indeed, the primary function of the comments on the cancer blogs is to provide or seek support in the form of shared experience, advice, and encouragement. Examples of support include the following:

> Hi Sylvie,
> We don't know each other, but I do know what you're going through. What you're doing is called "participating in life"—it's what keeps you

alive, keeps you going during this tumultuous time. What you need to know is that this is a special time . . . a you time.

(Comment on Sylvie's blog)

In turn, the support from the audience is acknowledged in the blog posts and shapes the events that are reported.

A few of you wanted me to let you know how things went today, on my first day of chemo. I appreciate your support more than I can explain. I thought I'd let you know how things are going.

(David Hahn, July 29, 2005)

Clearly, the interaction between the blogger and audience influences not only what gets written in the posts, but also the blogger's experiences in the offline world. Pragmatically, the comments seem to have a co-constructive influence on the narrative development. The co-tellership of the illness narratives is not equal between the blogger and commenter but is asymmetrical. The blogger alone retains the right to author the posts and to moderate which comments get published. Nonetheless, the audience's comments are a visible trace of their active involvement in the process of storytelling as the blog posts unfold. Like the Second Stories in discussion forums, the interwoven comments and posts influence the relational work that takes place in the cancer blogs, resulting in a sense of mutual support and involvement between narrator and their audience.

An empirical analysis of the cancer blog comments provides a more detailed profile of the interaction between the bloggers and at least a portion of their audience. Comments were categorized according to the gender of the blogger and the commenter. There was considerable variation in the number of comments generated by posts, ranging from posts that provoked no comment at all to posts that gained up to 191 responses (although such a high response was unusual). In light of this extreme variation, the aggregate figures in Tables 3.2 and 3.3 must be taken as suggestive tendencies only, not a consistent picture of this sector of the blogosphere. The gender of the posters includes an "anonymous" category for individuals who did not disclose their gender identity online. Several observations are prompted by these results. First, it is notable that the cancer blogs written by women attracted on average more than double the number of comments than any other blog subgroup. Second, women tended to post over twice as many comments as men (59 percent compared with 25 percent of all comments). The difference in commenting interaction on cancer blogs supports the pattern found in earlier studies of CMC that women were more likely to post messages to a cancer support group list, and felt more compelled to offer help and support to others (Wen et al. 2011), while men saw help as a "burden to be endured" (Gray et al. 2000, 276). However, it is too simplistic to suggest that gender alone can be used as an explanation for patterns of interaction. Instead, the tendency for a commenter to respond to a blogger of the same sex merits further consideration.

Table 3.2   Average Numbers of Comments per Post for Cancer and Travel Blogs

	Male Bloggers	Female Bloggers
Cancer Blogs	2.6	12.7
Travel Blogs	5.3	4.6

Table 3.3   Average Numbers of Comments per Post According to the Gender of the Commenter

	Male Commenter	Female Commenter	Anonymous
Male Blogger	46	39	16
Female Blogger	18	66	16
Overall Totals	25	59	16

One explanation is that the interaction occurs primarily between users with a common experience. E-health research has suggested that patients being treated for cancer are most likely to seek out someone who has had the same diagnosis as a means of advice and information (Gray et al. 2000; Balka et al. 2010). As some types of cancer are gender specific (e.g., prostate cancer) and readers comment on blogs relevant to the illness of interest to them, this gives rise to a gendered correlation between commenter and blogger. Thus, it would seem that it is the appeal to a shared experience that primarily determines these interactive patterns, not the gender of the user in an abstract sense.

Hyperlinks

The hyperlinks within a blog have a different interactive potential, manipulating the reader's movement in the blog, not the blog itself. Indeed, hyperlinks are primarily intertextual, connecting web pages rather than blog users. However, hyperlinks have a social dimension and may indicate what the blog is perceived to be "good for" (Beaulieu 2005, 35), through both the hyperlink's point of reference and its position within the blog. Hyperlinks may be found both on the sidebar of the blog homepage and within individual entries. Links on the homepage are deemed more significant due to their permanent presence (once individual posts are archived, they disappear from view) and because of their function in identifying the social network to which a blogger belongs (Nilsson 2007, 8). Both types of links are included in the following analysis. The distinction made by Herring et al. (2004) between personal blogs and knowledge logs suggests a contrast between hyperlinks that emphasize sources of information (an online form of annotation) and those that promote a user (through their own personal blogs). Examples of both types are given here:

> After some discussion it is decided to do a Tru-Cut <u>biopsy</u>.
> (Kelly, May 11, 2006)

> Please, I implore you, even if you are a complete stranger or a lurker, please in the spirit of Christmas, reach out and give <u>Minerva</u> some love.
> (Jeanette, December 23, 2006)

The links in each blog were analyzed for their point of reference, and the results summarized in Tables 3.4 and 3.5, which show that women's blogs contain more hyperlinks than the men's. On closer examination of the links' functions, it is notable that the women's homepages contain more than double the number of links to personal blogs than the men's. It would seem that the women used these links to identify themselves within a community of personal bloggers to a greater extent than the men: presenting their blogs as personal writing rather than a source of medical knowledge. Moreover, the women's cancer blogs were more frequently linked to other personal blogs than the men's. Calculated on the basis of searches taken from Technorati, on average, 133 blogs linked to each of the women's blogs, while 61 blogs linked to each of the men's. The hypertextual profile of the blog sidebars thus presents a clear picture of women's cancer blogs that align themselves with personal blogs, emphasizing their densely connected positions within a network of users.

Table 3.4 Average Number of Sidebar Hyperlinks per Blog (Cancer Blogs)

	Information Site	*Personal Blog*	*Total*
Male Blogger	3	3	6
Female Blogger	3.9	8.3	12.6
Total	6.9	11.3	18.6

Table 3.5 Average Number of Hyperlinks per Post (Cancer Blogs)

	Information	*Personal Blog*	*Total*
Male Blogger	0.53	0.21	0.74
Female Blogger	1.1	0.16	1.26

EVALUATION AND STORY GENRES: REFLECTIVE ANECDOTES

The interactive nature of blogging is not limited to its digital resources, but also influences the linguistic choices made by narrators. The narrative framework employed to explore this here is that developed by Labov (1972), with a special interest in evaluation devices. According to Labov, evaluation is the resources a speaker uses to make her or his narrative vivid and of perceived relevance to their audience and corresponds to the narrative dimension that Ochs and Capps describe as tellability (2001, 33). In Labov's work, the identification of the evaluative highpoint, usually coinciding with "the most reportable event," demarcates the transition between Complication and Resolution and functions to engage the audience, warding off the withering question, "so what?" (Labov 1972, 366). The distribution of evaluation thus also contributes to the perception of a narrative's linearity or structural progression (Ochs and Capps 2001, 41). Labov's seminal work identified a range of markers that typically occurred to signal the speaker's evaluation in their narratives of personal experience. Labov grouped these markers into intensifiers, comparators, correlatives, and explicatives.

Labov's methods for categorizing and interpreting evaluation clearly reflect the interest in quantifying linguistic variables and identifying structural patterns current in the variationist sociolinguistics and structuralist narratology of the late 1960s. Since then, both sociolinguistics and narrative research have moved on, and it is clear that evaluation is not a neutral, de-contextualized phenomenon that can simply be "read off" on the basis of identifying a set of grammatical cues. Nor is there one, universalized narrative schema that is characterized on the basis of a central, climactic turning point. Instead, Labov's evaluative categories are best regarded as part of an open set that might be extended and refined in the context of stories from different cultures, periods, and modes. Indeed, the evaluative forms identified by Labov are trans-generic phenomena that do not always appear to signal evaluative stance on every occasion. Conversely, the speaker's evaluative perspective might also be indicated by lexical choices not covered by the Labov's categories. This presents the analyst with a dilemma: how to interpret evaluative marking in a way that is both transparent and replicable but also sensitive to the sometimes ambiguous, culturally specific, and idiosyncratic manifestations evaluation might take. In the analysis that follows, Labov's categories provide the starting point, but are not regarded as the only means by which the narrator's attitude might be indicated.

As might be expected, the distribution of the evaluation devices in the cancer blogs is quite different from that described in the Labovian paradigm. Labov predicted that evaluation would typically cluster at the climactic high point of a fully formed narrative, but could also be dispersed throughout the narrative (1972, 369). The cancer blogs by both women and men contained a wealth of evaluation devices, but these are distributed in a complex manner, not concentrated around a single turning point in an overarching narrative sequence that marks a definitive move toward closure. A partial explanation for this is that although cancer blogs certainly contain stories of personal experience, they are much lengthier and more complex than the minimal narratives considered by Labov. Even while narratives of illness embrace notions of mortality and recovery, they deal with a range of experiences, many of which do not offer the teleological release of resolution or closure realized by a narrative climax and resolution. In terms of Frank's narrative voices, the structures implied by evaluative patterning do not suggest the contained coherence of the restitution voice. Instead, a more heterogeneous and polyvocal mixture of illness narratives emerge in this sample of cancer blogs. This heterogeneity is not random but rather can be compared and contrasted on the basis of the bloggers' use of evaluation.

A more flexible approach to narrative evaluation draws on Martin and Plum's (1997) typology of story genres. Working from a Systemic Functional Linguistics perspective, they position the classic Labovian model as one of four story genres, which also include Anecdotes and Recounts. These story genres are categorized pragmatically (according to their social purpose) and structurally (dependent upon the position of evaluation in the narrative sequence). Thus Recounts are a temporal sequence of events where the evaluation is less prevalent and ongoing rather than found in a concentrated climax (Eggins and Slade 1997, 269). A typical example is as follows:

> The chemo is done for today. I've had fluids, anti-nausea medication and the chemo drugs and now I'm home. The whole process took about 4.5 hours, and **the worst part** was the needle stick into my port. With the exception of **one little scream** when that happened, **I think I was a pretty good patient.** I have a **private** room with a **private** bathroom and my own TV. Tracey stayed with me **the whole time** and my mom came by too. I **even** had a visit from Larry Shyatt, one of the UF basketball coaches and player David Lee.

> (Jackie, January 21, 2005)

In this extract, the narrator evaluates her experiences, drawing attention to "the worst part" of the treatment, and her positive ability to endure the experience, where "one little scream" is the only contrast to her assessment as "a pretty good patient." The point is not that Recounts are free of evaluation, but that this is dispersed throughout the narrative episode rather than clustered in a single textual point.

In contrast, Anecdotes are stories that report a remarkable event, characterized by an evaluative punch line.

> Then I was subjected again to the blue stirrups where I had another <u>color Doppler ultrasound</u>. There is a large flat panel color screen **right** over your head and you can see what the doctor sees. Last time I had

this procedure there were several red clusters **all over** my prostate that indicated the blood flow that was feeding the cancer. **This time NADA!!! I can tell you that it was a powerful image for me. NADA cancer!**

(Dan, March 27, 2006)

In Dan's Anecdote, he also evaluates his experiences, including intensifying descriptions of the proximity of the equipment "right" over the patient's head, and the indications of cancer "all over my prostate." But the most concentrated cluster of evaluation appears in the last three sentences where he emphasizes the impact of seeing that there is no sign of cancer in the ultrasound screening. The evaluation intensifies the narrator's reaction through repetition ("NADA"), multiple use of expressive orthography (exclamation marks and capitalization), and the direct address to the audience ("you"). It is the increased, localized concentration of evaluation and its placement at the end of the narrative episode that characterizes it as an Anecdote.

Rather than forming a unified narrative that follows a single teleological progression (like Frank's restitution model), these blog posts contain a myriad of Recounts and Anecdotes that capture the author's fluctuating experiences of cancer interwoven with his or her everyday life. Both women and men used a range of story genres in their cancer blogs. However, men tended to use more Recounts, while women made greater use of Anecdotes. The difference in the use of story genres is important, for the function of Anecdotes is to generate a shared affectual response to an event, leading to solidarity between narrator and audience (Martin and Plum 1997, 310), while the emphasis of a Recount is simply the retelling of events. The women's greater use of Anecdotes hints at a more affective style of storytelling, in line with their tendency to promote a shared and supportive experience through commenting on and linking to other personal blogs.

The material marked out as tellable reinforces this gendered difference. Although not exclusively, the men tended to use evaluation in a dispersed way to describe events, whereas the women often used evaluation to highlight an emotional response or to reveal their internal thought processes. The contrast between a masculine focus on events and feminine self-disclosure is demonstrated in the following extracts where the narrators describe getting their initial diagnosis:

Jim's Diagnosis
I was diagnosed with prostate cancer on the Friday before Memorial Day, 2004. This was completely unexpected and has turned my life upside down. The whole affair started when my doctor referred me to a local urologist because my PSA blood test was slightly above normal (4.9). I got another blood test a few weeks later that came back 6.6. Next was a prostate biopsy that took 20 minutes and was not

very comfortable. I found out the bad news three days later. Cancer detected on both sides of my prostate with a Gleason level of 7. That scale indicates the cancer is growing and active and needs to be dealt with quickly.

(Jim, June 28, 2004)

The male narrator, Jim, evaluates the external events such as the diagnosis ("This was completely unexpected"), treatment ("a prostate biopsy that [. . .] was not very comfortable"), and cancer itself ("the cancer is growing and active"), but he does not then provide any internalized reaction to these events other than that these have "turned my life upside down," locating the impact of the illness externally on "my life" rather than introspectively on him.

The women's accounts tend to be different, with evaluation that highlights both their emotions and thought processes. An eloquent example of this is found in the writing of Sylvie Fortin. The full account of her initial diagnosis is lengthy (1,487 words). I include here a small extract from what she describes as the "internal dialogue" that occurred during her diagnosis:

Sylvie's Diagnosis

Modified Scarff Bloom Richardson Grade: 3/3 with a Total Score of 8/9

OK, this doesn't sound good at all. So, let me understand this correctly. You're saying that out of all the types of breast cancers, mine is the worst it can get? I have to look this up when I get home to see what this really means. (*Please tell me this didn't spread to my lymph nodes*)

(update: I did look it up when I got home. It means I have a 50% chance of surviving another 5 years.)

Lymphatic/vascular invasion: Extensive
Oh crap! It spread to my lymph nodes! Oh my god, oh my god, oh my god! OK, now what? What does this mean? Does this mean I'm going to die? Is that what this means? (*Please tell me you can fix me!*)

(Sylvie, 20 October 2006, underlining, emboldened and italicized fonts in the original)

The evaluation in this example is extensive, again including intensifiers (repetition and ritual utterances: "Oh my god, oh my god oh my god!" and exaggerated quantifiers: "at all") and comparators (superlatives: "the worst"; negatives: "doesn't," "didn't"; modals: "can," "have to"; and questions). What is significant is the way that these dramatize Sylvie's internal reaction to the diagnosis, juxtaposing the official terminology with her attempts to understand what is being said and her hope that the medical profession will be able to treat her, graphically intensified by her use of bold font, italics, and parentheses. The focus is not on the event itself but rather on Sylvie's attempt to come to terms with the diagnosis.

The women's use of evaluation is not limited to highlighting remarkable events, but also characterizes further stretches of reflective commentary that are interwoven with their narratives. I give typical examples of these evaluative passages here:

> Another recent conversation with another person. . . . In a reference to a male worker in a workplace—"He chases after **anything** with breasts." Granted, I found this to be a comment that I have heard in various forms over the years. **This time when I heard it, I couldn't help** but take note. It was the criteria and the plural; breasts. **Once again** I found myself mulling over the role a woman's breasts (yep, there is **that plural again**) play in our society. Yes, I have always been aware of this, **but now it is taking on a much different slant** as I my unilateral mastectomy is approaching a week from today.
>
> (Jeanette, May 30, 2005)

> This, my dears, is **not a life**. This is a drudge, a waste of energy. I am **not a wonderful, caring, lovely, all encompassing mother** with my arms open wide for my darling babies, **I am a ghost, a bald spectre** who is **barely** moving around the rooms, whose path **barely** disturbs the flow of air.
>
> (Minerva, February 14, 2007)

> His words **shattered my confidence and belief** in my own ability to live forever. In a single moment, **my life flashed in front of me, my plans for the future were called into question, and the happiness I had begun my day with was suddenly and completely overshadowed** by these terrifying words.
>
> (Sylvie, August 9, 2006)

The women's reflections are rich in evaluation, particularly the device described by Labov as comparators. These are characterized by modality, negation, metaphor, questions, superlative, and comparative forms and function by comparing present events "with events which might have happened but did not" (1972, 381). The implicitly dual nature of comparators makes them an apt device for narrating the fragmentation of self undergone by those experiencing severe illness. The change in perspective articulated by Jeanette and despairing frustration of Minerva seems typical of the illness narrative as a genre described by Frank, where the author is dislocated from the illusions of their previous "normal experience" and instead forced to recognize their own lack (1994, 15). The comparative passages particularly draw attention to the rupturing effect of illness and its treatment on the narrators' gendered identities. For example, Minerva constructs the distance between the de-familiarized image of herself as a "ghost, a bald spectre" and the idealized description of a "wonderful, caring, lovely, all encompassing mother." Likewise, Jeanette contemplates the symbolic gap between the hegemonic ideal of femininity that operates within a heterosexual economy: the two-breasted woman and her physical condition that will follow breast surgery.

These passages are significant not just for exposing the ruptures to the narrator's identity brought about by illness but also because they do not readily conform to the heuristic typology set out by Martin and Plum (1997). What emerges from these women's stories is a distinctive subgenre I am calling the Reflective Anecdote. As the name suggests, this is most closely related to Martin and Plum's Anecdote, for the evaluation is typically located following the report of a narrative event and may be tied cohesively to it. In the earlier examples, this is signaled by the *cataphoric* references: "I found this to be a comment" (Jeanette), "This, my dears, is not a life" (Minerva). However, the excess of evaluation extends far beyond the evaluative punctuation described by Martin and Plum, and the reflective passages are marked by a deictic shift from the past event to the present time of narration: "now it is taking on a much different slant" (Jeanette), "and now, I face an uncertain and frightening future" (Sylvie). In narrative terms, the evaluation signals that the raison d'être of the story lies not so much in the reported events but with the act of narration itself. These Anecdotes are thus reflective in their content (emphasizing introspection), in their pivotal structure (interfacing between events and evaluative narration), and in their linguistic concentration of comparators, all of which illustrate the liminal boundaries of the narrator's past, present, and future in critical flux (Rimmon-Kenan 2002, 20).

The Reflective Anecdotes are also significant, because in this data sample, they are absent from the cancer blogs written by men. Far from being dismissed in derogatory terms as a feminine digression, Reflective Anecdotes perform an important social purpose. The blogger Minerva explains the motivation behind her writing as follows:

> So why am I going on about this? It isn't, surprisingly to those who know me, (*grin*), a cry for attention but I want you, you on the other side of this fence to understand what it is like if you have someone going through this and where their anger and frustration comes from.
>
> (Minerva, February 16, 2007)

The point of the Reflective Anecdote is thus to provide emotional education for the audience. Unsurprisingly, the emphasis on emotional disclosure is similar to that of Anecdotes generally, which are told so as to share an affectual response. It is certainly not the case that Anecdotes are exclusively told by women. But the relative amplification or absence of emotional expression in these Anecdotes echoes the pattern of self-disclosure that has been found frequently in conversational stories told between women friends but rarely in all-male talk (Coates 2003). At a superficial level, the lesser emotional expression from the men's blogs might then be interpreted as indexing the scripts of hegemonic masculinity. As Coates writes, in men's stories, emotional vulnerability is usually concealed behind what she describes as the "masculine mask of silence," a discourse strategy that promotes a view of conventional, Western masculinity as being "tough" and "achievement focused" (2003, 75). Men do self-disclose in their narratives of illness, but in this data sample, the absence of Reflective Anecdotes and greater use of Recounts in the men's posts suggest that gendered discourse styles found in offline cancer support groups and in earlier forms of CMC have been carried over into illness narratives in the blogosphere. As one of the male bloggers puts it, in a blog post tellingly headed by an image of a disintegrating mask:

> Men suffering PCa do not speak up.
>
> Men suffering PCa remain silent.
>
> Men suffering PCa hide their disease.
>
> [. . .]
>
> Hundreds of thousands of men die every year from Prostate Cancer.
>
> In silence.

SUMMARY

The analysis in this chapter has shown that gender persists as a salient category in sociolinguistic accounts of narrative in social media contexts. Despite early claims that identities constructed online were separable from those performed in offline situations, the analysis of interaction as shown through length of posts, commenting, and distribution of hyperlinks found a pattern where the women's cancer blogs were characterized by a larger number of comments, with more hyperlinks to and from the blog than the men's. This finding echoes the conclusions repeated across many studies in the medical humanities and e-health where women were more likely to participate in cancer support groups than were men, and that women used support groups for mutual emotional support while men used the support groups to seek and share information.

The greater engagement between the women bloggers and their audience was also manifest in the storytelling style used by the women bloggers and their choice of story genre. Women employed more evaluation than men, which they used to mark as tellable their emotional reflections on the process of being diagnosed with and treated for cancer. These stylistic choices have important implications for the narrative dimension of linearity, for the increased quantity of this evaluation placed at the end of a narrative episode (rather than a climactic mid-point) combined with a stated purpose of fostering affective empathy between narrator and audience reconfigures the offline story genre of the Anecdote as a new subtype of story genre: the Reflective Anecdote.

Despite its prominent use by women in this data sample, the Reflective Anecdote should not be understood as a universally feminine form. Orgad (2006) points out that the belief in emotional expression as a therapeutic strategy is ideologically salient in North American contexts, and may not be carried over into other national cultures. It is notable that eight of the ten women bloggers were North American. Examining blogs from other cultural contexts and in other languages might reveal other patterns of evaluative distribution. Of course, the stigma associated with particular illnesses makes it more or less easy for narrators to tell their stories in public contexts like the blogosphere, and even more so to reflect emotionally on such personal experiences. It may well be that the stigma associated with prostate cancer is still more pressing than the stigma associated with breast cancer, which in turn prohibits the likelihood that men might write Reflective Anecdotes on this topic. More research needs to be done on narratives about other kinds of cancer, and by narrators who tell stories in different cultural contexts before more definitive conclusions can be made. Nonetheless, the importance of gender as a speaker variable deserves further attention, as does the role of signaling emotion in storytelling contexts. Both of these topics are taken up in the following chapter, but focuses on data taken from a different social media genre: the social network site Facebook.

4   Storytelling Styles in Facebook Updates

FACEBOOK IN CONTEXT

Social networking sites (henceforth SNS) began to emerge in the last decade of the twentieth century and have since proliferated in range and application. SNS typically combine features that boyd and Ellison (2007) define as offering participants a public or semi-public profile within a bounded system, an articulated list of other members with whom the participants shares an interest, and the ability to traverse the list of connections made by themselves and others within the system. Facebook was first launched as a network for a niche community in 2004, when it was made available to Harvard college students only. In the years following, it achieved remarkable uptake outside that original community such that by 2010 it was the most frequently used SNS in the United Kingdom and boasted 500 million active users worldwide (Gadsby 2010).

Like other SNS, Facebook enables users to create a personal profile for themselves that itemizes demographic information, interests, an uploaded photograph, and a list of Facebook Friends, and may be enhanced by bespoke Facebook applications such as games and quizzes. Facebook clearly operates within a participatory culture (Jenkins 2006) where the more static display of personal profile information is framed by a variety of communicative channels for interaction. Friends can send each other e-mail messages, use instant messaging (chat), join discussion threads, share and tag photographs, post public messages on another member's profile (in Facebook terminology, their "wall"), take part in various games or quizzes, and send messages about their current activity via a status update to all the Friends on their list.

The participatory, convergent nature of Facebook is highly dynamic. The contexts for communication change continuously as the participants interact with each other and the site. For example, Friend lists fluctuate as contacts are added or removed; members update their profile information, play games, and communicate with others. Similarly, the **RSS feeds** that draw together the Facebook activity of a Friend list are updated continually as an ever-changing constellation of those Friends' most recent Facebook activities. The contexts created by Facebook also change dynamically as developers continue to update the interface and infrastructure of the site. Large-scale examples of changes to the Facebook interface include streaming Facebook activity so that it distributed activity into RSS feeds for each Friend list (September 2006) and changing the format for the status update template (July 2008).

Prior to July 2008, the template for status updates asked members to respond to the prompt question, "What are you doing right now?" Writers could publish accounts of their life experiences by completing a template that began with the user's profile name followed by "is," for example, "Ruth is . . ." After July 2008, the verb particle "is" was removed, and the prompt question was replaced by the instruction to "Share what's on your mind." In the earlier template, status updates did not have a direct feedback mechanism, although it was possible for Friends to write on the updater's wall, e-mail, message, or talk in the offline world in response to information in a status update. But in July 2008, Facebook developers added a "Like" button and a comment function to the update template. Together, these changes increased the expressive range and interactive potential for updating. Although the ongoing changes in Facebook's interface pose challenges for capturing comparable data samples, they also present us with useful opportunities to examine how specific changes in the online textual context (such as the template development) might impact the style of the stories told in these updates.

Increasing the opportunities for interaction between Facebook Friends reflects the emphasis on social connection that underpins Facebook's generic context. From the outset, Facebook was designed to replicate and strengthen social connections that existed in the offline world: it is a relationship-oriented SNS (Zhang and Wang 2010). Unlike the publically available discussion forums and blogs that we have examined in earlier chapters, the social context of Facebook interaction is distinctive in that members can apply privacy settings to their accounts (boyd and Hargittai 2010), creating a semi-public environment with an audience vetted by, if not known to, the Facebook member.[1] The nature of Friend relationships in Facebook also contrasts with the online communities where members only ever meet in virtual contexts. Facebook Friends usually already know each other in the offline world before connecting via the Facebook site.

The Facebook Friend relationship is reciprocal (once a Friend is confirmed to a Facebook member, both can see each other's profile) and mimics peer-to-peer interaction. However, Facebook "Friends" should not be taken as synonymous with offline friendship, and the social ties between a Facebook member and the individual people on their Friend list will vary considerably. Like other networked publics (boyd 2008), Facebook Friend lists are characterized by collapsed contexts, where groups normally segmented in the offline world are brought together in a single online distribution list. For example, a Friend list might include close friends, family, current work colleagues, or more distant acquaintances like old school friends. The difficulties of negotiating the collapsed context of a Friend list are brought into focus by the practice of posting status updates. On the one hand, posting an update is one measure that can mitigate the necessarily discontinuous nature of offline relationships, acting as one means by which members can make social realities like relationships "real" (Leeds-Hurwitz 2005), and potentially building social capital (Ellison et al. 2007). On the other hand, the collapsed contexts of a Friend list present risks for the updater who may not wish to disclose the same levels of personal information to all the members aggregated in the single audience of the list. The strategies and styles that members use to negotiate the socially interactive challenges and opportunities of updating their status in Facebook are the focus of this chapter.

DATA SAMPLE

This chapter presents a longitudinal analysis of the storytelling styles found in Facebook status updates.[2] The data consists of 2,000 updates contributed by 100 White British participants, divided equally between women and men and from 13–50 years of age. The participants were separated into groups according to age: 13–18, 19–24, 30–39, and 40–49. The participants were not a convenience sample of my own contacts, but were second-order contacts from my Friend list (i.e., they were Friends of my contacts, but previously unknown to me). The updates were sampled in early 2008 and again in 2010, resulting in two datasets of 1,000 updates each.[3] As far as was possible, updates from the same participants were used in both datasets. Seventy-three participants remained in the same age categories for both datasets. In 2010, twenty-seven participants either withdrew from the study or were excluded because they had changed age categories, in which case they were replaced by participants who had not been included in the 2008 sample. The gender of the participants was inferred from their names and profile information, confirmed by the first-order contacts on my Friend list and, where possible, by questionnaire return.

The narrative analysis charts stylistic developments in the updates, encompassing the period before and after the change in update template in July 2008. Prior to July 2008, it was not possible to provide direct feedback to Friends' updates. However, the analysis of the later updates incorporates a quantitative comparison of the "liking" and commenting practices that accompany the updates. In order to gain an ethnographic perspective on the participants' own perspectives on their Facebook use, participants were invited to complete a questionnaire about their preferences for different kinds of Facebook activity and the factors that they felt influenced their updating behavior. The return for this questionnaire was low (20 percent) and so is used only to provide anecdotal evidence of the participants' perspectives.

FROM STATUS UPDATES TO SMALL STORIES:
TELLABILITY IN FACEBOOK

Status updates are heterogeneous forms of communication. The updates in the datasets included reports of the updater's experiences and opinions, messages directly addressed to the Friend list (questions, greetings, thanks), quotations, and jokes (see Bolander and Locher 2010 and Lee 2011 for similar content analysis of updates). Among the communicative diversity of updates, self-reports are a dominant type of activity, accounting for approximately 70 percent of the updates in the data samples. Typical examples include reporting day-to-day activities such as watching a film, preparing food, or carrying out domestic chores.

> <F34–08> has watched star wars episode 4 with her boys for the first time, and i liked it!
> (Female updater, 25–29 years of age, May 19, 2008 at 20:01)

> < F43–08> will prepare a 'nutolene' salad tonight will let you know.
> (Female updater, 30–39 years of age, June 13, 2008 at 17:12)

> <F46–08> cleaned the litter tray, only to have Whiskers pop back in minutes later. . . . :-(.
> (Female updater, 30–39 years of age, June 23, 2008 at 20:24)

The narrative dimensions of the self-reported stories in status updates are shaped by the generic context of Facebook and the relationship between participants within the collapsed contexts of Facebook's Friend lists. In particular, the tellability of the updates is constrained by the need to indicate social connection with members of a Friend list, but to avoid disclosure that might be judged inappropriate for Friends who are acquaintances, rather than intimate friends.

Ochs and Capps (2001) contrast the polarities of high and low tellability. Highly tellable stories are assumed to be of great interest to the teller and audience, reporting unusual, out-of-the-ordinary events that capture the attention of the audience. Such stories are often polished, rhetorical performances. Stories of low tellability are said to report mundane events, where the narration is marked by unevenness, hesitation, and the lack of a clear punch line that emphasizes the narrative relevance. Tellability thus entails at least two dimensions: subjective judgments that relate to the choice of subject matter (unusual versus everyday topics) and rhetorical finesse (polished versus hesitant styles).

The subject matter of the self-reporting updates typically focuses on the minutiae of everyday events. Writers update about a range of topics, including the weather, their mood, travel, leisure, or domestic activities.[4]

<F27–08> enjoyed the fitness training and tactics at Netball this evening. Bring on 2mo's game.

(Female updater, 19–24 years of age, May 20, 2008 at 21:19)

<M35–08> is waiting for a train &guess what its late! Now there is a surprise!!!

(Male updater, 40–49 years of age, June 21, 2008 at 17:29)

In the 2010 dataset, the subject matter also referenced well-known, national public events, such as political announcements, sports events, or television shows.

<M24–10> is watching the live Spending Review to see if Nick Clegg actually starts crying. At the moment, he doesn't look too far off.

(Male updater, 25–29 years of age, October 20, 2010 at 11:55)

<M96–10> Gutted for Mahut . . . what a match to lose!

(Male updater, 25–29 years of age, June 24, 2010 at 17:00)[5]

These references to shared, public events occurred when updaters were commenting on events broadcast through the mainstream media. Like Twitter, Facebook seems to be changing the way that media is consumed (Anstead and O'Loughlin 2010).

The characteristic tellability of the updates in terms of subject matter suggests they tend to be positioned as low rather than highly tellable stories. Ochs and Capps argue that stories with low tellability are "geared less to narrative as performance and more to narrative as a social forum for discovering what transpired" (2001, 38). In line with this, the range of tellability and social orientation of status updates are also highly suggestive of the genre described by Georgakopoulou (2007) as small stories. Like Martin and Plum's (1997) work, Georgakopoulou's category of small stories moves beyond the Labovian paradigm for canonical narratives of personal experience. Small stories are characterized by fluidity, plasticity, and open-endedness, usually occurring in the small moments of talk, rather than as distinct, fully fledged units (2007, 36). In contrast to the narration of landmark events, small stories, like status updates, are interwoven with the participants' daily experiences, emphasize some kind of immediacy, and are heavily embedded in their surrounding discourse. While Martin and Plum distinguish between story genres according to the narrative's pragmatic function, Georgakopoulou identifies a range of small story subgenres on the basis of the relationship between time of the story events and the time of narration. In addition to the past tense events reported in personal narratives, she includes *Breaking News Stories* where "tellers seem to wish to share the reported events straight away, as they are still unfolding" (2007, 42), such as,

<M31–10> is now starting to understand why graduates don't get jobs having read some truly awful applications in the last hour.
(Male updater, 25–29 years of age, October 20, 2010 at 11:21am)

<F30–10> is studying in starbucks, but it's not quite the same without the lovely [name deleted].
(Female updater, 19–24 years of age, October 16, 2010 at 10:18am)

Projections contrast with the present tense of Breaking News Stories. Instead, the speaker constructs a taleworld of events that have not yet happened (2007, 47).

<F11–10> is not looking forward to waking up at 7am tomorrow to go into hospital for my operation. tonsils: I will miss you. just kidding you keep making me ILL.
(Female updater, 13–18 years of age, October 15, 2010 at 23:24)

<F62–10> will be getting to see White Lies, Biffy Clyro & I Am Arrows at the Muse gig at Wembley this weekend. . . . eexxcccciiittted! :-)
(Female updater, 40–49 years of age, October 13, 2010 at 14:45)

Finally, *Shared Stories* is an umbrella term for stories that recall or retell in skeleton form an experience of interaction shared by the group of speakers (2007, 50). Shared stories can refer to events either in the past or the present moment. Shared stories describe the reports of national or international events found in the 2010 dataset, events that were usually disseminated through mainstream media channels.

<M14–10> has been watching the mine for several hours now. I think the rescuers that went down at the beginning are ridiculously brave, actually choosing to go down, and being the last to come up. Wow
(Male updater, 25–29 years of age, October 13, 2010 at 11:14)

<M28–10> Gotta love the Chilean Miners—What legends!
(Male updater, 13–18 years of age, October 13, 2010 at 19:10)

<M44–10> Five words I didn't ever want to hear . . . "dancing the Salsa, Anne Widdecombe . . ."
(Male updater, 40–49 years of age, October 9, 2010 at 19:08)[6]

The small stories foster the sense of social connection between participants that is privileged in the generic context of Facebook. Georgakopoulou describes small stories as "fundamental acts of sharing, and through doing so, reaffirming closeness in positions and viewpoints, putting them to the test, or revisiting them" (2007, 40). However, the communicative context of posting a status update is quite different to the face-to-face contexts discussed in Georgakopoulou's work. While the imperative to indicate relational closeness remains for both face-to-face and computer-mediated contexts, the aggregated nature of a Friend list (bringing together participants normally separate in offline environments) means that the way in which that relational closeness might be expressed operates within particular constraints.

One such constraint is the level of personal disclosure exposed in the story content. While intimate disclosure might be appropriate for face-to-face conversation between close friends, this is not a usual practice in the datasets from this study. In order to avoid levels of self-disclosure that might provoke social awkwardness or unwanted reactions, writers seem to elect relatively inoffensive story topics about daily events that carry less potential threat of misappropriation. In the questionnaire responses elicited in this study, the writers consistently mentioned modifying the content of status updates in order to reduce levels of personal exposure. One teenager said,

> I keep significant information about me minimal [. . .] whereas superficial stuff such as where I drink coffee or what computer I use, I'm not too bothered about them as that information can't be used against me.
>
> (Male updater, 13–18 years of age)

When asked about what they would avoid putting in status updates, another writer said,

> I would not put in anything that I would only share with close friends. I want it to be shallow and light hearted, so I keep my privacy.
>
> (Male updater, 25–29 years of age)

The low tellability typically found in small stories might be interpreted as a social strategy that enables writers to connect with their Friends online, but also mitigates the threat of undesirable levels of self-disclosure in a networked public.

BEYOND EVALUATION: AFFECTIVE DISCOURSE AND TELLABILITY

Despite the somewhat lightweight, everyday nature of the small stories, writers do not leave their updates as bald, factual reports. Instead, the updaters also write about their opinions, reactions, and emotional responses to their life experiences, drawing on some of the rhetorical strategies associated with highly tellable stories. In particular, the updates are characterized by their use of expressive resources associated with affective discourse.

Affective discourse is particularly important because the generic context of Facebook promotes a sense of social connection between participants, and earlier research has stressed the important role played by displays of emotion in achieving this kind of face-enhancing relational work. Far from prohibiting the expression of emotion, computer-mediated contexts seem to enhance the opportunities for writers to express affect of various kinds (Derks et al. 2007). This echoes Biber and Finegan's (1989) observation that expressing feelings is most often found in interactive genres (like personal letters) that do not carry the face-threatening risks of face-to-face conversation. The perception that communicating via Facebook status updates as an asynchronous, and so less face-threatening, mode for social interaction was supported by the questionnaire responses from the participants in this study. One updater wrote that they liked

> being able to keep in touch with people in a very non threatening way [. . .] It has definitely improved relationships within my family as we now all follow status updates and write on walls. It's a much better form of communicating with people like that than awkward "what do I say now" phonecalls.

(Female updater, 30–39 years of age)

In addition, Derks and her colleagues argue that the expression of emotion tends to be increased when the type of communication is social rather than task oriented, when the participants know each other rather than being among strangers, and that the kinds of emotions favored in such high-sociality settings are positive in nature (Derks et al. 2008). Given that the infrastructure of Friend lists in Facebook promotes social connection, where Friend networks consist of members who are usually known to each other, it is perhaps no surprise that the affective dimensions of evaluation in storytelling come to the fore so prominently in this form of social media.

The linguistic features used to signal the writer's opinion and emotional responses have been described in various ways in sociolinguistic and discourse-analytic research, including affect (Ochs and Schieffelin 1989) stance (Biber and Finegan 1989) and APPRAISAL[7] (Martin 2000, 2003; Martin and White 2005). Within narrative analysis, the importance of the speaker's emotional reaction was incorporated in Labov's concept of evaluation (1972). The analysis of the cancer blogs in Chapter 3 illustrated the flexible set of evaluative devices that serve interrelated semantic and interpersonal functions in storytelling. In this chapter, the category of intensifiers provides my starting point for analysis. In the early description of these devices, Labov includes exaggerated quantifiers and qualifiers, repetition, ritual utterances, and expressive phonology (1972). If we take typographical emphasis (use of fonts, capitals, exclamation marks) as a mode-specific substitute for expressive phonology, all of these features are found readily in the small stories told in updates.

<F62–10> had a fab afternoon/night with some lovely friends and her 2 favourite siblings, found a new gig venue, enjoyed Suzerain's gig, walked/danced 3 blisters into her feet and finished off "the visit" with a trip to the chocolate room in Harrods. . . . **very expensive but ooohhhh sooo good..**

(Female updater, 40–49 years of age, October 10, 2010 at 15:10)

<M9–10> **ARGH**—leg cramp!! *squirm* **ARGH**—now my laptop is slipping away *squirm* **ARGH**—awkward crab like position . . . the tribulations of laptoping in bed :/

(Male updater, 19–24 years of age, October 15, 2010 at 00:20)

<M18–10> Manchester United 2–2 West Bromwich Albion! **Over paid fuckers ain't so fucking smooth** are they really! To all you Utd fans. . . . **HAHAHAHAHAHAHAHAHAHAHAHAHAHAHAHAHA!**

(Male updater, 25–29 years of age, October 16, 2010 at 16:48)

But Labovian intensifiers are not the only means by which updaters express their opinions. In order to capture a fuller picture of the kinds of evaluative stance found in the updates, we must move beyond Labov's categories and also include analysis of other expressive resources.

In a later study, Labov (1984) focused more closely on the forms of intensification used to emphasize emotional response in personal narratives. Ochs and Schieffelin (1989) point to the critical role of affect in supporting the social and interactional functions of the language system. However, the linguistic representation of emotion and attitude is richly multifaceted, subjective, and notoriously difficult to analyze systematically. A recent attempt to model the system of expressing opinion and emotional response is set out in Martin's work on APPRAISAL (Martin 2000, 2003; Martin and White 2005). While still an emergent framework, Martin's work is compatible with Labov's findings on intensification (Page 2003) and provides the means by which we might chart the kinds of emotional reactions that are expressed in the updates.

APPRAISAL

APPRAISAL is a recent framework developed in Systemic Functional Linguistics that explains the way language is used to evaluate, to adopt stances, to construct textual personas, and to manage interpersonal positioning and relationships (Martin 2000). The area of APPRAISAL that is applied in this analysis is that of ATTITUDINAL positioning. The subcategories in this system are

AFFECT, which is understood as relating to the speaker's emotional response:

<M58–10> has just finished referencing an essay for tomorrow! **feels overjoyed!**

(Male updater, 13–18 years of age, October 15, 2010 at 00:18)

<F50–10> Just **got very irrate** with customer service operater for a credit card company! Useless lot!

(Female updater, 40–49 years of age, September 30, 2010 at 16:00)

JUDGMENT, where the speaker expresses their moral evaluation of behavior:

<F61–10> has a **very clever** friend called [name deleted]! **almost too clever** for this world!

(Female updater, 40–49 years of age, June 21, 2008 at 9:24am)

<F8–08> is **really stupid** . . . and still cant tell north from south . . . even with a satellite navigation system!!

(Female updater, 19–24 years of age, April 27, 2008 at 9:27am)

and APPRECIATION, which concerns the speaker's aesthetic opinions of entities (including people) or processes:

<F5–08> can still fit into **my stunning dress** . . . 2 weeks til the wedding.. will it still fit then?!

(Female updater, 30–39 years of age, May 23, 2008 at 9:26)

<M7–08> cannot get over **the tacky dullness of Indy 4. It was like an extended cut-scene from Tombraider but without the tits.**

(Male updater, 25–29 years of age, May 26, 2008 at 20:57)

Martin points out that these categories are interrelated because they "all encode feeling" (2000, 147). As the examples show, the systems of AFFECT, JUDGMENT, and APPRAISAL can be further subdivided according to whether the sentiment or opinion is positive or negative, relative to the cultural position of the updater and their audience.[8]

A quantitative comparison of the attitudinal APPRAISAL in the status updates shows that the proportion of updates with are marked by some form of AFFECT, APPRECIATION, or JUDGMENT had increased from 39 percent of the dataset in 2008 to 48 percent of the updates in 2010. Of the different subtypes of Attitudinal APPRAISAL, AFFECT was by far the most frequently occurring in both datasets, accounting for 83 percent of all APPRAISAL in the 2008 updates and 70 percent of all APPRAISAL in the 2010 updates. Likewise, positive APPRAISAL was used more frequently than negative forms for all subtypes, with 59 percent of all APPRAISAL being positive in 2008 and 64 percent being positive in 2010. The relative proportion of APPRAISAL subtypes in the 2008 and 2010 datasets is summarized in Figure 4.1.

Analysis of the APPRAISAL according to the gender of the updater shows that women writers were responsible for contributing a greater proportion of the APPRAISAL than men. In 2008, 59 percent of all APPRAISAL was authored by women, 41 percent by men. In 2010, 62 percent of all APPRAISAL was authored by women and 38 percent by men (summarized in Figure 4.2).

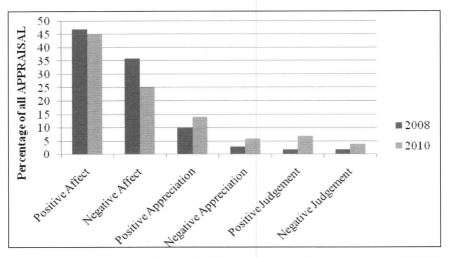

Figure 4.1   Comparison of Attitudinal APPRAISAL subtypes in 2008 and 2010 updates (as a percentage of all APPRAISAL).

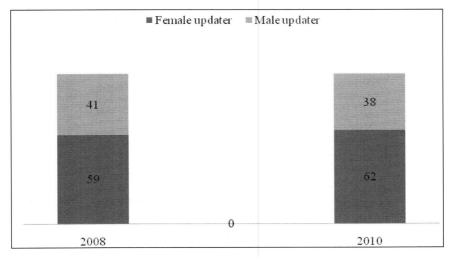

Figure 4.2   Authorship of updates with APPRAISAL according to gender (as a percentage of all updates).

Nonverbal Displays of Affective Style: Emoticons, Kisses, and Laughter

A speaker's emotional stance toward a given event or person can be expressed in lexical choices, as indicated through APPRAISAL choices. It may also be expressed implicitly through the nonverbal resources used in the updates. Because participants in CMC are not usually co-present when they communicate, people have developed forms of textual representation to compensate for the absence of nonverbal, paralinguistic resources that might signal emotional response in face to face settings. These resources include written signals of laughter,

> <F19–08> cant wait to get through this week and be off for a week. It gives him the chance to laugh at those of you who will be working. **HAHAHAHA . . . hahah . . . hehehe . . . ha.**
> (Male updater, 19–24 years of age, May 18, 2008 at 15:44)

Other displays of affection include equivalents to haptic intimacy such as kisses and hugs:

> <F35–10> Has just had a lovely a lovely meal with her hubby 2 b! Thats rite peeps, he popped the question and I said yes! Yay! **X**
> (Female updater, 25–29 years of age, October 8, 2010 at 22:10)

Finally, emoticons (emotion+icon) represent facial expressions by using keyboard symbols. These expressions can indicate positive emotions, such as smiling or happiness, and negative emotions, such as anger, tiredness, or sadness.

> <F17–08> Ashamed to take last place in the Shitehouse quiz. Too much wine methinks :-).
> (Female updater, 30–39 years of age, July 6, 2008 at 22:31)

> <F61–10> Spent most of the day at hospital with [name deleted] had an abscess in his ear which has left a nasty infection. Antibiotics pain relief and dressed with gauze needs to go back again tomorrow to change the dressing poor man :(
> (Female updater, 40–49 years of age, September 22, 2010 at 19:08)

Emoticons and their allied resources can indicate the current mood of the updater and clarify or accentuate the meaning of a message. Like offline paralinguistic signals (such as facial expressions), these resources are an important component of impression management in online discourse, and their use varies according to the age and gender of the updaters. Each of the updates was coded according to the number of nonverbal displays of affection they contained. Hence an update like the example from updater

<F80–10> was classified as containing two signals: the emoticon (crying face) and the kiss.

> <F80–10> My whole body aches thanks to that stupid man crashing into our car on Monday :'(X
>
> (Female updater, 13–18 years of age, August 20, 2011 at 15:43)

A quantitative comparison of the datasets shows that the number of updates that contained at least one nonverbal affective display (emoticons, kisses, laughter) increased over time, from 67 updates in 2008 to 201 updates in 2010 (summarized in Figure 4.3) In line with the variation in APPRAISAL, women wrote more updates that contained these nonverbal displays of affection than men in both datasets. In both, 76 percent of the nonverbal displays of affection were authored by women and 24 percent by men.

When these results are disaggregated for age, and the total number of nonverbal displays of affection is quantified, a rather more complex picture emerges (Figures 4.4 and 4.5). In 2008, women between 13–18 and 19–24 years of age authored the most nonverbal displays of affection. This produced gendered differences in the styles of the updates for the two youngest age groups, but not in the style of the updates written by those in the category for 30–39 years of age. In 2010, women between 30 and 39 years of age authored the most nonverbal displays of affection. It appears that the expressive style used first by young women was later adopted by women of older age groups too. However, the use of

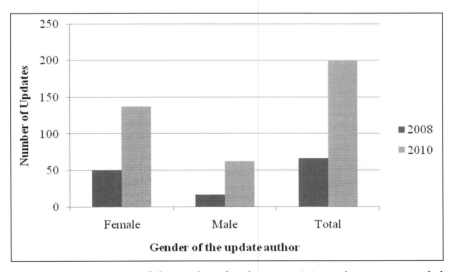

Figure 4.3 Comparison of the number of updates containing at least one nonverbal display of affection in 2008 and 2010, according to the gender of the update author.

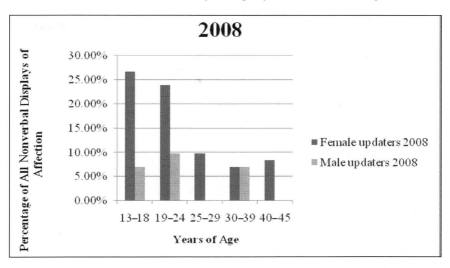

Figure 4.4 Total nonverbal displays of affection according the gender of the update author (as a percentage) for 2008.

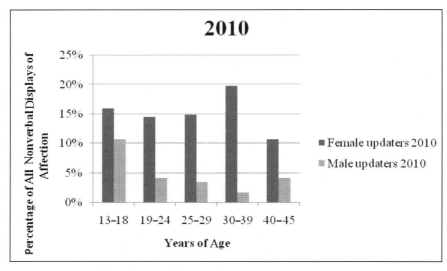

Figure 4.5 Total nonverbal displays of affection according the gender of the update author (as a percentage) for 2010.

nonverbal displays of affection was not adopted in equal measure by the male updaters. When these resources (emoticons, kisses, and laughter) are used by men, these updaters are mostly in the youngest age group: 13–18 years of age.

Intensification

The APPRAISAL and evaluation found in the small stories told in status updates are gradable resources, that is, they can be represented with varying degrees of force or commitment. Earlier studies have categorized the features used for scaling up evaluation in various ways, including amplification (Eggins and Slade 1997), intensification (Labov 1984), and Graduation (Martin 2003). As Martin (2003) notes, there are many more features that tend to be used to increase the intensity of Graduation than those which might reduce it, which include the markers of intensification suggested by Labov's categories (repetition, expressive typography, ritual utterances, exaggerated quantifiers, and qualifiers).

The updates were first compared according to whether or not they contained any intensification devices. A quantitative comparison shows that the proportion of updates containing at least one form of intensifying device had increased from 474 updates in 2008 (47 percent of updates intensified) to 602 updates in 2010 (60 percent of updates intensified). As the results summarized in Figure 4.6 show, updates authored by women were intensified more often than were updates authored by men in both datasets.

The concentration of intensifiers within a given update was also quantified, so that an update like that written by updater <F13–10> was classified as containing one instance of intensification, the exclamation mark.

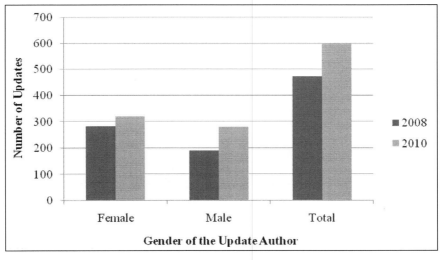

Figure 4.6 Comparison of the number of updates containing at least one intensification device.

<F13–10> Got 500 points on my boots card after my little e-mail mentioning some issues with customer service. They have gone back up in my opinion again. Thanks j for the tip! :-)

(Female updater, 30–39 years of age, October 13, 2010 at 17:22)

Other updates were more densely intensified, like the post from updater <M98–10>, which contained capitalization, repeated exclamation marks, repetition, exaggerated quantifiers "all" and "everyone," and an exclamation "woop," so was classified as containing six intensification devices.

<M98–10> FINISHED A LEVEL EXAMS!!! woop! All I need now is my 3 A's baby! FUSION Next week thursday!!!! everyone remember and come to [name of school deleted]!

(Male updater, 13–18 years of age, June 25, 2010 at 16:31)

The distribution of intensifiers varies according to the characteristics of the updater (their age and gender), and changes over time. In 2008, 62 percent of the total number of intensification devices were authored by women; 38 percent by men. In 2010, women were still responsible for 55 percent of intensifications, but the gendered difference in use was reduced, with men authoring 45 percent of the intensification (summarized in Figure 4.7).

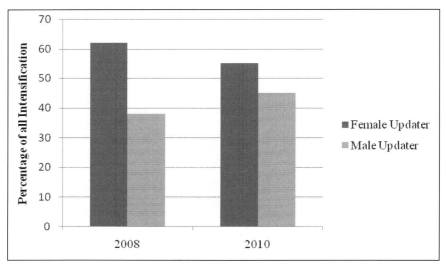

Figure 4.7 Comparison of intensification devices in 2008 and 2010 according to the gender of the updater (as a percentage).

When the results are disaggregated for age, a more complex pattern of variation emerges (summarized in Figures 4.8 and 4.9). In 2008, the intensification resources were concentrated in the updates written by women 19–24 years of age. This produced a gender difference in the distribution of intensification for that age group, a difference that is reduced for other groups, and in fact almost disappears for the participants in the category of 30–39 years of age.

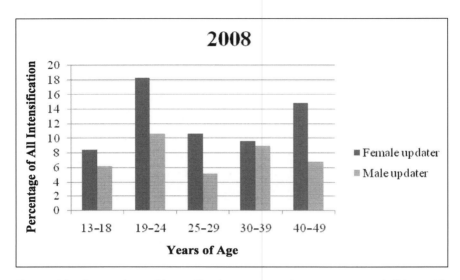

Figure 4.8   Comparison of intensification resources (as a percentage of all intensification) according to the age and gender of the updater in the 2008 dataset.

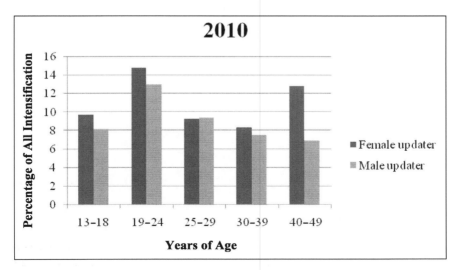

Figure 4.9   Comparison of intensification resources (as a percentage of all intensification) according to the age and gender of the updater in the 2010 dataset.

In 2010, although the women between 19 and 24 years of age still authored the most intensifiers, intensification devices were distributed more evenly between women and men in each age group, with only very small differences in the intensification levels of the women and men updaters in the age ranges of 25–29 and 30–39 years of age. The outcome is that the gender differences in updating style for each age group was smaller than in 2008, with the exception of the intensifiers used by participants in the 40–49 years of age category. It would seem that young women were in the vanguard of using a highly intensified style in 2008—a style that was later adopted more widely by women and men of other age groups.

Boosters: *Very, Really,* and *So*

Within the broader category of intensifiers, adverbs that amplify or scale up the meaning of a following adjective or adverb have been identified as a good place to observe linguistic change (Tagliamonte and Roberts 2005), a process that can also reveal the role of certain participant groups in promoting innovative use of language. Although a wide range of intensifying devices and adverbs were found in the status update stories, here I focus on the use of *very, really,* and *so*. These three adverbs are the most commonly occurring intensifying adverbs in contemporary English (Ito and Tagliamonte 2003; Tagliamonte and Roberts 2005) and demonstrate differing degrees of innovation over time. Examples of these intensifiers were found to scale up APPRAISAL in the datasets, where the women updaters used *really* and *so* particularly to emphasize positive sentiments.

> <F80–10> **So glad** to be back at home with a bed and a proper toilet :)
> (Female updater, 13–18 years of age, July 1, 2010 at 19:43)

> <F73–10> is **so proud** of her A Level students' results and has new carpet in classroom . . . BRILLIANT!
> (Female updater, 25–29 years of age, August 24, 2010 at 10:48)

> <F100–10> I am **really looking forward** to my party tomorrow nite—hope you are all coming along too!
> (Female updater, 40–49 years of age, June 26, 2010 at 19:43)

> <F61–10> Survived my first day at uni. . . . . . **really enjoyed** it. . . . going to be a busy 3 years!!
> (Female updater, 40–49 years of age, September 20, 2010 at 21:07)

The limited size of the corpus in this study means that any conclusions about the frequency and use of the intensifying adverbs in the datasets can only be provisional. Nonetheless, an initial survey of how these forms have changed between 2008 and 2010 is suggestive. The relative frequency and distribution of *very*, *really*, and *so* in the datasets of the updates in this study varies over time and across different participant groups (summarized in Table 4.1 and 4.2). In line with the general increase in intensification, the combined relative frequency of the three adverbs rose from 111 tokens per thousand words (2008) to 168 tokens per thousand words (2010). The overall increase was generated fairly equally by the behavior of women and men, who contribute thirty and twenty-seven words to this total respectively.

In 2008, the most frequently used adverb was *very* (fifty per thousand words), while in 2010, the most frequently used adverb was *so* (sixty-four per thousand words). As the numbers in Table 4.2 indicate, between 2008 and 2010 the frequency of *very* increased the least. However *so* and *really* show a rise in frequency, with the greatest increase contributed by the women's use of *so* (an increase of twenty-seven tokens per thousand words). These findings are consonant with developments documented in other research that also identifies women as initiators of change in the use of these intensifiers (Tagliamonte and Roberts 2005, 288).

Taken together, the analysis of APPRAISAL, nonverbal displays of affection (emoticons, kisses, and laughter) and intensifiers shows a complementary pattern of development. The three features all occurred with increased frequency in the later dataset and, overall, women were more likely than men to use these stylistic resources in their updates. However, women and men did not fall into homogenous categories and their updating styles changed over time. In 2008, the affective discourse features were found most frequently in the updates written by young female updaters. In particular, nonverbal displays of affection (emoticons, kisses, laughter) were used by female updaters of 13–18 years of age, and intensification was used most frequently by female

Table 4.1   Relative Frequency for *So*, *Very*, and *Really* in the 2008 Facebook Dataset (per Thousand Words)

	So	Very	Really	Total
Female	25	29	15	68
Male	12	20	9	41
Total	37	50	24	111

Table 4.2   Relative Frequency for *So*, *Very*, and *Really* in the 2010 Facebook Dataset (per Thousand Words)

	So	Very	Really	Total
Female	42	29	29	100
Male	22	25	20	68
Total	64	54	49	168

updaters of 19–24 years of age. The distribution of these resources produced a pattern of gender difference in writing style for the participants in the younger age groups, but that difference was not sustained for all other age groups. In 2010, the stylistic features associated with affectively oriented discourse were still used more by women than men, but the features were adopted increasingly by women in the older age groups and by men. The results support earlier studies in CMC, which found that men adopted the rate of expressing emotion characteristic of women (Wolf 2000). The results of the update analysis suggests that young women are trend setters of an affective discourse style in Facebook that is now being used in that context more widely by the participants in this study, at least. In the next section, I discuss why the changes in affective discourse might occur and what the use of expressive resources in storytelling might mean in the context of Facebook.

PERFORMED SOCIALITY: IDENTITIES AND INTERACTION IN FACEBOOK

Although sociality characterizes the generic context of Facebook as a site that enables its members to "connect and share with the people in your life" (Facebook homepage), the extent to which a member might use an affective style to narrate a small story in a status update is not a simplistic measure of actual relational closeness between that member and their Friend list, nor of the emotional states of the updaters. The increase in the use of affective discourse devices between 2008 and 2010 does not mean that the participants in this study began to experience more emotions or that their social relationships had necessarily changed within that time span. Instead, the small stories in status updates are rhetorical performances, not transparent representations of reality. Deborah Tannen (2011) describes the resources I have grouped together as symptomatic of affective discourse in the description of expressivity, which she argues is interpreted by young North American women as indicating camaraderie, emotional warmth, and sincerity. Similarly, I suggest that the use of APPRAISAL, nonverbal displays of affection and intensification can be interpreted as a type of performed sociality.

The performance of sociality is shaped by the way in which interaction is enabled and valued in Facebook. Throughout this chapter, I have argued that updating enables a one-to-many form of communication between the updater and the network of their Friend list. It enables the updater to project social connection with others but also presents risks in negotiating the collapsed contexts of the Friend network. Within this context, interaction with others operates within a system of exchange, where appropriate language use enables the updater to gain social capital (i.e., social acceptability). The interpersonal interaction projected through the performances of sociality in status updates is one means by which social capital can be gained (or lost).

Drawing on the work of the French sociologist, Pierre Bourdieu (1977), Herring and Zelenkauskaite (2009) describe the ways in which computer-mediated environments can function as linguistic marketplaces, where certain discourses acquire differential values. In the metaphor of linguistic markets, when a highly valued style is used appropriately, this can bring social (or economic) value to the language user. In Facebook, the benefits gained by interacting with a Friend list via updates are primarily social in nature, including the maintenance of an online identity approved by others and improved social networks.[9] Participants in this study were asked to reflect on the benefits they gained from using Facebook. Their responses suggest that updating is one means by which the ties within a social network can be strengthened, especially those ties that are deemed weak (Granovetter 1973). Excerpts from their questionnaire responses illustrate this point.

> It's nice to know little bits and pieces from status updates and be reminded when birthdays are so that even with people I don't know really well and maybe had pretty much lost touch with (such as old school friends) are on the radar again.
>
> (Female updater, 30–39 years of age)

> I use it for keeping in touch with friends whom I don't see very often because they now live too far away.
>
> (Male updater, 25–29 years of age)

> Facebook is good for talking to people I haven't seen for ages.
>
> (Male updater, 13–18 years of age)

The stories in status updates operate as tokens to be exchanged within the relational market places constructed in Facebook, where the value of a network is all the more important because interaction between Friends is interwoven tightly between online and offline contexts. The tellability of a status update must be managed appropriately in order for the story to gain value within this system. In terms of subject matter, the tellability of the story must be sufficiently low as to avoid unwanted personal disclosure, but in terms of rhetorical style, tellability must be high enough to gain and maintain the attention of the audience. This prompts a further question: does the performance of sociality result in actual interaction with others?

Status Updates and Interaction

The practice of "liking" and commenting on an update can be used as one parameter to measure interaction between an update and members of the updaters' Friend lists. A comparison of the interactive profiles of the updates in this sample shows that these practices vary according to the age and gender of the updater. In the 2010 dataset, updates authored by women attracted slightly more comments (53 percent) than those authored by men (47 percent). Similarly, updates authored by women attracted slightly more "likes" (56 percent) than those authored by men (44 percent). A closer analysis of the updates shows that more comments are made by women than by men, and that commenting seems to privilege interaction between participants with the same declared gender. In other words, women comment more frequently on updates written by women and men comment more frequently on updates written by men (summarized in Figure 4.10).[10]

When these aggregated results are separated by age group, a slightly more complex picture emerges (summarized in Figures 4.11 and 4.12).

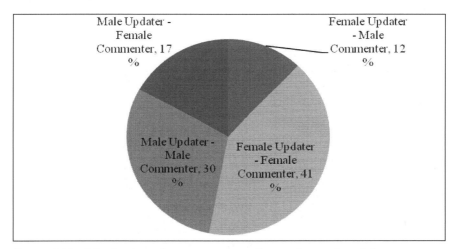

Figure 4.10 Distribution of comments according to the gender of the commenter (as a percentage of all comments).

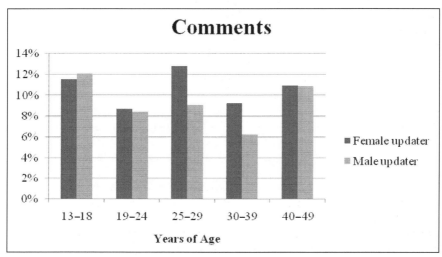

Figure 4.11 Percentage of comments appended to updates, according to the age and gender of the updater.

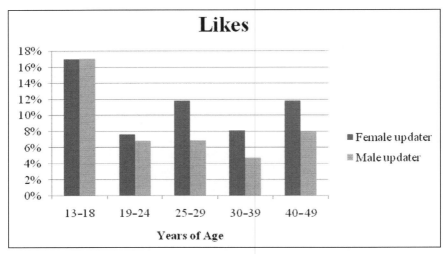

Figure 4.12   Percentage of "likes" appended to updates, according to the age and gender of the updater.

The results of this analysis show that there was almost no difference between the number of "likes" and comments attracted by updates written by women and men in the category of 13–18 years of age. Similarly, there was negligible difference in the number of comments attracted by female and male-authored updates for participants in the categories of 19–24 and 40–49 years of age. Where differences in interaction patterns did occur, they were generated by the "likes" appended to updates written by female authors in the age categories of 25 years old and above. Similarly, updates written by women attracted more comments for the age ranges 25–29 and 30–39 years of age.

The analysis of the comments and "likes" appended to updates in the 2010 dataset suggest that there is a broad similarity between the frequency with which the expressive features of affective discourse occur and the amount of interaction that an update attracts, where, overall, women use more APPRAISAL, nonverbal displays of affection, and intensifiers than do men, and where the updates written by women attract more interaction as signaled by comments and "likes." However, this aggregated correlation masks differences in the distribution of both discourse features and interactive patterns.

Moreover, there is not a causal relationship between discourse style and interaction patterns. That is to say, writing in an affectively oriented style does not automatically entail that the update will also be responded to by "likes" or comments. Conversely, not all updates that were commented on were intensified, carried APPRAISAL, or contained emoticons, kisses, or laughter. In fact, the updates with the most comments and "likes" contained

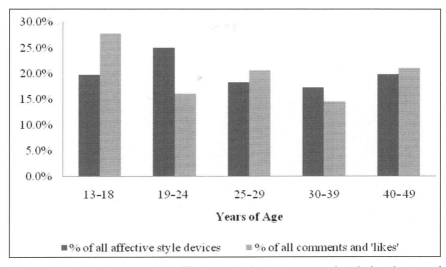

Figure 4.13 Distribution of all affective style devices compared with distribution of all interaction (comments and likes) across updates in 2010.

only small numbers of intensifiers. Figure 4.13 shows the combined frequency of comments and "likes" as compared with the combined frequency of APPRAISAL, intensification, and nonverbal displays of affection for the updates written by participants in each of the age ranges.

As the trends in this chart show, there is no simple correlation between discourse style and amount of interaction prompted by updating. In particular, there is a mismatch between the group associated with the most frequent interaction (updaters in the group of 13–18 years of age) and the group associated with the densest concentration of affective discourse (updaters in the group 19–24 years of age). This could be because the comparison of updating style with commenting and "liking" is based on the activity generated by two different participant groups: the style is produced by the updater and the interaction is produced by other participants. In addition, choosing to interact with an update may well be influenced by multiple factors that are less tractable and not included in this study (such as whether the participant's updates are being distributed to a Friend's account via a cell phone, the frequency with which an updater might comment on the wall posts of other Friends, etc.).

Status Updates and Identity

While the use of an affective discourse style does not prompt interaction in a mechanistic fashion, the variation in the use of APPRAISAL, intensification, and nonverbal displays of affection suggest that the storytelling style used in status updates is used a resource to construct the updater's identity. Bolander and Locher (2011) describe updates and their comments as acts of positioning, in which the updater can align his- or herself more or less closely with their Friends. The stylistic choices used to perform sociality can be interpreted similarly as a rhetorical strategy of positioning the updater as engaged with their Friend list. However, as the analysis of these resources as shown, performances of sociality are not homogenous. In the case of the datasets considered in this study, gender persists as a salient variable.

The symbolic value of the resources associated with affective discourse seem to echo those associated with hegemonic, Western femininity in other online contexts that interpret the use of nonstandard typography (repeated letters and punctuation) as indicating sociability and playfulness (Herring and Zelenkauskaite 2009). In the datasets considered in this chapter, the typographical features are part of the affective discourse that was associated with the rhetorical style used most frequently by female updaters in the younger age groups (13–18 and 19–24 years of age) in 2008 and was later adopted by women in older age groups and by some men. Sociological studies documented that women in the age range of 19–24 years were most heavily engaged in Facebook use during 2008 (Lenhardt et al. 2010), and that women remain the main users of SNS (Boland Abraham et al. 2010), while in the United Kingdom, women in the age range of 30–39 years have nearly gained parity in representation on Facebook with the younger women who were early adopters (ClickyMedia 2011). It seems plausible that the style used by the demographic group initially spending the most time interacting with Facebook (women in the age range 19–25 years of age) would set the trend for what could be regarded as appropriate linguistic behavior in updating, and that their style would then be adopted by others. This is not to say that APPRAISAL, emoticons, and intensification are used only by female updaters. They are found in updates written by male authors, but not to the same extent as these stylistic resources are used by women.

The linguistic trends found in these status updates suggest that gender differences in Facebook are becoming reified, where expressivity as performed sociality continues to be an index of playfulness associated with young, Western femininity. This conclusion is in line with other recent studies that depict Facebook as a heterosexual marketplace in which women are particularly sensitive to the needs of self-presentation in order to compete for attention (Stefanone et al. 2011). Clearly, there are other strategies for performing sociality that extend beyond the use of affective discourse, including the use of taboo language, in group jokes and sports talk. Camaraderie can be performed linguistically in a variety of ways and further research that explores the small stories found in status updates told by other demographic groups would be fertile ground for further research.

SUMMARY

The analysis of the small stories told in Facebook status updates has important implications for the narrative dimension of tellability. It draws attention to the interrelated but separate aspects of tellability as a subjective judgment concerning a narrative's subject matter and as a rhetorical resource for creating interpersonal involvement between a narrator and their audience. Both dimensions of tellability have bearing on the face needs of the narrator and audience, such that the maxim that a narrator must make his or her story relevant to their audience can be spelled out as the requirements to (1) tell your story in such a way so as to enable face-enhancing involvement with others, and (2) avoid telling stories that result in face-damaging outcomes for teller and audience.

The means by which a narrator meets the dual requirements to avoid damage to face and foster face-enhancing involvement are negotiated according to the specific context in which the story is situated. The asynchronous contexts of Facebook alter the face-threatening risks of communication in two ways. First, communicating via a status update avoids the risks of expressing emotion in a face-to-face context, enabling high levels of affective discourse to be used by members in order to meet the site's demand for sociality. Second, the collapsed contexts of Facebook Friend lists, which bring together members of a narrator's audience who would usually be separated from one another in offline contexts, increase the face-threatening risks of personal disclosure. The need to perform sociality in collapsed contexts thus puts pressure on the dimensions of tellability in specific but separate ways. In order to avoid damage to the face of self or others, the updaters in this study elected to tell stories about seemingly inoffensive, day-to-day topics: subject matter that would conventionally be regarded as low tellability. But in order to project face-enhancing involvement with others, the narrators also used rhetorical strategies of performed sociality that are associated with high tellability. In particular, the use of evaluation as indicated through APPRAISAL, intensification, and nonverbal displays of affection were used to give emphasis to the events and opinions reported in even the most mundane of small stories.

The use of APPRAISAL, intensification, and nonverbal displays of affection has been recognized in other contexts as resources that index sociality, especially for young women. In this study, the distribution of the affective style resources was not uniform. Initially, it tended to be used most in the writing of female updaters between 19 and 24 years of age, the group that was at that time also the most frequent user of Facebook more generally. Over time, the style was adopted increasingly by women in other age groups and by some men, as the frequency of site use has dispersed similarly. Although there is not a mechanistic relationship between the presence of APPRAISAL, intensification, and nonverbal displays of affection in an update and the amount of interaction that the update attracted, there are also gender differences in the interactive patterns of updaters and commenters. Updates written by female updaters attracted more comments and "likes" than did updates written by men, and more comments were written by female participants. These findings echo the conclusions in the analysis of the cancer blogs, namely, that gender persists as a meaningful category in computer-mediated contexts and that offline values do not disappear in online interaction.

However, it is clear that gendered differences in storytelling style do not arise in a universal or essentialist manner. The stylistic and interactional differences reported in this chapter are matters of comparative tendency, not exclusive and categorical use of linguistic forms by one social group only. The male updaters in this study did use APPRAISAL, intensifiers, and affective displays of emotion, but the female updaters tended to use these more frequently. As the longitudinal comparisons indicated by the results in this chapter suggest, styles can change over time and may take on different meanings. But in this context, the meaning associated with the rhetoric of high tellability is the need to promote sociality within a market where the attention from and interaction with a Friend list is all important. The need to compete for status and interaction within a linguistic market is by no means exclusive to Facebook. In the next chapter, I move on to consider the role of updating in a rather different environment: the microblogging site of Twitter.

5 Celebrity Practice
Stories Told in Twitter

TWITTER AS A CONTEXT FOR PRODUCING CELEBRITY

Twitter was founded by Jack Dorsey in 2006. Although it has been burgeoning since its inception, this growth has increased exponentially since January 2009 (Wilhelm 2010) such that at the outset of 2010 the site boasted over 100 million users (Owyang 2010).[1] Twitter is a microblogging site, in which members communicate with each other by posting messages known as tweets. The characteristics of a tweet reflect Twitter's evolution within *SMS* constraints (Huberman et al. 2009). Tweets can be no longer than 140 characters in length, do not allow comments to be appended, and are multifunctional.[2] They can be used to send a message to another individual or to an indefinite number of others, to report on daily activities, forward messages or information from others, share links, and so on. Twitter is potentially a "noisy environment" (Cha et al. 2010), where communication is fast-paced and ephemeral. In order to mitigate this, users have developed a number of conventions to assist in keeping track of the communication threads: using the @ symbol to indicate a public message directly addressed to a particular individual or a Twitter username (Honeycutt and Herring 2009), the # symbol to trace topic threads, and the abbreviation "RT" to signal that a message is being retweeted (boyd et al. 2010), that is, forwarded from another user.[3] This results in three main types of tweets analyzed in this chapter: addressed messages, retweets, and updates.

An *addressed message* is a public tweet that begins with an "@username" address, and so will be registered in the *@mentions* folder of the user's account. The following tweet was written by the presenter, Philip Schofield, but addressed to the twitter account for George Benson (@GBGuitar). Unlike Direct Messages (DMs), which are not included in this study, addressed messages appear in the public timeline of a Twitter account.

> @GBguitar Thanks for coming on the show today, always great to see you. Have a great tour
> Schofe: Thu, 27 May 2010 11:41

Retweets are tweets that have been forwarded without amendment and begin with the abbreviation "RT." In the following tweet posted by Sarah Brown, she forwards a message originally posted by the Twitter user @KathViner, which recommends an article by Margaret Atwood.

> RT @KathViner: Sweet piece by Margaret Atwood on how she loves Twitter; 'it's like having fairies at the bottom of your garden'
> SarahBrownUK: 08 Apr 2010 09:23

Updates are all other publically available tweets that appear in a tweeter's timeline, like this tweet from the actor Stephen Fry.

> On my way to the BBC R4 Today studio to bore the poor world further on the subj of Richard Wagner. Maybe they'll want to talk darts instead.
> StephenFry: May 2010 07:07

The information posted in Twitter can be posted publically so that anyone, even if they are not a member of Twitter, can view the content on the tweeter's home Twitter page. Alternatively, privacy protocols can be set so that the tweet is only seen by the individuals who have been accepted as Followers of the tweeter in question. Unlike Facebook, where privacy protocols are widely applied, only 7 percent of Twitter accounts are private: the default assumption of public communication dominates instead. The relationship between Twitter users is also distinctive. Unlike in most human social networks, Kwak et al. (2010) found that the relationship between individuals and their Followers was low in reciprocity. In other words, in Twitter, most users do not follow the same people who are following them.[4] This asymmetry is mirrored in other communicative dimensions typical of Twitter, specifically, the balance between one-to-many compared with one-to-one exchanges and whether or not users and their Followers are known to each other. So although Twitter is still sometimes defined as a social network site, its interpersonal dynamics suggest a rather different pattern of communication from those that might occur in semi-private, peer-to-peer environments like Facebook.

The public, one-to-many capacity of communicating via Twitter makes it an apt tool for promoting awareness of a topical event or subject with great rapidity, such that it has been dubbed an electronic form of "word of mouth" (Jansen et al. 2009). Recent studies suggest that Twitter discourse can be an accurate predictor of election outcomes (Tumasjin et al. 2010) or box office success (Asur and Huberman 2010), connecting public opinion as indicated via tweeting sentiments with "real world" social actions. Twitter's potential to share and shape audience response is also exploited by a media ecology characterized by "connectivity [and] real-time participation"

(Anstead and O'Loughlin 2010) and is deemed to be changing the way in which mainstream media is consumed (Johnson 2009).

Like other forms of social media, Twitter's audience is characterized by collapsed contexts (boyd 2008). In part, this is because like the audiences of discussion forums and blogs, the Twitter audience can lurk rather than making themselves known or participating in the discussion. As in Facebook Friend lists, Followers are aggregated into single online contexts that are normally segmented in offline contexts (such as work colleagues, family members, or more remote, professional contacts). In addition, Twitter collapses contexts that have been described as front and back stage regions. The sociologist Erving Goffman described the settings in which people perform their social identity as falling into separate regions: the front stage and the back stage (1959). The front stage is governed by protocols that maintain moral and social standards for decorum, where the audience is co-present with the performer. In contrast, the back stage is the space in which "the performer can relax: he can drop his front, forgo speaking his lines, and step out of character" (1959, 115).

In some respects, Twitter demonstrates some of the characteristics of a back stage region. Tweeting appears immediate and spontaneous and allows access to apparently privileged information about other tweeters, including public figures whom the Twitter audience might never meet in offline contexts. Given that Twitter is increasingly produced and consumed through intimate, mobile technologies, the capacity for Twitter to foster a sense that the audience is "behind the scenes" with the tweeter in their daily experiences is a tantalizing illusion that fosters a sense of assumed relational closeness between the tweeter and their Followers.

In other respects, Twitter is quite different to the privacy suggested by a back stage region. The Twitter audience is always present, and its scope is expansive. In February 2011, the UK Press Complaints Commission ruled that material posted on Twitter had a public status and that tweets could be reproduced without constituting an invasion of privacy. The ongoing need to negotiate between apparent back stage freedom of expression and the restrictions of front stage public consumption is a tension that tweeters confront regularly. In high-profile cases, this has resulted in celebrity figures like pop star Miley Cyrus withdrawing from Twitter. Sanctions have been applied against sports personalities tweeting during competitive events, and there have also been debates about using Twitter in contexts like the Supreme Court in the United Kingdom.[5] The legalities that govern the publication of private information in Twitter remain an ongoing source of controversy. In May 2011, an anonymous Twitter account released a series of celebrity names that had been embargoed in mainstream media publications by super injunctions, calling into question the power of the legal system to protect individual privacy in the age of social media.[6]

Given its reach and potency, it is no surprise to find that celebrity figures now dominate mainstream Twitter use.[7] The accounts with the highest number of Followers (over a million) are all recognized as celebrities in main-stream media (Kwak et al. 2010), and celebrity names rather than other user names tend to appear as trending topics (a facility that promotes the most talked about subjects on Twitter). The recent changes in celebrity culture, of which Twitter is now a part, place the very definition of celebrity under scrutiny (Turner 2004). Celebrity is not an attribute that an individual has or may be acquired on the basis of exceptional skill, achievement, or elite status. Rather, celebrity identities are discursively produced and need to be maintained by complex manipulations of the mainstream media.

The advent of social media offers new opportunities and challenges for the way celebrity culture is practiced. The discursive construction of celebrity has shifted beyond the controls of an institutionalized system to contexts like Twitter, where celebrity figures can interact directly with their fans. Marwick and boyd (2011) describe celebrity practice in social media contexts as including the "ongoing maintenance of a fan base, performed intimacy, authenticity, and access [to] and construction of a consumable persona." These strategies are similar to the processes that Senft (2008) describes as micro-celebrity, whereby "ordinary" people can gain popularity and fame in online contexts. The production of celebrity through micro-celebrity practices is embedded in wider media trends, preceded by the rise of other genres such as reality television shows (Stefanone and Lackaff 2009) and the subsequent democratization of celebrity status (Couldry 2002). But while fame exists on a continuum, the celebrity practices in Twitter do not collapse the hierarchical poles of this spectrum. Instead, the communicative dynamics of Twitter are well placed to boost celebrity status and reinforce the distinction between elite and nonelite identities. In Twitter, the prominence of a person or subject depends on the number of tweeters talking about them, as indicated by trending topics and "top tweets." In this way, celebrities may leverage the trending topics so that their status, products, and performance are promoted to an audience far beyond their immediate Followers. At the same time, the illusions of intimacy (Shickel 2000), interaction, and reworking the distinction between front and back stage regions for celebrity performances offset the promotional tactics celebrity practice entails. In this chapter, I will examine the role of storytelling in amplifying celebrity status while simultaneously constructing celebrities' identities as authentic and accessible individuals who are engaged with their fans.

DATA SAMPLE

The dataset that forms the basis for analysis and discussion is taken from sixty publically available Twitter accounts. This includes the accounts of thirty celebrities, of whom fifteen are women and fifteen are men, all English speaking and frequently mentioned in the British or American press, or both. They were chosen because their use of Twitter had been discussed in mainstream news reports. The celebrity figures selected have achieved prominence across a range of different spheres:

- Sport: Andy Murray, Lance Armstrong, Shaquille O'Neal
- Acting: William Shatner, Ashton Kutcher, Mischa Barton, Demi Moore, John Cleese
- Music: Britney Spears, Lady Gaga, Katherine Jenkins, Lily Allen, Dita von Teese, Amy Lee, Dave Matthews
- Presenters: Jonathan Ross, Philip Schofield, Holly Willoughby, Oprah Winfrey, Stephen Fry, Ellen de Generes, Paris Hilton, Dannii Minogue, Amanda Holden, Jimmy Fallon, Jamie Oliver, Charlie Brookner
- Politics: Arnold Schwarzenegger, Boris Johnson, Sarah Brown[8]
- Journalism: Charlie Brooker

Using the Twitter *API*, the most recent thousand tweets were selected for each of the celebrities in the first week of June 2010. In order to see how far the celebrity Twitter discourse was typical of Twitter in general, a parallel dataset from thirty randomly selected public Twitter profiles (fifteen men, fifteen women) was also taken. The total dataset consisted of 51,643 tweets, totaling 939,540 words.

As with all online contexts, the question of speaker authenticity remains controversial. Unlike the Friend networks in Facebook, where the members usually know each other in the offline world and where authenticity is strongly encouraged, there is no guarantee that the celebrity tweets are written by celebrities themselves. While many celebrity tweeters claim authenticity for themselves and rebuke tweeters who have falsely appropriated their celebrity name, other celebrity tweet streams are clearly written by a promotional team rather than a single individual, with individual tweets signed by managers or assistants, such as those included in the Twitter accounts for Britney Spears and John Cleese.

> We have a new video straight from Britney tomorrow on www.Britney-Spears.conm . . . just a few more hours. . . .~posted by Lauren~
>
> BritneySpears: Mon, 20 Oct 2008 10:39

> From Garry: Back in Santa B. JC off to see Sienfeld tomorrow night (he's performing here). Should be fun.
>
> JohnCleese:Thu, 05 Mar 2009 23:33

Because the focus of this study is on narratives of personal experience, the third-person narratives where a tweet was clearly authored by someone other than the celebrity themselves were discarded. In all other cases, where the tweet was represented as if authored by the celebrity figure, it was included as part of the identity performed by that figure.

FROM FOLLOWERS TO FANS: THE INTERACTIVE
CONTEXT OF TWITTER NARRATIVES

The stories that construct celebrity identity in Twitter are shaped by their interactive context, including the relationship between the narrator and his or her audience. Twitter homepages contain scant biographical information about narrators.[9] Instead, the interaction between tweeter and their audience is a critical factor that distinguishes between the identities of mainstream celebrities and "ordinary" tweeters. One difference concerns the size of the tweeter's known audience. Each Twitter homepage lists the number and details of people whom the tweeter is following, along with the number of Followers the individual has. This information was collated for each of the Twitter profiles considered in this study and is summarized in Table 5.1.

As might be predicted, celebrity tweeters have many more Followers than "ordinary" tweeters. All of the selected celebrities were being followed by over 20,000 individuals each: nearly half of them by more than a million. In contrast, the "ordinary" tweeters in this sample had between 65 and 3,017 Followers. There is no overlap between the sizes of the Follower lists for celebrity and "ordinary" tweet accounts. The smallest Follower list on a celebrity account in this sample (23,285 people) was over seven times the size of the largest Follower list for an ordinary account (3,017 people). Moreover, while both celebrities and "ordinary" tweeters were being followed by a greater number people than they in turn were following, this difference was more strongly marked for the celebrities. The mean number of Followers accrued by a celebrity figure was approximately one and a half times bigger than the number of Followers gained by the "ordinary" tweeters. The ratio between Followers and the number of people a tweeter follows makes plain this contrast. The Follower list for celebrity tweeters was nearly sixty times the size of the Twitter population the celebrities were

Table 5.1   Average Number of Followers and Following Participants for Celebrity and "Ordinary" Tweeters

	Celebrity Tweeters		"Ordinary" Tweeters	
	Mean	Range	Mean	Range
Followers	1,575,859	23,285–5,075,521	619	26–3,017
Following	26,287	24,000–418,352	386	28–2,228
Ratio of Followers to Following	60:1		6:1	

interested in receiving tweets from: a ratio ten times the size of that found on "ordinary" accounts. These figures would seem to confirm the nonreciprocal relationships observed in Twitter more generally, but show that the scale of this disparity is increased sharply for celebrity figures.

The asymmetrical relationship between tweeter and audience is reflected in the choice of whether to use addressed messages or updates. Addressed messages suggest peer-to-peer conversation, while updates are one-to-many broadcasts. The relative proportion of types of Twitter behavior suggests subtle contrasts between the ways in which celebrity and "ordinary" figures in this dataset interacted with their Followers. Table 5.2 summarizes the percentage of each group's updates, retweets, and directly addressed tweets.

These results suggest that the most frequent type of Twitter activity is the posting of an update. Update tweets may ask a question; report on activities, conversations, and locations; or share a link. With such varied functions, it is perhaps not surprising that this is the most frequent type of posting behavior, and further analysis may reveal greater variation in use of Twitter. Nonetheless, even at a surface level, the relative balance between the one-to-many messages (updates) and one-to-one communication (addressed tweets) for the celebrities and regular tweeters is notable. Like "ordinary" tweeters, celebrities tend to favor updates more than addressed messages but this preference is more marked for celebrity twitter practice. For "ordinary" tweeters there is 6 percent difference between the updates and addressed messages for regular tweeters (48 percent and 42 percent, respectively), while there is 31 percent difference between updates and addressed messages in the celebrity dataset (63 percent and 32 percent, respectively). The general patterns of Twitter behavior surveyed in this study thus suggest that celebrities favor one-to-many communicative practices, a dynamic well suited to broadcasting information to a sizeable fan base rather than conversing with a smaller number of peers.

As with the Facebook updates discussed in Chapter 4, tweet updates are a highly varied and multifunctional genre. In this dataset, 39 percent of celebrity updates reported events or told a story. But like the stories found in other social media contexts, the kinds of narratives found in Twitter contrast with canonical narrative in terms of their linearity, embeddedness, tellability, and tellership, all of which are reworked by the celebrity practices of constructing intimacy, authenticity, and consumable identity.

Table 5.2 Percentages of Tweet Types Used by Celebrity Figures and "Ordinary" Tweeters

	Updates	*Retweets*	*Addressed Messages*	*Total*
Celebrity	63%	5%	32%	100%
"Ordinary"	48%	10%	42%	100%

NARRATIVE TWEETS AND LINEARITY

As with many other forms of social media, the linearity of narrative tweets is derived from the representation of time generated from the timestamp in the tweet template, the position of the tweet within an archive of updates and the content of the tweet itself. Tweets are posted in a standard template that automatically generates the minimal narrative cues of a timestamp and the tweeter's username and profile photograph, as shown in Figure 5.1.

Because tweeting is assumed to occur in close proximity to the time that the reported events takes place, the audience can use the information from the timestamp as the basis for inferring the chronological context for the events too. This is crucial information as narrative production is removed from the time of narrative reception, and although the tweets are distributed in chronological order, they are sequenced so that the most recently updated posts appear first in the archived RSS feeds. Both the asynchronous nature of Twitter interaction and the priority placed on recency are connected to the linguistic representation of temporality within the content of the tweets.

Unlike past-tense verbs, which were taken to be definitive of canonical narratives of personal experience, the abbreviated style typical of Twitter discourse relies on verbal phrases that are often truncated. Typically the verb forms in Twitter omit the auxiliary particle, leaving only the *nonfinite* forms of the past or progressive participle.

> Excited to break ground on our second veterans home this week. Watch at http://tweetcast.in
>
> Schwarzenegger: Fri, 21 May 2010 17:29

The effect of truncating the verb phrases in this way is that the tense of the clause becomes ambiguous. Although there is not a direct correlation between verb tense and narrative time, the absence of the tensed auxiliary means that the tweets could be interpreted as referring to events that take place in the past,

> Just landed in Egypt! :)
>
> ParisHilton: Wed, 02 Jun 2010 10:43

 ruthtweetpage Ruth Page
rewriting my chapter on celebrity twitter.
14 minutes ago

Figure 5.1   An illustrative example of the Twitter update template.

or nonfinite participles could refer to events in the present or future,

> Roasting in paris today. Hitting with pablo cuevas at 2pm . . .
> Andy_Murray: Sun, 23 May 2010 10:34

This temporal ambiguity is a highly appropriate strategy for bridging the asynchronous nature of Twitter discourse, eliding the gap between narrative event, report, and reception.

Despite the temporal ambiguity of the nonfinite verb participles, the tweeters locate the reported events chronologically by making reference to points in time through temporal adverbs, deictics, and conjunctions. Using Antconc concordancing software (Anthony 2011), I compared the twenty-five most frequent terms of temporal reference from the word list of the celebrity dataset with their frequency in the general Twitter dataset and two reference corpora: the *British National Corpus* (BNC) and the *Corpus of Contemporary American English* (COCA) (Davies 2011).[10] The relative frequencies of the ten most frequently occurring temporal terms from this list in each of the datasets and reference corpora are summarized in Figure 5.2.

These results demonstrate that the references to time favored in this Twitter dataset occur on average approximately three times more frequently than in either the British or American reference corpora, and that this difference is even greater in the celebrity tweets. In part, this might be explained by the high number of narratives in the celebrity updates that might concentrate temporal marking more than would be expected in general language use. But the increased frequency of temporal marking does not apply to all

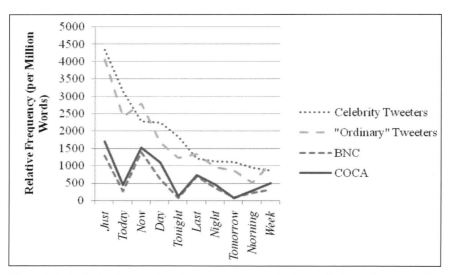

Figure 5.2   Relative frequencies of temporal terms in Twitter talk (per million words).

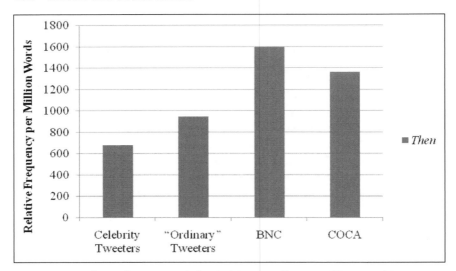

Figure 5.3   Relative frequency of *then* in Twitter talk (per million words).

temporal references. The adverb *then*, which typically signals a chronological sequence, occurs less frequently in the Twitter datasets than in general British or American language use (summarized in Figure 5.3).

In contrast, the temporal terms used with the highest preference in Twitter are the three adverbs *tonight*, *today*, and *tomorrow*. The overuse of these three temporal adverbs is striking when we compare them with other, similar forms. For example, the relative frequency of *yesterday* in the celebrity Twitter dataset is 311 per million words, ten times less frequent than *today* (3,131 per million words) in the same dataset. While this is still slightly more frequent than the occurrence of *yesterday* in the BNC and COCA corpus (195 and 66 occurrences per million words, respectively), the difference between occurrences in Twitter use of *yesterday* and the reference corpora is much less pronounced than the differences that exist for *tonight*, *today*, and *tomorrow*. The greater frequency of the adverbs *tonight*, *today*, and *tomorrow* suggests that the Twitter updates are less retrospective (reporting what happened yesterday) and more grounded in the events of that particular day and the immediate future.

The emphasis on the present moment is supported by a comparison of the reciprocal deictic pair *now* and *then* with the pair *here* and *there* (summarized in Table 5.3). In each case, the adverb which indicates close proximity to the time and place of the speaker (*here* and *now*) occurs more frequently in the celebrity Twitter dataset than those that indicate distance (*then* and *there*). In addition, both *here* and *now* are overused in the Twitter updates compared with the reference corpora. In contrast, *there* and *then* appear

Table 5.3   Relative Frequency of *Here*, *There*, *Now*, and *Then* (per Million Words)

	Celebrity tweets	BNC	COCA
Here	2,663	699	1,031
There	1,369	746	1,961
Now	2,284	1,382	1,515
Then	795	1,595	1,360

underused in Twitter (with the exception of *there* compared with the BNC). On the basis of these results, we might conclude that the temporal deictics center the celebrity updates in the *here* and *now*, in line with their emphasis on *today*, *tonight*, and *tomorrow*.

The combination of nonfinite verb forms, which generate a free-floating temporal frame of reference, and the high frequency of temporal adverbs, which anchor the tweets' chronological context in *here* and *now* of *today* and *tonight*, gives rise to a sense of an ongoing present in which the narrative tweets are continuously situated. Any sense of retrospection is diminished, as each episode is received within the context of an ever-present *now*. The sense of an ongoing temporal present in the Twitter stories is entwined with the use of Twitter to create an ongoing sense of *presence* between the speaker and the audience. Previous work has noted the effect of shared time on human relationships, such that they encourage an illusion of relational proximity (Bennett 2000), one that is in keeping with the celebrity practice of projecting intimacy with their audience. However, the collocational patterns associated with the most frequent temporal adverbs in the Twitter datasets suggest that the sense of shared time constructed in celebrity practice has less to do with personal intimacy centered on the celebrity's private life and more to do with promoting mainstream celebrity performance.

The association between narrative immediacy and the promotion of mainstream celebrity performance is suggested by the repeated co-occurrence of temporal adverbs and lexical items that are related to media performance, such as *show*. The repeated co-occurrence of these terms, known in corpus linguistics as collocation, is seen in the three most overused temporal adverbs (*tonight*, *today*, and *tomorrow*). The term *show* collocated strongly with all three adverbs. It was ranked seventh most frequent collocate for *tonight*:

> Mannequin's going **into the show tonight** for the first time. I'm really excited for everyone to see it!–Britney
> Britneyspears: Sun, 05 Jul 2009 19:35.

Show was the fifteenth most frequent collocate for *tomorrow*,

Nighty nighty! Just arrived in Manchester ready for my very early performance **on the Andrew Marr show tomorrow.** Up in less than 5 hours! Xxx

(KJofficial: Sat, 03 Oct 2009 23:44)

and the twenty-first most frequent collocate for *today*,

I always love having Kid Inventors **on the show and today** is no exception. http://su.pr/23ZYZ0

(Theellenshow: Mon, 01 Mar 2010 17:43).

The stories told in Twitter associate narrative immediacy with mainstream celebrity activity, rather than their private life. The connection between immediacy and performance is distinctive to celebrity practice rather than being characteristic of Twitter in general, for in the updates tweeted by "ordinary" figures, the temporal adverbs occurred with high frequency, but did not collocate with terms like *show* at all. Like the celebrity figures, "ordinary" tweeters talk about the professional activities that are taking place in temporal proximity to the present moment, like coding data or preparing a presentation.

Taking a break from coding **today,** need a break from all those letters & numbers. Instead I am spreadsheeting. Oh, damn #itsjustasbad

Male tweeter: Fri, 14 May 2010 09:59

Finally nailed my presentation for **tomorrow.** Got it down to 5 minutes exactly. Now all I've got to do is suppress my nerves!

Male tweeter: Mon, 26 Apr 2010 16:37

But these professional activities are not public displays that are promoted as mainstream media events. We might conclude from this that celebrities are exploiting Twitter's emphasis on the *here* and *now* as a means of promoting their mainstream activity and so presenting themselves as a consumable commodity.

NARRATIVE TELLABILITY: FRONT AND BACK STAGE PERFORMANCES

The tellability of social media stories can vary considerably. In earlier chapters we have seen how blog narrators might reflect on life-transforming topics like critical illness, which contrasts with the scale of tellability found in Facebook updates, where mundane, everyday topics are elected in order to avoid the risks of unwanted personal disclosure. Mainstream media has sensationalized celebrity use of Twitter as a means of accessing the intimate details of their private life, for example, that Shaquille O'Neal had just worked out (Johnson 2009) or that Demi Moore had steamed her husband's suit while dressed in a bikini (*Telegraph* 2009). However, glimpses of personal disclosure are by no means the only kind of story found in celebrity tweets. Instead, the tellability of narratives used in celebrity practice is negotiated within the collapsed contexts of Twitter, which blurs an easy distinction between front and back stage regions for performance.

Goffman's dramaturgical metaphor of front and back stage regions suggests that these settings are distinct environments. There is a clear boundary separating the front and back regions, with the back stage region "cut off . . . by a partition and guarded passageway" (1959, 115) that conventionally excludes the front stage audience. Although Twitter is an environment that is outside the institutional media systems, it functions as a public environment in which the audience is still present. In this sense, Twitter is not an authentic back stage region (in Goffman's use of the term), but an environment in which pseudo–back stage performances are broadcast publically to fans. I use the term *pseudo*–back stage for these Twitter performances, not because the content is necessarily false or untrue, but because the reports remain mediated, publically staged constructions of authenticity for the front stage audience. Twitter is not a space where the performer can "relax" as if the audience were not present. Instead, Twitter is an additional environment in which celebrities can manage their communication with their fans.

How far back behind the scenes the celebrity allows their fans to see via Twitter can vary. Back stage performances on Twitter can include reports from immediately before a mainstream performance takes place (e.g., from a performer's dressing room, or pre-performance rehearsal), travelling to or from a performance, or training for an event.

> Standing in the middle of an empty River Plate Stadium, Buenos Aires, about to start my soundcheck. Very VERY cool x
>
> KJOfficial: Mon, 24 May 2010 13:35

Back stage also includes the social events surrounding a performance, such as meals with co-performers or teammates.

> Went to players party last night with the guys, was good fun, won a new putter in the putting competition, miles was very jealous
>
> Andy_Murray: Fri, 12 Mar 2010 17:16

Still further away from the mainstream performance, celebrities might also document aspects of their private life, including meals, the activities of family members, and daily activities such as going to bed.

> I am going to bed to watch a film about Leningrad while my wife lies next to me dreaming up dialogue for mutants ! Da, comrades.
>
> Wossy: Tue, 25 May 2010 20:50

right I'm taking a leaf out of @Amanda_Holden 's book, just got a bowl of cereal and a glass of wine . . . x

hollywills: Thu, 06 May 2010 22:15

There is a clear relationship between back stage information and constructions of intimacy: the further behind the scenes the fan is allowed to see, the greater the illusion of intimacy.

In order to assess the relative emphasis that celebrity practice in Twitter places on mainstream performance as compared with the most personal back stage information, I analyzed a random sample of a thousand narrative updates from the celebrity accounts. I coded each update according to whether the subject matter reflected the private life of the tweeter, or was related to their professional activity (including rehearsals for or social events directly related to a mainstream performance). The comparison of professional and private life stories in the dataset is thus a heuristic gesture rather than an absolute measure. As Figure 5.4 suggests, personal disclosures of mundane, everyday activities such as watching television, cooking a family meal, or going to bed are by far in the minority of this dataset. Instead, the majority of stories (73 percent) are told about the celebrity's professional activities. There are some tweeters who do not disclose any personal information, such as Arnold Schwarzenegger and Boris Johnson, but there were no celebrity tweeters who talked only about their private life.

The tellability of stories in the celebrity tweets is clearly centered on the narrator's professional activities. The results suggest that celebrity practice on Twitter is mostly used as a means of extending front stage celebrity performances, and emphasizes the events, products and activities which

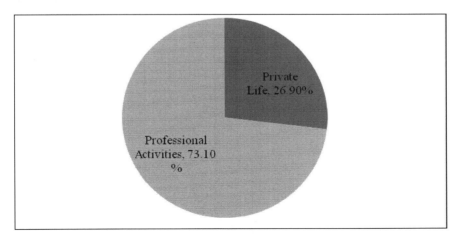

Figure 5.4 Comparison of tweets from celebrity figures about professional or private-life activity (as a percentage).

are associated with a celebrity's professional identity. This is not to say that celebrity practice on Twitter is not used to perform intimacy. It does do so, but to a lesser measure than the mainstream media lead us to believe, and not necessarily through disclosures of a celebrity's private life. Instead, the tweets are another mechanism by which these celebrities promote their mainstream activity, harnessing the news-sharing function of Twitter where broadcasting information is more important than generating social connectedness. Together with the one-to-many communicative patterns and disproportionately large number of Followers garnered by the celebrities in this dataset, it would seem that the celebrities are functioning as information sources for their fan base, not as Friends within a network of peers.

EMBEDDEDNESS: NARRATIVE TWEETS IN CONTEXT

Ochs and Capps describe the narrative dimension of embeddedness as the extent to which a narrative can be detached from its surrounding rhetorical, discourse and social context (2001, 36–37). Although it is quite possible for a narrative to be told in its entirety within a single tweet, there are also many occasions where one tweet is not enough to tell the whole story. When a narrative is dispersed across multiple tweets or between a tweet and additional online material, it becomes very difficult to detach the emerging story from its textual and extrasituational contexts.

Shared Stories: Real Time Commentary on Mainstream Media Performances

The real-time reporting of narrative events in Twitter enables narrators to produce an ongoing, episodic series of consecutive tweets that appear to relay events as they are happening. Typical uses of this real-time commentary for celebrity tweeters include counting down the minutes immediately preceding a performance, thereby reminding viewers that a show is about to begin. The following extract illustrates Ashton Kutcher encouraging his fans to tune in.

> broadcasting LIVE around 10:00 a.m. PT at http://bit.ly/2zQhjI #rustechdel
> Aplusk: Thu, 25 Feb 2010 17:54

> hey guys . . . running a few mins late on our broadcast. going live soon at www.ustream.tv/ashton
> Aplusk: Thu, 25 Feb 2010 18:08

> about to go LIVE www.ustream.tv/ashton
> Aplusk: Thu, 25 Feb 2010 18:17

We are LIVE from @katalysthq—TUNE-IN http://bit.ly/V4ov #rustechdel
Aplusk: Thu, 25 Feb 2010 18:24

The real-time commentaries also emerge as the celebrity is watching another performance (such as a sports match or television show). Examples include Stephen Fry who tweets about darts matches, Lily Allen who is an avid cricket fan, and the many celebrities who post their opinions on talent show contests.[11] The celebrity commentaries share some similarities with other sports broadcasts. Ryan argues that broadcasts favor the structural features of the chronicle, which "requires no retrospective point of view, no global design, and consequently no teleological principles" (2006, 81), all features that are ideally suited to the immediate and emergent characteristics of social media. But the celebrity commentaries in Twitter are quite distinct from the radio broadcasts that Ryan examines. The purpose of the celebrity commentary is not to document events for the benefit of an absent audience who cannot view them. Instead, the celebrity commentaries provide an evaluative perspective on events that are assumed to be shared with a co-spectating, although remote, audience. An example from the Twitter account of the British television celebrity Amanda Holden illustrates this point. The following sequence of tweets was published on Saturday May 29, 2010, during the period that an episode of the television show *Britain's Got Talent* was aired. Holden was a judge on the show.

Sat, 29 May 2010 19:00	Got my tweeting fingers flexed for BGT!X
Sat, 29 May 2010 19:03	I've got butterflies!
Sat, 29 May 2010 19:04	Thank god I eat veggie sausages!
Sat, 29 May 2010 19:06	HYSTERICAL
Sat, 29 May 2010 19:09	watch this!!!
Sat, 29 May 2010 19:10	Xmas Party??
Sat, 29 May 2010 19:12	Cheap gag but it worked!
Sat, 29 May 2010 19:12	That was a number one by the way
Sat, 29 May 2010 19:25	Hope she's insured x
Sat, 29 May 2010 19:26	My hubby loved that
Sat, 29 May 2010 19:29	I think the Pet shop boys are safe!
Sat, 29 May 2010 19:30	Lovely chap
Sat, 29 May 2010 19:30	Won't be booking him for Lexi's b day x
Sat, 29 May 2010 19:37	Might borrow one of those outfits for the live shows next week!
Sat, 29 May 2010 19:43	Get your tissues ready
Sat, 29 May 2010 19:47	I'm welling up
Sat, 29 May 2010 19:57	See I can move my eyebows! No botox!
Sat, 29 May 2010 20:06	Who's going thru do you think???!!!!

Holden's tweets make little sense without the context of the screened television show. The tweets contain unglossed pronominal and deictic references that point beyond the text, for example, "watch *this*," "my hubby loved *that*," "one of *those* outfits" (emphasis added). Similarly, her evaluations do not make plain who or what is being evaluated. Without seeing the show, we do not know who the "lovely chap" is or what was "HYSTERICAL" or constituted a "cheap gag." The Twitter commentary is supposed to be consumed in conjunction with the mainstream media, not in isolation from it.

Evaluative commentary like Holden's does not constitute a story in itself, at least if narrative is understood as a sequenced series of events because the tweets report sequenced evaluation, not sequenced events. However, the commentaries are akin to the small story subgenre of shared stories (Georgakopoulou 2007). As we saw in the discussion of Facebook updates in Chapter 4, shared stories are references that call attention to a narrative communally known to a narrator and their audience. These shared stories are an important resource for celebrity practice, as they foster the performance of intimacy through the projection of a shared perspective. Through shared stories, the celebrity repositions their identity as a performer who is also a viewer along with the "ordinary" audience at home. This shift is an entirely apt strategy for talent shows like *Britain's Got Talent*, which are embedded in the demotic trends in media where the viewing public's voting behavior determines the outcome of the competition and the elevation of an ordinary person to celebrity status. Once again, performed intimacy is tightly bound up with the celebrity practice of promoting their products, for the more the audience is engaged with the show (through viewing figures and voting activity), the more revenue can be generated. Encouraging audience participation, harnessing the power of what Anstead and O'Loughlin (2010) call the "viewertariat," is not a neutral, altruistic measure that celebrates participatory culture. More cynically, it reflects the ways in which mainstream media celebrity practices symbiotically use social media to shore up rather than destabilize its own values, commodities, and hierarchy.

Intertextual Stories: Linking in the Tweets

The narratives told in Twitter are also embedded in intertextual contexts of the World Wide Web. The original purpose of blogging was to list the various sites that the user had visited (Myers 2010, 30). Microblogging retains this function, and disseminating links to other material is widespread in Twitter. Twenty-three percent of the tweets in the Twitter dataset as a whole contained a link to an external URL. As with the personal blogs discussed in Chapter 3, the relative frequency of linking and a qualitative analysis of the links achieve important identity work for the tweeter. For example, the sites that are linked to tell us about the position the tweeter adopts within a wider network of online resources, and what the tweeter's interests, areas of expertise and authority are related to.

The conventions for embedding links in Twitter contrast with those found in the cancer blogs in Chapter 3. In personal blogs, links are usually embedded via hyperlinked words in the text and function as annotations to the narrative. In Twitter, the URLs for the links are included explicitly and the usual practice is to accompany this with a caption of some kind that annotates the link.[12]

> Mick Jagger went all Desmond last night on "LATE" http://bit.ly/ ddO6Zb
> Jimmyfallon: Wed, 12 May 2010 12:48

> The hypnotic sounds of @johncmayer put some kind of hilarious spell on my husband . . . http://tweetphoto.com/6405730
> Amyleeev: Mon, 14 Dec 2009 05:41

These captions need not be narratives in themselves (although some are), but when understood in the wider context of the linked material, they can take on a narrative function. The captions function in a similar way to a headline for a news report as a means of attracting the viewer's attention and directing them toward additional information, or a further story to be told. As Bell (1991) pointed out, when news headlines function in this way, they become a centre of evaluative focus for the story that follows, a "nucleus" around which the satellites of the news report follow (White 1997). Three main relationships between the tweet nucleus and the linked material emerge, each of which foregrounds a different aspect of narrative structure.

Abstract

Like the Abstracts that Labov (1972) described in relation to personal narratives, tweets can compress and restate the main events that are given in more detail elsewhere.

> Just went with GB to opening of Poetry for Haiti event at Westminster Central Hall: amazing line up and still going on http://bit.ly/cGhvcQ
> SarahBrownUK: Sat, 30 Jan 2010 15:20

> Had a really busy morning. Been out in Charlton where I met some inspiring apprentices—http://bit.ly/NTkf6
> Boris Johnson: Wed, 28 Oct 2009 14:47

Orientation

Even if the text accompanying a link does not contain a complete narrative, often, and especially when the link is to a photograph, the link will contain contextual information that gives more temporal and spatial information. It is these additional contextual cues of time and space that prompt an interpretation of narrativity.

> In the green room with Michael Buble http://twitpic.com/slf3m
> Kjofficial: Mon, 07 Dec 2009 23:44

> Behind the scenes video in Cape Town with Marks & Spencer ! http://bit.ly/aSqgvs
> DanniiMinogue: Wed, 24 Mar 2010 13:28

Evaluation

The caption prefacing a link may also indicate the celebrity's stance toward or evaluation of the events that are reported or depicted. The tweeter might state whether they like the material, find it funny or offensive, or whether it is useful to their audience.

> The USDA & Milk board MIGHT find this interesting when they feed the kids the choc milk@school jox www.mayoclinic.com/health/calcium/an01294
> Jamie_Oliver: Sun, 25 Apr 2010 20:19

> hahaha http://bit.ly/jxe6S
> Lilyroseallen: Wed, 16 Sep 2009 12:03

The intertextual links that follow the captions amplify and extend the narrative potential of the tweets. The amplification has two dimensions. First, it amplifies the content of the tweet by sending the viewer to additional online materials that provide more detail about the story. Second, they may amplify the status of the tweeter by directing the viewer to more resources that document the celebrity's activity, but also by constructing the celebrity as an authority who can filter the wealth of online material and endorse specific sites or content.

A quantitative analysis of the links suggests that linking serves an important role in celebrity practice on Twitter. The simplest observation is that celebrities link to other sites more frequently than do the "ordinary" tweeters in this dataset, where 27 percent of all celebrity tweets contained links, compared with 19 percent of the tweets from the "ordinary" Twitter accounts. Most of the links occurred in the update tweets (rather than in directly addressed messages or in retweets), summarized in Figure 5.5. A qualitative analysis of links suggests why linking might be an important amplification strategy for celebrity status. The web pages to which the audience is directed from the tweets are of many multimodal stories: YouTube

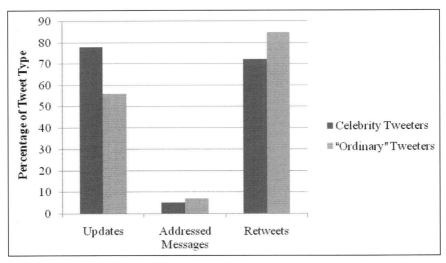

Figure 5.5 Comparison of tweets containing links in celebrity and "ordinary" Twitter accounts (as percentages of each type of tweet).

movies, podcasts, online news pages, blogs, photographs, and so on. It is beyond the scope of this chapter to provide a full analysis of all the links in the dataset, but a corpus-based approach allows us to isolate the links to photographs (twitpics and tweetphotos) and to audiovisual material hosted on YouTube. From these searches, we can observe that celebrities link to images more frequently than do the "ordinary" tweeters: 27 percent of all celebrity links were to images, compared with 8 percent of the links from the general Twitter dataset. Photo sharing, especially from mobile devices like smart phones, is said to create an increased feeling of co-presence between tweeter and audience (Ito 2005), and the interplay between text and image produces a heightened sense that the tweeter is "real" (Suler 2008). The higher number of links to images might be interpreted as examples of performed intimacy and authenticity, supporting the illusions of back stage access to the celebrity constructed in the public context of Twitter.

Beyond the obviously multimodal resources, the links in tweet streams direct the audience to a variety of other sites. Some ask the viewer to do something (purchase goods or join a petition), but most contain additional information, such as links to mainstream news, movie trailers, or blog posts. One hundred links were taken from the celebrity and noncelebrity tweets to gauge an initial impression of what content was represented in the linked sites. Both celebrity and "ordinary" figures linked to external resources that reflected the areas of expertise associated with their professional identities.

"Ordinary" tweeters linked to external news reports or adverts for events in their field of interest, for example, a vicar might link to a podcast of a sermon, a solicitor to news of a recent legal ruling, and a food critic to reviews of a restaurant. In contrast, the celebrity tweets linked to resources where the celebrity figure was the focus of the news report or the resource. For example, Katherine Jenkins and Lily Allen linked to mainstream news reports in which they figure, and Paris Hilton linked to celebrity gossip reports. Other celebrities disseminated movie trailers for films in which they star (Ashton Kutcher, Arnold Schwarzenegger), promotional videos for their products (Demi Moore), or music videos (Lady Gaga). Promoting products and recirculating mainstream news of celebrity activity are strategies which present the celebrity as a consumable commodity—again suggesting celebrity practices of amplification that prompt the increased use of links in their tweets.

TELLERSHIP: RETWEETS AS CO-CONSTRUCTED NARRATIVES

The need for celebrity practice to project back stage illusions of intimacy as a front stage strategy for maintaining and managing a fan base shapes the tellership of co-constructed narratives found in retweets. Retweets are messages that are forwarded to all the Followers on a tweeter's account. Retweets involve at least two parties in the act of discourse creation: the original tweeter (who authors the first message) and the retweeter (who forwards on the message). As boyd et al. (2010) point out, the conventions for retweeting are still in flux. A tweet can be forwarded without any additional information, or the original text may be transformed by the retweeter, for example, by adding new detail or compressing some of the original.

The co-tellership of modified tweets is distinctive from the other forms of social media we have seen in earlier chapters. The contributions from the original tweeter and retweeter are compressed into the same textual unit, rather than separated into distinct forum posts or blog post and comment. In addition, the attribution of the multiple contributions is not always easy to signal within a single tweet. A common convention is for the retweeter to add their contribution at the start of the message, separated from the original message by the abbreviation "RT." Hence the structure for a modified retweet is "[Retweeter's comment] RT [original message]." An example of this structural pattern is seen in the retweet provided below. The retweet was made by Dannii Minogue, and the opening phrase, "Enjoy Tabs. You deserve a break," has been added by her. The original message written by Tabitha Webb (@tabswebb) follows to the right of the message, with the authorship indicated by the use of her Twitter name immediately after the abbreviation "RT."

> Enjoy Tabs. You deserve a break! RT @tabswebb: http://twitpic.
> com/1cllck—The sun is shining, the snow is calling . . . hurrah! So
> good to be out of town . . . x
> DanniiMinogue Fri, 2 April 2010

The principal of recency that shapes the linearity of Twitter narratives and their archiving sequence is also applied to the horizontal arrangement of material in a retweet. The retweet places the most recently written comment first, rather than sequencing the segments in the chronological order that they were written.

Although retweeting is a multigeneric form of communication, one aspect involves co-constructing narratives. This process occurs when a story is retweeted with later material added. There are no restrictions on the kind of comment that might be added to a retweet, and further information or requests for clarification occur as appended material to narratives. But in this dataset, a common practice is for the retweeter to add an evaluative assessment to the start of a retweet, for example, that Lady Gaga was "outraged."

> Outraged. RT @Laurapalooza: Staff at the MEN aren't letting people into the arena with cans in their hair. So many sad Little Monsters :(
>
> Ladygaga: Wed, 02 Jun 2010 15:08

Or that Demi Moore had seen and enjoyed the trailer promoted by fellow tweeter, Kevin Rose:

> Saw it yesterday awesome! RT @kevinrose Square (@square) is going to kick some major ass, my video demo: http://bit.ly/79XgBJ
>
> MrsKutcher: Mon, 18 Jan 2010 01:31

It is by no means unusual for the audience to add evaluation to a narrative. Evaluative assessments occur commonly in conversational narrative as a means of showing audience response and engagement between speaker and listener (Norrick 2008). They also appear in forum posts and in comments appended to blog posts or Facebook updates. As in other contexts, evaluation is an important resource that can modulate the speaker's stance toward the reported event. The evaluative comments also achieve important relational work. In many cases, the evaluative comment is a mechanism for constructing the retweeter's attitude toward the initial tweeter. For example, they might commend the tweeter on their reported achievements, or tease them about misfortunes.

> FANTASTIC!! RT @Graceahhh I'm a 16 yr old who watched yr show and got encouraged to eat better an all natural. Lost 10lbs so far. Thanks!
>
> Jamie_Oliver: Thu, 06 May 2010 12:29

> That is SO you! :-) RT @fifi_box: locked myself out, credit cards cancelled, flat tyre now my phone just died . . . someone please put the voodoo doll down!!
>
> DanniiMinogue: Wed, 28 April 2010

The appended comments often build the positive face of the tweeter, for example, by giving a compliment or aligning the celebrity's view with the sentiment of the original tweeter.

> Nice work T! RT @taylorphinney: Bunch sprint today . . . Got 7th!!! Pretty excited about that.
> Lance Armstrong: Tue, 09 Feb 2010 15:38

> Agreed! RT @NickKristof: "I am for sale" for 20k; horrifying LAT story of educated Afghan girl peddled by her brothers. http://shar.es/aQr31
> Aplusk: Wed, 06 Jan 2010 20:21

The social function of the evaluation is in line with other forms of face-enhancing discourse, namely, to build solidarity between speaker and listener.

"Ordinary" tweeters also modify retweets, but not as frequently as the celebrity figures in this dataset did. Five percent of the updates authored by "ordinary" tweeters were modified retweets, compared with 12 percent of the updates from celebrity Twitter accounts. The contrast suggests that celebrity figures amplify the tendencies seen in general Twitter behavior. Perhaps this is not surprising, as the co-constructed tellership of retweets is an apt mechanism for performing intimacy as a front stage form of celebrity practice. On one level, adding a comment in a retweet is a way for the celebrity to display engagement with their audience and to endorse the value of contributions made by other tweeters. The evaluative assessments project solidarity with their audience through the use of face-enhancing relational work (compliments and alignment), and in this dataset rarely showed points of disagreement or criticism. However, the tweeter could achieve this relational work through interactions that are one-to-one, like private or directly addressed messages. Instead, these modified retweets are conversational exchanges that are disseminated as one-to-many broadcasts to the large scale audience of Followers: they are front stage performances of what might be interpreted as back stage behavior.

SUMMARY

The narrative dimensions of linearity, tellability, embeddedness, and tellership are reshaped in line with conventions of Twitter use that emphasize immediacy and information sharing in a public domain. The stories told in Twitter prioritize the present moment (as signaled through the use of temporal adverbs like *today*, *tonight*, and *tomorrow*). The tellability of Twitter stories does not focus on introspective reflection (like the bloggers in Chapter 3) or everyday domestic or leisure activities (like the Facebook updates in Chapter 4). Instead, the norms for tellability in Twitter suggest that this is a front stage environment, where the public, professional identity of the tweeter is of greater importance. The stories told in tweets are embedded in a wider discourse, which makes use of linking as a strategy for disseminating news and amplifying a tweeter's identity. Retweets provide a new format for co-tellership practices, where the dyadic turn-taking pattern of adding an evaluative assessment to a narrative report is compressed into a single textual unit which positions the most recently added comment first. The narrative dimensions of stories told in Twitter are different in every respect from the canonical examples of past tense, single teller, landmark stories recorded in narrative interviews or life histories. Instead, the narrative dimensions of Twitter stories are shaped by the emergent, collaborative character of social media forms that are heightened in the specific environment of Twitter itself.

The salience of recency, professional activity, dissemination of material through linking to external sources, and collaboration by means of retweets are important for Twitter stories generally, but are amplified in the practice of celebrity figures. The celebrity figures in this dataset had distinctively large Follower lists and favored one-to-many communication through updates (rather than addressed messages). They used temporal adverbs associated with the present moment more than did "ordinary" tweeters (associating this with their mainstream performances and products), included more links in their updates than did "ordinary" tweeters and posted more modified retweets than did "ordinary" tweeters. Celebrity practice thus harnesses the affordances of Twitter as a public site for promoting immediate dissemination of information in order to construct a persona that is situated firmly in the commodified systems of mainstream media. So while it may appear that Twitter gives fans unparalleled opportunities to interact directly with celebrities, this pseudo-interaction is one where the celebrities broadcast their identities to their fan base as a carefully managed strategy that shores up their offline activity and status, not a social interaction between peers.

6 Narrative and Commentary in Collaborative Storytelling

This chapter examines the collaborative characteristics of social media, with a focus on the co-constructive possibilities for narratives that are written by multiple tellers. The collaborative interactions explored here differ in several important respects from the personal storytelling that has been considered in earlier chapters. First, the discussion of tellership focuses on projects where communities endeavor to create a single narrative text, rather than on the dialogic co-tellership dispersed across different textual segments (such as separate forum posts, blog posts, and comments). Second, the kinds of collaborative stories I analyze are not reports of personal experience but explicitly fictional storyworlds. Finally, the narrative dimension of tellership is shaped by the generic contexts of the social media considered in this chapter, which includes the editing capabilities of wiki software. I begin by reviewing the collaborative storytelling associated with digital fiction, and then move on to examine the narrative identities that have emerged as stories were told in two recent online projects: *A Million Penguins* and Protagonize.

MULTIPLE TELLERSHIP AND COLLABORATIVE FICTION

The contrast between single and multiple tellership is not limited to conversational narratives of personal experience. It also applies to the tellership of literary narratives. Collaborative authorship has a long established history (Rettberg 2011), including examples of fictional narrative that predate the advent of digital media (Richardson 2006). More recently, the connective power of networked computers combined with the asynchronous nature of CMC have enabled many examples of online collaborative fiction to emerge that exploit different kinds of technical, narratological, and social formats. The forms of multiple tellership used to create collaborative fiction vary. For example, a closed group of writers might work together in one location to create an artistic work of hyperfiction such as *The Unknown* (Rettberg et al. 1998–2002). In contrast, an open-ended group of writers might submit stories to a single archive, such as *Mr. Beller's Neighborhood*. While the archived stories might be thematically connected and reflect a wider collaborative enterprise, the individual stories are not interdependent: it is the project that is collaborative, not the storytelling.

Some online collaborative genres have grown out of print origins, such as writing circles (*Dargonzine*), round robins, or *"choose your own adventure stories."*[1] Other collaborative genres are "born digital" and include role-playing games, or adaptations of sites like Twitter (*140 Novel*), Facebook, and Del.ici.ous. Many collaborative projects use audience response in the form of rankings to direct the stories' evolution (as does *One Million Monkeys Typing*), while others promote contributions according to recency (e.g., the Ficly project that replaced Ficlets). Some require compliance with strict constraints (e.g., in word length), while others do not. As with all online projects, some collaborations run for many years and attract a significant audience, while others are short lived and pass with little comment.

Early theorists of new media drew attention to the ways in which hypertextuality destabilized the notion of a single, authoritative textual creator promoted by print culture by endowing the reader with co-constructive narrative power (Landow 1997).[2] While the redistribution of creative potential in hyperfiction has been fiercely debated (Miall 1999), collaborative fiction moves away from conceptualizing the identity of a narrative author as a single figure or function. Online collaborative fiction in particular draws attention to the distributed process of storytelling more than its offline antecedents (Klaiber 2010). With this in mind, we might ask what storytelling enabled by digital media (and in particular social media) allows us to see about the processes of narrative production and reception that offline forms of storytelling do not. I will answer this question by examining the interactions of two collaborative storytelling communities and, in so doing, explore the expanded range of discourse identities that are entailed in telling stories in online communities.

COLLABORATIVE STORYTELLING CONTEXTS: *A MILLION PENGUINS* AND PROTAGONIZE

The two textually oriented examples of collaborative storytelling considered in this chapter are large-scale projects that bring together geographically distant authors in shared online spaces. One case study is the wikinovel *A Million Penguins*. The other is the storytelling community known as Protagonize. In both projects, the creation of a narrative text is interwoven with conversation between the multiple storytellers found in appended discussion forums similar to those discussed in Chapter 2. However, there are several important differences between the generic contexts of the two projects that influence the storytelling process, the coherence of the emerging narratives, and the characteristics of the communities of tellers.

A Million Penguins

A Million Penguins was an experiment in collaborative writing launched by the faculty of De Montfort University in the United Kingdom, in partnership with the international publishing house Penguin. The project was open to contribution between February 1 and March 7, 2007, attracted 75 000 viewers, and had 1,476 registered users. The project used wiki technology as the basis for the collaborative storytelling. A wiki is a web page that users can edit as well as view. The first example of a wiki was developed by Ward Cunningham in 1995, who coined the term "wiki wiki" from the Hawaiian word for "quickly," reflecting the rapidity with which users could edit content. Wiki design is strongly influenced by open-source principles, where the emphasis is on the emerging contribution of a community rather individual authorship. Authorship of wiki content is not usually attributed on the main pages by the individual writer. Instead, individual interaction is identified by the page histories that document all revisions to that part of the wiki. The revisions to a wiki page have to be negotiated in an interactive process taking place on the talk pages of the wiki site. The structure of *A Million Penguins* thus consists of a number of wiki pages that can be categorized as main pages with narrative content (491 pages), 50 talk pages (appended directly to the main narrative pages), 73 user pages (i.e., pages that contained the profiles of the contributors), and 47 talk pages appended to the user profiles (Mason and Thomas 2008).

The editing capacities of wiki technology might seem at odds with conventional print narrative production as a top-down process, for narrators could add new content and edit (including deleting) the contributions of other writers. The wiki technology enabled innovative tellership practices, where the freedom to make or change narrative contributions of others was not constrained by technological formats (such as "locking" a page) or social convention. The project team did not define or limit the creative scope of the contributors by providing specific guidelines on what kinds of stories could or should be told (although ethical guidance was given and moderators intervened to avoid vandalism or inappropriate content such as pornography).

The sentence used to initiate the story was the opening sentence of Charlotte Brontë's novel *Jane Eyre*, "There was no possibility of taking a walk that day." This sentence was deliberately nonformulaic, so as to avoid predetermining any particular narrative genre or style. What followed was the creation of a wikinovel that appeared the antithesis of narrative form and practice. When the project finally closed on March 7, 2007, it did not contain a single narrative thread. Instead, the wiki was divided into twenty-one sections, containing what Mason and Thomas (2008) describe as "multiple versions and variants of plot lines and characters . . . In addition, there are nine 'choose your own' adventure stories and unaccountable fragments of plots, characters and ideas."

The initiating sentence of the wikinovel was embedded finally in the fourth section, "Brain Food."

> *There was no possibility of taking a walk that day* . . . a swim, perhaps, but not a walk—for <u>Artie</u> was a whale, a humpback whale, to be precise, at least in these moments. It was a sunny day, and Artie would have worn his sunglasses, but being a whale meant he didn't have ears, which made it difficult for his sunglasses to stay on.

The somewhat flippant tone of this section was echoed throughout the wiki. But there was no coherent set of characters that created a narrative frame of reference that continued from one section of the wiki to the next. For example, in the immediately preceding part of the wiki, Section 3, "Dark and Deep," there is no mention of a whale, but the story focused on two characters, Tony and Jim, located in an Internet Café.

> Tony took a deep breath and paused from his writing. He was focusing on his deadline. "Deadline"—such a harsh word, like the <u>walk</u> of the damned, or the equally damned proof of sobriety with a pistol aimed at your temple. Tony was a writer. One of thousands. He was also 46 years old, paunchy with a body like a doomed hillside and a slightly receding hair line. He had acne scars like a moonscape, and a gentle introspective expression that belied his time in youth as a once promising football player.

By the time the wiki reached Section 6, "Schrödinger's Copy Cat," the storyworld had shifted to a setting in Copenhagen with four completely new characters: Mike, Gina, James, George, and Fluffy the cat who was "both alive and dead."[3] These shifts in content, character, setting, and event line continued across and sometimes within the twenty-one sections of the wiki. Although the final output of *A Million Penguins* appeared a far cry from the characteristics of canonical narratives, the patterns of participation in the experiment and the comments that the contributors made in the talk pages offer us interesting insight into the constraints and possibilities of collaborative narrative production.

Protagonize

Protagonize is an international creative writing community that draws together amateur writers from North America, Canada, and Europe.[4] Founded in December 2007, Protagonize is an ongoing community, which in February 2011 boasted over 15,000 registered authors and some 80,000 pages of story writing. The stories published in Protagonize are categorized by their authors into genres (including Children's Fiction, Crime/Detective, and Chick Lit). Unlike the generic openness of *A Million Penguins*,

Protagonize promotes a particular form of collaborative writing: ***addventure stories***.[5] In addventure genres, the contributors can only add new episodes to an existing story stem; they cannot edit existing text written by others. This results in an episodic form that resembles the linearity of canonical narrative, in that stories have a recognized beginning, and move towards a carefully managed point of closure.

The generic constraints of the writing in Protagonize are managed in a number of ways. The main site contains guidance for new authors about the genre, and how to engage with the community as a whole. Each individual story also has an Author Guidance panel, which provides inspiration and advice for new contributors. Protagonize is also a profoundly discursive community, and like *A Million Penguins*, the episodes in addventure stories are accompanied by comment pages, and members of Protagonize have their own profile page which also has comments enabled.

Rather than analyze the entire output of Protagonize, I focus here on one story in particular: *Free Your Mind*. This story was begun by the Protagonize member Asheyna on April 23, 2009, and ended, some 125 chapters later, on September 3, 2009, as the collaborative product of seventeen authors. The story and its episodes had been commented on 556 times, by thirty-four members of Protagonize (including the seventeen story authors). In contrast to *A Million Penguins*, *Free Your Mind* has a coherent storyline. The narrative was a playful take on an alternative reality game, where the story characters were named after the authors who contributed. The premise for the story set out in the Author's Guidance was that the authors were members of a community, where "creative/artistic minds are the outcasts of society. They're shunned, even hunted by the rest. And we, a literary society known as the Protagonizers, have formed a resistance movement."

In the first episode, *Free Your Mind* introduced the first main character, Asheyna, and set out the narrative conflict which would generate future story episodes:

> Once there had been a vibrant community. The most creative minds from all over the world had gathered together to practice and perfect their craft. Ideas and wit passed like lightening in messages that only fueled the fire of their artistic souls. They laughingly called themselves The Protagonists. The name a bittersweet reminder of the artistic mecca Nick had so painstakingly created for them.

The stories are playfully self-referential, creating a fictional storyworld that used the name of the website for the community itself ("The Protagonists") and individual usernames for characters in the story ("Nick" refers to Nick Bouton, who created Protagonize). The generic context of Protagonize promoted narrative coherence for *Free Your Mind*. The author panel instructed new contributors to "aim for continuity, whether it's character personality or events in the story" and to collaborate with other contributors, "Confer with them before committing them to a course of action." The result was a series of story episodes, in which the narrative characters and frame of reference was maintained (with more or less success) from one section to the next. For example, the first episode, authored by Asheyna ended, "Asheyna jumped as the single door to the room flew open, the sunlight turning the lone figure into a sillouette." The second episode, "Fresh from the Border," authored by G2Lapianistalrlandesa, began,

> Both the figure and Asheyna gasped in shock, then sighed in relief.
> "Geez, don't *scare* me like that!" the latter hissed. The figure came into the dim, grimy light, shrugging.
> "Didn'mean to," the figure, who Asheyna recognized as Gwen, muttered appologetically. "Guess you're doing a good job keeping quiet, huh, f'y'scared me like that?"

The story ended with the final episode, "Should We Stay or Should We Go," by author Spockeh, in which the (fictional) Protagonists debated whether or not to establish a new community in another setting. Although the linearity of the final narrative product of *Free Your Mind* was very different to the internal inconsistencies of *A Million Penguins*, the attendant commentary found in the talk or comment pages appended to each project illustrates the practical and social processes that were negotiated by multiple tellers who tried to tell single stories in social media contexts.

NARRATIVE, COMMENTARY, AND EMBEDDEDNESS

In *A Million Penguins* and Protagonize, talking about storytelling seems to be just as important as telling the story itself, and the emergent narratives are embedded in a surrounding discursive context of discussion threads. However, the status of the commentary and narrative are not the same. Comments will not necessarily influence the text of the narrative, and the stories can be read without reference to the comments that accompany them. But while the completed story can be *read* as a detached artifact without reference to the commentary, the story could not have been *produced* without the commentary. Narrative production is inextricably linked to the surrounding talk that evolved episodically along with the story content. In *A Million Penguins* and Protagonize there are two discursive spaces where the contributors could talk about the story under construction: (1) on the talk pages/comments appended directly to the segments of narrative content or (2) on the comments/discussion pages attached to a member's profile. These spaces differ in their proximity and subsequent influence on the narrative text. The talk pages directly appended to the narrative content are the main focus for analysis here.

In Protagonize, the commentary was organized as discussion threads appended to individual chapters or to the global story. Authors characterize their comments using the given headings "Praise," "Critique," "Editorial Note," "Tips and Advice," or "Just Chatting," and post's author is clearly shown by displaying the member's name and profile photograph. The structure of the talk pages belonging to *A Million Penguins* was less clear. The talk pages began as empty spaces without any guidelines about what or how to contribute. As a result, contributors added responses above and below an initiating question, different topics were not always clearly flagged up as distinct from the surrounding co-text, and contributors did not always leave a signature.

Although the discussions that evolved in the process of creating *A Million Penguins* and *Free Your Mind* are different in structural format, the commentary in each case served three main functions: to provide (1) retrospective evaluation, (2) prospective suggestions, and (3) reflections on the writing process.

Retrospective Evaluation

The commentary was used by writers to evaluate the existing narrative content. Unlike the comments appended to blog posts or status updates, the commenter appraises the narrative text rather than the author's life experiences. The evaluation offered by other project members may either be positive or negative, in similar manner to the APPRAISAL discussed in relation to Facebook updates. Examples include posts such as these:

> I Have to say, I'm LOVING how the novel looks and reads now It's been almost 2 weeks since i last dropped by, and was expecting more wacky plots twists than a 70's stoner movie, but WOW! What a great read!
>
> *A Million Penguins*: Beldarin 17:35, 2 March 2007 (EST)

> I didn't feel your sentence structure/ description was quite up to it's usual par in this one. The chapter it's self is good, but a lot of times you used the same sort of word over and again: 'It was simply decorated, a few pieces of furnature decorated the room. A simple tan carpet covered the floor,'
>
> Just, ya know, pointing it out so you can keep a-top of that sort redundancy.
>
> *Free Your Mind*: posted Jun 20, 2009 by *Druidx*

Prospective Suggestions

However, the commentary is far more than just an evaluation of the work in progress. It is also a space in which contributors make plans for the story's future development. In this sense the commentary serves a prospective function. Examples of prospective comments include making suggestions about content or previewing segments before they are finally posted:

I'm thinking it might be prudent for us leaving and finding/founding a new Safe to pass by Dru and Archi, being the car that was mentioned in Dru's last post perhaps unless anyone has any other ideas. Perhaps the car could be Spockeh driving away from the Safe after setting things up or could be a new arrival. Lots of things could happen though I would like to see my poor battered and twisted wife.

Free Your Mind: posted May 24, 2009 by darkliquid

It would make more sense if Carlo is sitting at the front door—there is less movement to negotiate that way so we can get on with whats in his head. I think we can make more of this—but it would probably take someone who has experience of this kind of mental state to describe it more vividly. I agree—we need to think where we are going to go from here . . .

A Million Penguins: Custard, 31 January 17.01 (EST)

Of course, the suggestions for narrative development were not always carried out. Much of the commentary in *A Million Penguins* indicated the levels of frustration that emerged when there was little if any consensus between contributors as to how the story content could be either managed or developed.

Too late for me. I left for a weekend, and *everything* was different when I got back. Really, only the URL and the underlying software was the same. There's really no point to staying involved if this project moves away from cohesion as it progresses. . . .

A Million Penguins: Gamblor856 00:10, 12 February 2007 (EST)

Reflections on Writing

The commentary also provided a forum for contributors to discuss the nature of online collaboration and the opportunities and challenges this posed for narrative writing. The values of wiki writing in particular seemed at odds with conventional principles of narrative production, and caused contributors to reflect on the advantages of improving writing through collaboration juxtaposed with the risks of incoherence brought about by unlimited editing.

This is an object lesson in living with Web 2.0. I also venture to suggest that it challenges all our ideas about how fiction is made. This is a long way from the lone genius in the attic. It's a new model, a different model, and decisions about whether or not it is working have to be reached by new rules and definitions.

A Million Penguins: Sunlight 03:37, 4 February 2007 (EST)

I was prepared for the pain of finding I'd been deleted; what's rather nice is to find I've been improved—a sentence extended, details added. That gives me hope for the whole concept, its wikiness making it more than just an enormous game of consequences.

A Million Penguins: Jeremyet 12:57, 1 February 2007 (CST)

NARRATIVE IDENTITIES

In narrative theory, paradigms of textual production conventionally separate the role of teller and their audience. For literary, written texts this is represented diagrammatically in the well-known schematic outline set out by Chatman (1978, 151), and reiterated again here:

Author—(Implied Author)—[Narrator—Narratee]—(Implied Reader)—Reader

The multiple tellership of collaborative fiction complicates this model in several ways. First, in this schematic model, authors and readers are distinct roles usually occupied by separate persons who undertake different kinds of activities. Authors write, readers read. However, in collaborative storytelling communities, although authoring and reading text remain distinct activities, they may be undertaken by the same person (readers can also become authors and contribute to the narrative production). In addition, the readers' responses may be formulated in writing, and there are different kinds of creative activity that may take place in the production of the narrative text. Lastly, Chatman's schema separates the identity of the author and reader from the textually created figures of the narrator and *narratee*, and from the projected identities of the implied author and reader, signaled in the schema by the use of parentheses that indicate the separate levels to which these identities belong. But the nature of identity performed online means that these distinctions are blurred, because the paratexts that provide cues about the author's identity are discursively constructed, just like the narrative text itself.

In narrative theory, the implied author is understood as a reading effect rather than a core role in narrative transmission (Toolan 2001, 66), an anthropomorphized figure who may be quite distinct from the historical author. The notional nature of the implied author has generated considerable controversy in narrative theory (summarized in Nunning 2005), but as Toolan goes on to point out, "[T]he pictures we have of authors are always constructions, so that all authors are, if you like, 'inferred authors'" (66). Indeed, the vagaries of online representation might tempt us to question the project of recovering historical authors for collaborative projects at all, when text is the only source for inferring identity. Readers construct identities for implied authors on the basis of the narrative itself (Richardson

2006) and the narrative's surrounding paratexts (Lanser 2003). In online collaborative fiction, neither of these resources can be taken at face value.[6]

Both *A Million Penguins* and Protagonize offer contributors the opportunity to represent themselves in a profile page. In Protagonize, the profiles follow a standard template where contributors supply an image, username, and information about themselves (which might include where they live, how long they have been writing, etc.). Individual contributors vary in the degree of self-disclosure they employ, for example, in whether to use an apparently realistic photograph (or not), a pseudonym, or a name that reflects their offline identity. From these paratextual cues, the audience might infer aspects of the member's transportable identity (including their age, gender, nationality), but the paratextual profiles cannot provide affirmation of the participants' offline identities. The possibility of creative identity play might be interpreted pejoratively as a hoax in some online contexts. But in the case of Protagonize, the discursive nature of identity appears to offer writers the opportunity to destabilize the ontological boundary between the author's identity and the fictional status of the characters within a narrative storyworld.

Free Your Mind illustrates the way in which authorial identities can merge with fictional characters. Authors were invited to write their Protagonize identities into the storyworld as characters to "[c]ome as you, come as your protag-self." Thus the characters in the storyworld bear the same names as the authors and display some of the attributes derived from the relevant Protagonize member profiles, attributes that could be later carried over into playful discussions in the commentary and that blurred a clear distinction between fictional and virtual identities. For example, the fictional character Dark Liquid is described in *Free Your Mind* as "a tall man, long hair spilling down his bearded face" with a "British accent," all characteristics that also applied to the persona described in the Protagonize user profile for the site member, Dark Liquid.

In contrast, the user profiles for *A Million Penguins* were more or less devoid of information about the contributor's offline identities. Like all the wiki pages, user pages could be edited by anyone, not just the writer themselves. Profiles of the story contributors were sometimes reconstructed by other writers. An example of a profile that was reconstructed in this manner belonged to a wiki participant named Pabruce. On February 3, 2007, Pabruce wrote a brief self description for his profile that linked to a MySpace page for Paul Allen Bruce, "pabruce, aka "bruce the fierce", aka uncle paul singer songwriter, construction worker, marble collector see examples." But this description was soon deleted and replaced by another contributor, Kate Fynn, who wrote an alternative profile for Pabruce: "May or may not own a piano. Well known as being a pretty cool guy. Suspected Communist." Before Pabruce finally deleted Kate Fynn's alternative a week later, he inserted dialogic commentary around her text, indicating willing acceptance for multiple versions of his authorial persona to be constructed.

But while Pabruce might have tolerated, if not played along with, other people authoring his authorial persona at this level, he objected strongly when his identity was treated as a fictional entity within the narrative pages of the wiki, as "just another wiki character" (Mason and Thomas 2008). When another contributor wrote a version of Pabruce into the wikinovel, Pabruce responded by leaving the project, stating, "Going to my myspace page and entering a thinly veiled version of my name INTO the novel is too weird." While the complex relationship between offline, online and fictional representation means that implied authors remain a useful heuristic, we should not forget that beyond the narrative discourse, historic authors continue to exist and may feel strongly about the status of their authorial identity.

The narrative identities that emerge in the creation of collaborative fiction include the discourse identities and situated identities that are created as members participate in narrative interaction (Zimmerman 1998). These identities extend the range of roles suggested by Chatman's schema and allow us to tease out the varied activities associated with the multiple tellership entailed in co-creating a single narrative text. Like the discussion forums discussed in Chapter 2, the sites for Protagonize and *A Million Penguins* were underpinned by a contextual infrastructure where the textual creation was controlled by an administrator. Similar to a site moderator, administrators were able to remove any or all content from the story, ban users from contributing or even accessing the site. Although an administrator may not create the story, they occupy the ultimate position of textual control, for without their support, the storytelling cannot take place. Other discourse identities arose as roles enacted in the patterns of participation created when members interact with each other and with the narrative text.

Analyzing the actual contributions to the commentary and narrative pages of *A Million Penguins* and Protagonize shows us more about how narrative identities emerge in practice. Looking at the frequency of contributions, it is clear that not all are equal: some members of the community contribute more than others, and do so in different ways. Mason and Thomas (2008) carried out an extensive analysis of participation in *A Million Penguins*. Their analysis showed that although 1,320 users were registered on the wiki, in fact the content of the wiki was generated by a much smaller proportion of those users:

Table 6.1 Participation Levels by Registered Users in *A Million Penguins* (from Mason and Thomas 2008, 31)

Participation Level	Number	Percentage
Never edited	814	55.4
Edited once	570	38.8
Edited 2–5 times	67	4.6
Edited 6+ times	18	1.2

Mason and Thomas interpret this data in terms of the "90–9–1 theory," that is, that 90 percent of internet users lurk but never contribute, that 9 percent contribute only occasionally, and that 1 percent of users contributes frequently. Drawing on a Bakhtinian metaphor of carnival, they conceptualize this theory so that lurkers are thought of as a "crowd" who occasionally react to a much smaller number of "performers." They go on to distinguish between the different kinds of performances that the more frequent contributors made, identifying *performers* (individuals who created narrative content on the most frequently edited main pages of the wiki), *vandals* (who destructively reworked narrative content on main and talk pages), *gardeners* (who attempted to assert order by bringing coherence to the narrative content, but made more contribution to the user talk pages), and *gnomes* (who made only very minor edits to narrative content and did not contribute to the talk pages at all).

We cannot draw direct comparisons between the participation in *A Million Penguins* and Protagonize, because Protagonize does not publish comparable figures about the site's use (such as page views for individual stories). However, we can compare the participation of contributors who added a story episode or made a comment to *Free Your Mind*.

As in *A Million Penguins*, the largest number of contributions to *Free Your Mind* was made by the smallest number of participants (see Table 6.2). But in contrast to the wikinovel, where 87 percent of the edits were only one-off interactions, only 24 percent of the contributions were one-off interactions in *Free Your Mind*, suggesting that there was a slightly more even distribution of interaction across the story collaborators in this context. However, these aggregate scores do not show what kinds of contributions the collaborators were making, that is, whether they were posting comments or creating story episodes and what relationship there was between commenting and posting narrative content. Each participant's contributions to the commentary and to the story content of *Free Your Mind* were calculated, and then the two sets of figures plotted comparatively. The scattergraph in Figure 6.1 shows that there is a clear trend between the frequency with which a participant comments and the frequency with which they contributed to the story content.

Table 6.2 Levels of Participation in Protagonize: *Free Your Mind*

Number of Contributions	Number of Participants	Percentage
1	8	24
2–9	11	32
10–49	11	32
50–99	2	6
100+	2	6

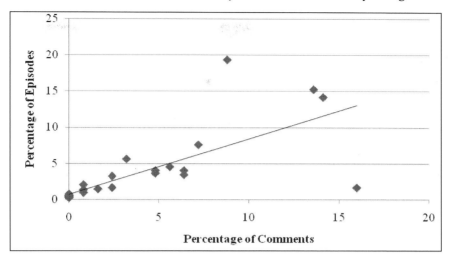

Figure 6.1 Correlation between commenting and creating content in Protagonize: *Free Your Mind* (as a percentage).

In most cases, the writers made very similar levels of contribution to the commentary and the narrative content, usually contributing slightly more comments than episodes. Engaging with the commentary thus acted as an index of general engagement with the storytelling itself (and vice versa). In general, the greater the contribution made to the narrative content, the greater the contribution to the commentary. The two most marked exceptions to this pattern were Blue Jay (who posted 16 percent of the episodes but only 1.6 percent of the comments) and Asheyna (who posted 19.4 percent of the comments but only 8.8 percent of the episodes). In order to explain these anomalies, we need to look more closely at the kinds of comments that the participants were making. These can be distinguished on the basis of the categories provided by the Protagonize site (Praise, Critique, Editorial Note, Tips and Advice, Just Chatting) and the kinds of relational work that the contributions achieved.

Although there is considerable overlap between the pragmatic function of any one post, and contributors often made comments in more than one category, it is possible to identify certain roles that the contributors adopted in relation to how frequently they contributed to particular categories of comment: the *Reviewer, Editor, Collaborator, Creator,* and *Convener.* These are not directly equivalent to the roles within the wiki discussed by Mason and Thomas (2008). For example, the wiki identities of vandals and gnomes cannot exist because editing text authored by others was not possible in Protagonize. Although the storyline of *Free Your Mind* could be disrupted by another participant, the text of another contributor could not. Nonetheless, key activities in collaborative storytelling relevant to both projects emerge.

The Reviewer

Members of the narrative audience may choose to lurk, that is, to view the story but leave no trace of their interaction other than a page view, or they may choose to express their response by adding a post to the discussion threads in the same way that comments can be added to blog posts or status updates. A typical role taken by those who leave comments is to review the emerging narrative. Reviewers tend to only make comments about the narrative. They do not add to the story episodes. Usually reviewers only make one-off contributions, rather than returning regularly with repeated evaluation of the text (or to see whether their recommendations have been acted upon). However, reviewing is a widespread behavior in the discussion threads surrounding *Free Your Mind*, accounting for 9 percent of the comments overall.

One of the main functions of the commentary is to provide retrospective evaluation of the narrative content. When reviewers make retrospective evaluation, this is most often a positive form of appraisal. Examples of reviewers included Belerama, who wrote,

> That was a very cool interesting intreging start to the story! off to read more!
>
> *Free Your Mind*: posted Jul 7, 2009 by *Belerama*

This positive evaluation does not suggest any changes to the narrative. In this sense, the reviewer appears to have little influence on the developing narrative text. But the reviewers' interactions perform important relational work for the storytelling community. The evaluation is similar to the face-enhancing work of compliments that foster a sense of involvement between the storytellers and their audience (Holmes 1995, 123). Like the comments made on blog posts, status updates, and the modified retweets, the reviewer's contributions are separate from and subordinate to the main narrative content, but they project an audience engaged supportively with the storyteller.

The Editor

Contributors who make comments do not just offer praise in their responses. They can also leave negative evaluations of the story. Unlike positive evaluation, which appears to have little influence on the narrative text, negative evaluations usually suggest that the story be changed in some way. These critiques include identifying typographic errors, suggesting improvements to a writer's style, and guiding the kind of events being depicted. Contributors who behave in this way adopt an editor's identity, checking and correcting the quality of the story rather than initiating ideas for new chapters. Editors contributed most frequently to the category of Critiques. A typical example of a Critique post was made by the Protagonize member Sly, who directed his comments toward the work of another contributor, Spockeh.

> I'm not trying to insult you, but your characters are like robots. I can tell from your writing that you can do so much better. People want to read about struggles, not accomplishments. [. . .] Your group shouldn't succeed at everything, as a matter of fact, the best characters are the ones that just barely make it through their adventures alive, or who never make it out alive at all!
>
> *Free Your Mind* posted Apr 24, 2009 by Sly

As this example demonstrates, making a negative evaluation is a face-threatening activity. It threatens the co-author's positive face by criticizing the quality of the author's writing, and threatens their negative face by imposing an alternative direction for the co-author's future activity. In contrast to the face-enhancing positive evaluation, Critiques were the least frequent of the comment types, accounting for 3 percent of the posts. In order to offset the face-threatening nature of Critiques, editors usually made at least as many face-enhancing posts of Praise too. There were exceptions to this pattern, but the editor's role generally mitigated the potential for social discord resulting from face-threatening critiques with other strategies which fostered involvement between the multiple tellers of collaborative fiction.

The Collaborator

The Just Chatting posts accounted for 70 percent of all the comments appended to *Free Your Mind*. Although the comments in this category were highly varied, there were many prospective suggestions about the narrative's future development and reflections on how the contributors should manage their contributions. The narrative identity that emerges from the participants' Just Chatting posts is the Collaborator. Unlike the Reviewer and Editor who make comments about the narrative writing, Collaborators show equal concern for the emerging narrative and the social process of working with others. The characteristics of a narrative Collaborator are exemplified in the interactive behavior of the most frequent contributors to Just Chatting: Spockeh and G2Lapianistalrlandesa. These Collaborators were equally engaged in creating the story content, being responsible for approximately 14 percent of the chapters each, and in contributing to the commentary (making 14 percent and 15 percent of the comments too).

The Creator

The writer who contributed the most story episodes was Blue Jay (20 percent of all episodes). Unlike Spockeh and G2Lapianistalrlandesa, who between them contributed 30 percent of the story chapters but also contributed nearly 30 percent of the comments, Blue Jay contributed fewer than 2 percent of the comments. This kind of contribution seems much closer to the performers that Mason and Thomas describe in *A Million Penguins*, where the interactive focus reflects a preoccupation with the act of narrative creation by an individual rather than enabling the contributions of others. Based on these results, Blue Jay seems to be a Creator of narrative content rather than a Collaborator.

The Convener

The writer who made the most comments was Asheyna, who authored one fifth of all contributions to the commentary. Based on the correlation that the greater the number of comments posted, the greater the engagement with story creation, we might predict that Asheyna would also author the most episodes. In fact, she authored only 9 percent of them. In contrast to Blue Jay's emphasis on story creation, Asheyna's concern seems to be maintaining the collaborative nature of the project. Asheyna occupies a special role in relation to *Free Your Mind*. She is the OP, which means that she wrote the first chapter and maintained the Author Guidance that accompanies the story. As in the discussion forums discussed in Chapter 2, the identity of the OP carries with it particular expectations that influence the emerging discourse. But rather than the OP being responsible for authoring the later story chapters, the OP appears to be responsible for co-coordinating the contributions made by others: he or she is a Convener.

The characteristics of the Convener can be inferred from looking at the frequency and quality of Asheyna's comments. Although Asheyna made many kinds of posts, her contributions dominate the category called Editorial Notes. Editorial Notes are, as the title suggests, posts that monitor and guide the narrative content. In these posts, Asheyna tries to prevent narrative inconsistency.

> Just a little note Spockeh, The Bard isn't a Protagonist exactly. In Scher's chapter when she introduces him he's got his own group and is trying to contact Ash, dark, gwen, etc to try and convince the Protagonists to join him.
>
> *Free Your Mind*: posted Jul 2, 2009 by Asheyna

The desire for narrative continuity and maintaining the original character of the story are themes that run through many other comments made by Asheyna.

> Author's Guidance has again been updated in an effort to keep everyone kind on top of what is going on. As always, if there's a mistake

put a note on my profile and I'll fix it! Great job everyone, we're the Featured Story this week!

Free Your Mind: posted May 26, 2009 by Asheyna

Asheyna's comments also attempt to maintain the social relationships between the multiple tellers. She welcomes new contributors to the project and intervenes to prevent narrative conflict occurring.

No problems for jumping in late Craziantix, we've had a few people do that lately. And it's cool.

Free Your Mind: posted May 27, 2009 by Asheyna

I'm not trying to be harsh, sorry if it comes out like that. I just knew that bluejay had a plan. Hopefully you can find a way to work that all out.

Free Your Mind: posted May 27, 2009 by Asheyna

As Convener, Asheyna's role serves a face-saving function. Her interventions are full of mitigating strategies, such as apologies and conditional constructions ("sorry if it comes out like that"), hedges ("just knew"), and acceptance of apologies ("no problems" and "it's cool"). Mitigating strategies are also present in Asheyna's more face-threatening posts where she orchestrates the pace of the other contributors' writing in order to enable collaboration. In the following post, she frames her request as a statement, opens with an informal greeting, "Heya!" downplays the scale of her request "a little bit," uses the inclusive pronouns "we," and provides justification for her instructions: "I'm afraid the story will start running away from the rest of the group."

Heya! I'm asking everyone who's posted recently in FYM to take a little bit of a break and allow some others to catch up a bit. We haven't seen a post from some of our author's in a while. Give it 2–4 days before those who have posted in the last say 10 chapters (that means me, bluejay, Craz, Spock, Chaos and Faltar) post again. I'm afraid the story will start running away from the rest of the group.

Free Your Mind: posted June 5, 2009 by Asheyna

The importance of a narrative Convener is not limited to the stories told in Protagonize. Indeed, the absence of a convening figure was one of the problems faced by the authors of *A Million Penguins*. Some of the writers expressed their desire for "an umpire of some description" to moderate the storytelling activities.

What started out as something quite exciting has de-generated into a blood bath of merciless editing and plot prostitution. Some restraints must be put in place. Some structure is needed. An umpire of some description, otherwise the whole project will never develop as it was meant to.

A Million Penguins: John K, 18:46, 7 February 2007 (EST)

The role of an umpire might seem to fall under the responsibilities of a site administrator, but administrators maintain only the generic contexts for a narrative and tend not to intervene in the development of the narrative texts (other than to ban users who contravene the rules of conduct for the site). The Convener appears to be a new role needed in order for collaborative storytelling to be both collaborative and story-like. Given that early hypertext theorists made radical claims about the diminished power of the author and increased power of the reader, and that social media appears at least superficially to be democratic and collaborative in nature, the need for a convening figure is perhaps quite surprising. It suggests that while online writing reworks the nature of narrative production to destabilize conventional ideas about authorship, certain aspects of the author's role remain crucial for narrative production to take place and these are fulfilled by the role of the Convener. When multiple tellership is intended to result in a single story, the content and its contributors need to be overseen by a single figure. This is true for collaborative fiction created within established generic constraints (like Protagonize) and those that appear to display minimal generic expectations (like *A Million Penguins*). Ironically, attempts to use the open-ended, bottom-up possibilities for storytelling enabled by social media seem to confirm that narrative production has to involve at least some top-down oversight.

COMPARING STORYTELLING COMMUNITIES

Expanding the narrative identities that emerge from narrative reception and production to include Administrators, Conveners, Collaborators, Editors, and Reviewers indicates that for these communities, the paradigm of narrative transmission is not a neat or symmetrical arrangement between authors and readers. There are more identities associated with narrative production than reception, but the productive roles are occupied by fewer people than the larger number of people involved in receptive processes. In other words, there are more Reviewers than Authors, and more Authors than Conveners. Conversely, it is the Authors and Conveners who make the most contributions to the storytelling production (both in terms of comments and narrative content). These narrative identities emerge from within the interaction generated as a narrative is constructed. They are not pre-designated and fixed roles. Tracing how the roles are adopted within storytelling communities can also indicate the nature of the community in question.

A Million Penguins and Protagonize are projects that show different kinds and levels of collaboration. *A Million Penguins* exhibited little collaboration, while Protagonize appeared to be a much more co-operative effort. The difference in degrees of collaboration is signaled by the narrative identities that emerged in each context. Both projects involved authors who acted in ways that I have characterized as Creators—or, in Mason and Thomas' terms, performers—who were primarily interested in generating narrative content. But in *Free Your Mind*, there was only one Creator, Blue Jay, who worked alongside a team of Collaborators (Dark Liquid, Druidx, Spockeh, and G2Lapianistalrlandesa) as the primary contributors responsible for writing the story episodes. *A Million Penguins* drew together a much larger number of contributors. Among these, there were multiple performers, including the most frequent contributor, Pabruce (Mason and Thomas 2008). In contrast to the wiki ethos that promotes negotiated textual production rather than individual authorship, the performers in *A Million Penguins* did not collaborate, but rather competed for authorial recognition in the narrative space. Pabruce marked this in numerous ways, for example, by documenting his authorial contributions on his user page, even pasting in copies of his writing to avoid it being lost in edits of the main wiki pages. Other performers included more disruptive contributions by vandals, such as Yellow Banana, who populated the wiki with references to fruit, and Leperflesh, who added highly critical material throughout the wiki that made his distaste for the early contributors' work clear.

The performers in *A Million Penguins* were without a Convener. The role taken by Asheyna in *Free Your Mind* is in some ways approximate to a wiki gardener, a participant who nurtures the growth of a wiki by seeding it with content and also by creating order (e.g., by correcting errors, arranging material so it can be accessed easily). Mason and Thomas (2008) identify participants who attempted to fulfill this role in *A Million Penguins*: Sentinel68 and Gamblor856. Both participants tried to create textual order, but they did not co-ordinate *social* order between the wiki contributors. In fact, quite the opposite of social harmony occurred, and Mason and Thomas point out that unlike typical wiki behavior, the gardeners in the wikinovel were contentious figures that came into direct conflict with the creative impulses of other performers.

In part, this might be explained by the generic contexts of the wiki, which did not predetermine particular roles for contributors: these could only have worked if they had been accepted by all contributors. In contrast, Protagonize's site establishes a recognized figure of the OP. Although Protagonize does not designate particular authority for the OP, it would seem that the community recognizes the special status of the role as entailing the both social and textual responsibilities. But even without an OP, Gardeners emerge as well-liked characters in other wikis, so we might question why this did not occur in *A Million Penguins*. One answer lies in the tensions between the principles of narrative transmission, which for canonical examples of print media is conventionally a creative process that operates in a top-down fashion. In contrast, wiki creative practices are bottom up, and allow editing that can disrupt linear coherence and encourage collective rather than individuated participation. In non-narrative wikis, the processes of revision include adding more information, and arranging this in different formats (Purdy 2009). Revising material in this way is feasible because the logical relations that hold between textual segments are not governed by chronological sequence, nor do they require consistent frames of participant reference. As Hoey (1995) points out, different principles of text organization apply to narrative and non-narrative texts. Gardening narrative and non-narrative wikis are thus quite different tasks that invoke different kinds and degrees of textual constraint.

The different constraints on textual production can also be seen in the way the editing activity was handled by each community. In Protagonize, authors retained editing rights over their own text. If another contributor wanted retrospective changes to be made, they had to recommend that the author make these. In *A Million Penguins*, anyone could edit the wiki pages, meaning that authors could not maintain a sense of ownership over their words. The lack of editing constraints and protocols made it very difficult to maintain narrative coherence, as essential information about narrative participants, events, and locations was constantly overwritten by new versions of the text. The radical editing capabilities of the wiki meant that the text was also susceptible to vandalism, a risk not present within the constrained membership of Protagonize.

The narrative identities of the Reviewer, Collaborator, and Convener that emerged from *Free Your Mind* emphasize the collaborative nature of the enterprise. In contrast, the generic context of *A Million Penguins* was ripe for potential conflict between contributors. The contrast between consensus and conflict is reflected in the relational work that characterized the commentaries in each project. The commentary for *Free Your Mind* exhibited a tendency toward face-enhancing rather than face-threatening talk. In terms of the types of comments made, face-enhancing Praise that reviewed the emerging narrative was far more frequent (124 posts) than face-threatening Critiques (16 posts). The balance between face-enhancing and face-threatening posts was not limited to this story and is typical of the Protagonize interactions as a whole. In April 2009 (the month in which *Free Your Mind* began), Praise comments occurred over ten times more frequently than Critiques (928 and 81 posts, respectively).[7]

Where Critiques were offered, the face-threatening potential of the editorial comments was usually mitigated by politeness strategies. Dark Liquid's contributions typify this face-saving style. An excerpt from one of his posts is given here. The criticism he offers that the "plot-setting" is "irksome" is mitigated with a great deal of negation, such as "not entirely sure," "can't really say why," "I'm not sure," and minimal quantifiers such as "mildly" and "a little." He offsets his advice with disclaimers ("It's probably just personal preference"), and the criticism is directed at the textual material, not the contributor who wrote it.

> I'm not entirely sure I'm happy with this, but I can't really say why. It's not the puppeteering I have issue with, that's fine, more so it's the plot-setting that goes on the the second half of the chapter I find mildly irksome. It feels a little, don't know, fake maybe, I'm not sure. It's probably just personal preference but I'd urge re-reading it aloud to see whether you get that kind of sense from it.
> *Free Your Mind*: posted May 28, 2009 by darkliquid

In contrast to the face-enhancing talk pages of Protagonize, *A Million Penguins* rarely contained any examples of praise. Instead, where evaluation was offered, this was largely negative. Face-threatening criticism was bald, on record, and unmitigated, such as that found on the many occasions where contributors came into direct conflict with each other. An example of this is found in the argument between the "gardener" Gamblor856 and the performer Leperflesh. The conflict between the participants emerged from a wider debate about how the multiple tellers might handle the problems posed by the editing capacities of the wiki software.

> Perhaps the whole page shouldnt be editable, only the chapters themselves . . . It is anoying to edit something in one chapter and not able to save it becuase of an edit in another chapter. With editing happening every few seconds this should be addressed.—Lincoln 18:10, 5 February 2007 (EST)

> I've started creating pages for each of the chapters so that this doesn't happen.—Gamblor856 18:45, 5 February 2007 (EST)

> you are not keeping up . . . —Leperflesh 19:43, 5 February 2007 (EST)

> You are substantially removing the humor in the chapter naming system (and, I should add, effectively removing whole chapters from the book) as you create your table of contents and sub-pages. Why? —Leperflesh 19:59, 5 February 2007 (EST)

> Just trying to add enough order that it takes. I'm going to leave it alone from now on. Reasons: the editing conflicts from trying to put everything on one page was driving me up the wall.—Gamblor856 20:08, 5 February 2007 (EST)

Leperflesh's face-threatening criticisms are direct and targeted at a fellow contributor's ability: "you are not keeping up." There is no modality or hedging to soften the charge against Gamblor856, "you are substantially removing the humor in the chapter," which instead is aggravated by the exaggerated quantifier "substantially," the *booster* "I should add," and the direct *interrogative*, "Why?" The result of the face-threatening attack on Gamblor856 is clear: the contributor stopped trying to create narrative order within the wiki—"I'm going to leave it alone from now on." In the light of such face-threatening commentary and the conflict between creative and convening narrative identities, the collaborative nature of multiple tellership did not arise nor did a coherent narrative emerge. Instead, there seems to be at least some correlation between the linearity of the narrative output and the participants' willingness to engage with the project. The more unstable the narrative coherence became, the less involved some of the authors felt.

> WHOA! A whole lot can happen in a day can't it? Seems like a totally different story now, and although I've made relatively few contributions thus far, seeing how much has changed makes me feel weirdly shunted out . . . hmmm
>
> *A Million Penguins*: Beldarin 15:35, 3 February 2007 (EST)

It is too strong to claim that the correlation between narrative coherence and social engagement held true for all wiki contributors. Others delighted in the creativity of continuous editing enabled by the wiki software. But, as the quotation from Gamblor856 indicates, there is at least some evidence that even in this most open of online environments, the preference for narrative constraints and coherence was strongly expressed. It is precisely these generic, technical, and social constraints that were set in place by Protagonize and that enabled collaborative storytelling to take place more successfully in a single social media textual space.

SUMMARY

In this chapter, we have observed how the multiple tellership involved in the creation of collaborative fiction gives rise to a range of discourse identities that rework and expand the roles involved in narrative interaction. The discursive nature of identity unsettles clear definitions of authorial identity, where the blurring of fictional and virtual boundaries opens up opportunities for creative play, albeit play that has consequences for the participants' sense of their identities offline. The distinction between the productive roles of authors and readers is reworked by the inclusion of situated identities established by the generic contexts of a site's infrastructure (such as administrators) and emergent discourse identities such as Reviewers, Editors, Collaborators, Creators, and Conveners. These roles indicate that multiple tellership entails co-coordinating textual contributions and relational work.

The relationship between the generic contexts of a particular storytelling site, the distribution of discourse identities and the kinds of relational work that occur between multiple tellers appear to bear on the quality of the narrative text that emerges. In the two projects discussed in this chapter, the participants expressed an ongoing preference for the kinds of narrative coherence associated with canonical narrative linearity, and for a single convening figure who orchestrated multiple tellership. While social media is characterized by the collaborative efforts of participatory culture, this does not mean that all the characteristics of single-teller, unilinear narratives are rejected out of hand. Rather, these characteristics are reworked by social media. In this case, when multiple tellers endeavor to tell the same story in a single textual space, they still need a Convener to help them coordinate their efforts.

7 Space and Identity in Stories on the Move

This chapter focuses on the narrative dimension of embeddedness. Ochs and Capps describe embeddedness as the extent to which a narrative is connected to its surrounding discourse and social activity (2001, 36). Social activity includes the physical situation in which the narrative is embedded, which I bring under the umbrella term behavioral context. The physical spaces embedded in behavioral contexts are an important resource for building storyworlds and positioning narrators and their audiences. Physical spaces, and the places found in them, are a central feature of the stories examined in this chapter, which are taken from an online archive of oral histories: the international project called [murmur].[1] These stories of everyday experience contrast with narratives found in earlier chapters in that the [murmur] stories are designed to be listened to (rather than read), preferably via a mobile device (such as a cell phone) in a geographical location that maps directly onto the locations projected from the storyworld. Thus the discussion in this chapter takes into account the multimodal, experiential nature of storytelling, and focuses less on the dialogic interaction between narrator and audience and more on the audience's identity as positioned within the behavioral contexts of narrative reception.

SPACE AS A NARRATIVE RESOURCE

Physical setting (including geographical space, place, and landmarks) did not figure in early attempts to define narrative. Instead, canonical definitions emphasized temporal sequence and eventhood as the primary criteria distinguishing narrative from other text types. Labov's definition exemplifies this tendency: "We define narrative as one method of recapitulating past experience by matching a verbal sequence of clauses to the *sequence of events* which (it is inferred) actually happened" (1972, 359–360; emphasis added). This emphasis on temporality and action has left a significant legacy in the relative neglect of studies of space in narrative analysis. The role of physical setting in narrative was relegated to an element of the narrative orientation, conceptualized as a pre-given backdrop that could be separated from the event skeleton built of narrative clauses. As later critics have pointed out, separating orientation and narrative in this way had the unfortunate effect of rupturing the interrelated dimensions of time and space (Schiffrin 2009) and of de-contextualizing the story content from its performance (Herman 2002).

More recently, the importance of space as a core property of stories and storytelling began to be recognized in both literary-critical and discourse-analytic narrative research traditions. Within discourse-analytic traditions of narrative research, the shift to a process-orientated treatment of narrative, paying closer attention to contexts of interaction, has given rise to more localized accounts of the role of space in storytelling production and storyworld content (Georgakopoulou 2003; Baynham 2004; Schiffrin 2009). Similar concerns have been raised in digital narratology, where the relationship between narrative and space has been debated in relation to the analysis of computer games as story (Ryan 2009) and the architecture of augmented reality experiences (Hatton et al. 2010), or employed in experimental forms of locative fiction that rely on *GPS* systems (Greenspan 2011). As yet, research on the personal storytelling that is emerging in social media has yet to explore the importance of physical space as a narrative resource, especially with reference to mobile technologies that enable stories to be told and produced creatively in different behavioral contexts.

The relationship between space and narrative is important for three reasons. First, storytelling performances are embedded in the physical spaces of behavioral contexts that can be described in geographic, interactional, social terms. Put simply, narrative tellers and their audiences are located somewhere when they tell and listen to their tales. Second, storyworlds are spatially constructed, with cues that construct multiple, dynamically unfolding locations and places that are meaningful in relation to the storyworld events and participants (Herman 2002). These two central relationships between space and narrative are interlinked: spatial resources found in the behavioral contexts of storytelling can be drawn upon as resources for locative and topographical referents for the storyworld. Conversely, the storyworld spaces and places might alter the narrator and audience's perception of the story performance setting. Third, space and narrative are inextricably connected to the identities that emerge in and through storytelling, for, as Schiffrin reminds us, "personal identity sits at the crux of time and space not just in narrative, but in all discourse" (2009, 423).

The discussion in this chapter builds on recent work in space and place from sociolinguistics, discourse analysis, and human geography. The interdisciplinary nature of work across these fields is rich and multifaceted, but underpinned by three key assumptions that I reiterate for their relevance to the analysis that follows.

1   Space and Place are Socially Constructed Phenomena

Researchers in human geography conventionally distinguish between abstract, geometrical *spaces* and lived, humanly experienced *places* (Tuan 1977, 1991), both of which might figure as locative resources in narrative.

This opposition defines spaces in "mathematical terms as a system of coordinates" (Ruston 2010, 107), while places are created by human interaction with particular sites. However, from a pragmatic discourse perspective, space is also conceptualized as a social phenomenon, dynamically configured by participants who orient themselves to others and to material artifacts (McIlveny et al. 2009), not a preexisting entity into which the storyteller inserts his- or herself. Spaces and their boundaries can be used to achieve important identity work in positioning the self in relation to others (Benwell and Stokoe 2006), while relationship to places can establish membership categories, be expressed flexibly according to the speaker's relationship with their audience (Myers 2006), and provide entitlement to tell a story (McCabe and Stokoe 2004).

2 Space and Place are Embedded in Localized, Multimodal Contexts

A storyteller's use of space and place is not abstract, but anchored in real localities and material situations of particular behavioral contexts. This includes the use of spaces and places constructed digitally, which in turn are manipulated by offline, embodied participants via technologies of various kinds. The interface between the storyteller's position in behavioral storytelling situations and projected spaces and places in the storyworld can be approached through frameworks of indexicality. This includes the study of deictics (Hanks 1992) and interaction spaces (Haviland 2000). As these studies point out, the evocation of space and place are not indexed through language alone. Instead, experiences of space and place involve multiple sensory modes of experience (sight, hearing, touch, taste, smell) and multiple semiotic modes of representation (oral, visual, kinesthetic, tactile), multimodal resources that operate simultaneously in layered ensembles (Lemke 2005).

3 Technology Mediates Space and Place in Creative Ways

Early theorists of the Internet predicted that digital technologies would dislocate, if not erode, the parameters of time and space in offline contexts (McLuhan 1964). However, rather than separating virtual and physical spaces as discrete zones, ethnographic studies suggest that interaction between virtual spaces and behavioral contexts are highly complex and overlapping (Arminen and Weilenmann 2009), and that interaction with online spaces can extend the use of offline space and place (Jones 2005). The impact of interacting with others via technology can vary in immersive and affective potential depending on the particularities of the speech situation. On the one hand, interacting with participants who are geographically removed from the immediate behavioral context of the speaker may give rise to a sense of displacement described by Gergen (2002) as the absent presence; on the other, use of mobile technology may open up new sites of engagement (Jones 2005) and intimacy (Arminen and Weilenmann 2009) between participants who move from one location to another, and between offline and online spaces.

The social, localized, and technological nature of space as an interactive resource comes to the fore in stories where space and place are central themes. The oral history project [murmur] is an archive of stories told by residents about their neighborhoods, where the social reworking of spaces into humanly lived places is enabled for speaker and audience by the creative use of mobile technology. Before describing the [murmur] stories in detail, I begin by setting the project in the context of oral history as a narrative genre.

ORAL HISTORY AS STORIED ACCOUNTS OF PLACE AND SPACE

Oral history accounts provide a rich repository of stories where the speaker's identity is intricately bound up with the spaces and places they have engaged with during the course of their life histories. Oral history is relatively under-researched from linguistic and narrative perspectives (but see Clary-Lemon 2010 and Schiffrin 2009), but has much to offer as a genre where everyday speakers use references to places and spaces to negotiate their individual identity in relation to collective identities (Riley and Harvey 2007). Oral history tends to favor the ongoing, open-ended linearity typical of chronicles (Ryan 2006), but these stories of personal, lived experiences often intersect with macro-level narratives of social change and can contest or internalize public myths or records of events (Seng 2009). As oral histories are made publically available in archives of different kinds, in turn, they function to become part of the collective memory for particular communities and locations. The digital technologies available from the 1990s onward marked a paradigm shift in oral history methodology, opening up oral history to new audiences and forms of engagement (Perks and Thomas 2006).

This chapter focuses on the online oral history project, [murmur]. [murmur] was initiated in 2002 by Shawn Micallef, James Roussel, and Gabe Sawhney. Originally based in Kensington Market, Toronto, [murmur] archives have since expanded across other neighborhoods including Calgary, and San Jose, California. International projects in Edinburgh, Dublin, and Australia were launched between 2007 and 2009, and other projects continue to be commissioned so that the [murmur] archive now consists of over one thousand stories. Although there is some diversity within this corpus arising from different projects' use of various production teams to elicit and publish the oral histories, the aim of the [murmur] project remains consistent: to capture personal anecdotes and recollections from everyday speakers, and to make these stories available both via the [murmur] web archives and mobile technologies so that the stories can be experienced by listeners engaged in exploring the place where the story events and story performances took place.

[murmur] brings together recent trends in oral history, along with participatory art (Orpana 2009), museology, and sound walks (Butler 2006). Unlike lengthy offline oral histories, the [murmur] stories are relatively short extracts, suitable for distribution as a podcast, with each fragment lasting between two and six minutes. In keeping with oral history's emphasis on the human voice, [murmur] is an expressly multimodal and multisensory project. The stories are available as sound files, and no written transcripts or summary documents are provided. The [murmur] web archive is also accompanied by visual resources, including hand-drawn maps of the neighborhood about which the stories are told and photographs of particular locations in relation to specific stories. In this multimodal format, and especially its privilege of the human voice, [murmur] is in keeping with other contemporary oral history archives like the *StoryCorps* project and community storytelling projects like those enabled by the Digital Storytelling Center (www.storycenter.org/).

In contrast to these other online projects, [murmur] focuses strongly on the stories told "about specific geographical locations" and encourages listeners to engage with the stories on-site via mobile technologies. In this way, [murmur] aims to bring the archive of the community members' personal stories "out into the street." Signs at the geographical site of the original telling encourage listeners to access the prerecorded stories by dialing a mobile telephone number as they inhabit the physical space in which the story belongs. The [murmur] stories foreground the central assumptions about space and place emerging from current research rehearsed earlier, that is, that space and place are not abstract, preexisting entities, but social, multimodal phenomenon that are situated in particular contexts and may be enhanced or engaged with through digital technologies.

In the analysis that follows, selected examples are taken from fifty [murmur] stories. Twenty-five stories were transcribed from the Spadina neighborhood section of the Toronto archive, and the remaining twenty-five stories were transcribed from the archive of stories for Leith, Scotland, in the United Kingdom. The two sets of stories contrast in national location, as well as diachronically, and are examples of earlier and later [murmur] projects. However, they retain the same generic format and are presented as everyday speakers' stories about their local neighborhoods that can be accessed either via a web archive, or through a mobile device on site. The narratives are preserved as audio files that were recorded by the speaker and a member of the [murmur] project team as they walked around the local neighborhood of a chosen landmark or location. The stories were not pre-scripted and were edited as little as possible. The stories cover a variety of topics, and focus on places that were elected as tellable by the speaker rather than the production team. The story's location is the central focus that must be conveyed to the listener, so that the audience can orient his or herself to the correct places and spaces being referred to by the speaker. But the audience's experience of the storyworld places and spaces will vary according to whether they access the stories remotely, via the [murmur] web archive, or whether they access the stories via a mobile device in the same setting in which the story was recorded.

Multimodal Interaction with the Storyworlds of [murmur]

The oral history stories told in the [murmur] archive sit at a three-way nexus of time. The first two temporal relationships are well documented in narrative studies, distinguishing between the time of the reported events and the time of story narration. In addition, the asynchronous nature of CMC means that the time of story narration is distinct from the time of storytelling reception, where the recorded story is played (and potential replayed) at multiple later points in time by different members of the audience. This three-way division of time for events, narration, and reception is familiar from storytelling in print literature, which is similarly asynchronous in its processes of production and reception. However, the mobile distribution of the [murmur] stories via cell phones means that the temporal split between reported events, narration, and reception does not have to be replicated in a similar three-way separation of the spatial dimensions of the projected storyworld and the spaces of the storytelling performance. Instead, the spaces referred to in the storyworld may be shared with behavioral context in which the story was recorded and later listened to.

Herman (2010) describes *endophoric storyworlds*, where the storyworld referents map onto the site of the storytelling context. Endophoric storyworlds are created when the narrator tells a story which is set in the same physical location as the behavioral context of the narrator's storytelling performance, such as a first-person account of a road accident, told on the site where the accident occurred. In contrast, *exophoric storyworlds* require a narrator and their audience to make a deictic shift from the storytelling context to a separate construction of time and space. In this case, the projected physical spaces of the storyworld are different from those found in the behavioral contexts of the storytelling performance, as when a first-person account of a traffic accident is told from a site away from where the events occurred (say, in a room inside the narrator's home). Herman's discussion of the differences between endophoric and exophoric storyworlds compared face-to-face, oral stories elicited in interviews that were either told on the same site where the story events took place or where the interviews took place in a geographically distinct situation from the inferred site of the story events. The possibilities for asynchronous storytelling in CMC (like that exploited by the [murmur] storytelling participants) add a further dimension to Herman's endophoric/exophoric distinction.

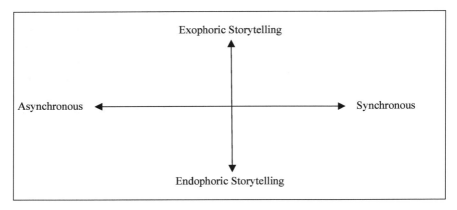

Figure 7.1 Options for storytelling in time and space.

Figure 7.1 represents the distinction between endophoric (on-site) and exophoric (remote from site) storytelling intersecting with the distinction between synchronous (same time) and asynchronous (remote time) communication. This yields a four-way contrast. Herman's (2010) discussion focuses on two of these: the resources made available in endophoric and exophoric synchronous storytelling, where both narrator and audience are present in the same temporal context. The asynchronous possibilities of CMC, combined with mobile devices that enable access to the communication in a range of geographical locations, presents two further options for storytelling. The first option is *asynchronous endophoric* storytelling where the narrator and listener share the same geographical context but are present on that site in different temporal contexts. An example of this would be when a [murmur] story is listened to in the same geographical location that it was recorded, and where the events of the storyworld are understood as taking place. The second option is *asynchronous exophoric* storytelling, where the storytelling performance is geographically and temporally removed from the contexts of the storyworld events. An example of this would include the listener's experience of accessing a [murmur] story remotely, via the web archive. The behavioral contexts of asynchronous endophoric and asynchronous exophoric storytelling can be quite different, and provide differing multimodal resources that enable the listener to connect the deictic centers of the storyworld and storytelling contexts.

Listening to a [murmur] story on-site and off-site contrasts in the quality and range of multimodal semiotic resources available in the narrative audiences' behavioral contexts, and in the relationship of those multimodal resources to the storyworld constructed in the narrative telling. At the heart of both on-site and off-site narrative experiences is an audio recording of the speaker recounting a past anecdote or report related to a particular location. The audio track consists of verbal resources (words) and sound (accent, prosody, voice quality, background noise). It is this audio-verbal track that projects the past experiences and identity of the narrator, the places and spaces from which the storyworld is constructed. However, the semiotic ensembles in which that audio track are embedded differ according to whether the narrative reception is exophoric, taking place off-site and via the web archive, or whether the narrative reception is endophorically situated in the same behavioral context as the projected story events.

Exophoric Off-Site Story Reception: The Multimodal Ensemble of the Web Archive

The audio files are embedded in the textual context of a web page within the [murmur] archive. Each file is represented by the icon for the Quick-Time media files. The icon appears in a bordered rectangle, with a header that contains the speaker's name. A typical example is provided in Figure 7.2, from the Leith [murmur] archive. The audio files are presented in a standard template on the left-hand side of the screen, accompanied to the right with a square, color photographic image of the location that forms the setting of the story. Above both photo and audio file there is a shaded banner, which contains the address for the location of the story events. Although it does not state so explicitly, it seems that the photograph is from the same time as the recorded story is told (i.e., it is not a document that relates from the earlier time of the reported events). The photographs are naturalistic and medium distance, shot in daylight, if not bright sunlight, as if the viewer is directly in front of the building, landmark or junction about which the story is told. The color saturation, sharpness

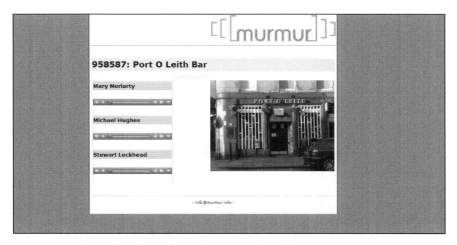

Figure 7.2 Screenshot from the Leith [murmur] archive.

of focus, and use of lighting all correspond to Kress and van Leeuwen's (1996) categories of high modality, suggesting that we are supposed to interpret the image as if the represented place were real. Where human figures occur in the photographs, these are usually too small to be identified and made subordinate to the main focus on a building, landmark, or pathway, by less sharp focus, perspective, or respective size. No images of the story narrator appear. Instead, the visual resources make plain that the focus of the communication is the places of the storyworld and how local history interacts with the present.

The behavioral context in which audience's interaction with the web pages are embedded will vary from listener to listener. For example, I could access the web archive and listen to the audio file of the [murmur] story while looking at the screen containing the photograph of a location in Toronto, Canada, but be sitting at my desk in a room inside my home in the United Kingdom, many miles removed from the geographical places and spaces described in the [murmur] stories. Sitting at my desk, I remain relatively static, apart from using the keyboard to start or stop the sound file playing, and in the meantime, I might sip a drink or make notes. In the background there might be ambient noise of different kinds that overlay the storyteller's voice, and in my peripheral view from the window other roads and buildings can be seen, but none of these situational features are interpreted as relevant to the story that I am listening to from the archive. Because of this perceived lack of relevance to the storyworld construction, the role of the audience's behavioral context is often a neglected aspect of human interaction with online stories. But, as work in mediated discourse analysis has shown, we interact with online and offline spaces and places simultaneously (Jones 2005). The potential of the physical context to contribute to narrative interaction becomes most apparent when we compare exophoric with endophoric asynchronous reception of the [murmur] stories.

Endophoric On-Site Story Reception

If the listener wants to hear a [murmur] story on the site of the story events, they can identify locations for storytelling by first using the hand-drawn maps that are available on the project web pages. Figure 7.3 shows a section from the map used to navigate the Leith [murmur] stories. Once in the vicinity of the story location, the listener must first find an iconic green symbol that marks the location of the [murmur] story events, dial the number on the sign, and then enter the code in order to select the correct prerecorded story. As the cell phone has to be held close to the ear in order to hear the sound, the relationship between the listener's body and the audio resources is literally closer than if accessed via a laptop or personal computer. But more significantly, no photographic image is needed

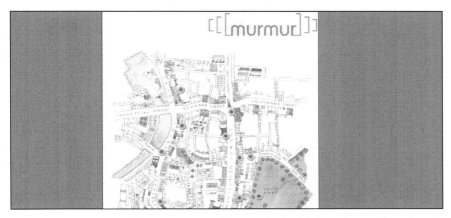

Figure 7.3   Screenshot from [murmur] showing the hand-drawn map of Leith.

to supplement the cues for the story's setting, for the listener can map the projected locations described in the storyworld onto the geographical locations of their own behavioral context, and cues provided by the narrators in their stories often help them to do this.

There are several differences between seeing a photograph of a location on a web page and being present on the site of the location itself. On site, the visual perception of the story location is co-temporaneous with the time of narrative reception, not production. The viewer sees the buildings, landmarks, and pathways without the mediation and the boundaries of a camera frame. The audience may alter their perspective, move closer to or further away from a landmark, or glance into the wider visual context available. The visual context is dynamic, not frozen as a still photograph would be, and changes uniquely and constantly as the light quality, climate, passersby, and other factors in the environment enter the space of interaction surrounding the listener with their phone. In this way, the on-site visual semiotic mode is intertwined with a multisensory combination of kinesthetic, tactile, auditory, and social resources made relevant to the story being told. The more expansive, dynamic, and embodied experience of the spaces and places is not only richer than an isolated photograph, but shares the same spatial deictic center as the storyworld constructed by the audio recording. This enables the listener to map the resources of their physical setting onto the mental map created by the [murmur] story. The differences in the multimodal resources involved in endophoric and exophoric storytelling contexts do not map onto a binary distinction between embodied and disembodied interactions. Both off-site and on-site listeners are having embodied experiences. However, the embodied setting of the on-site listeners provides a greater range of multimodal resources that map directly onto the spatial components of the storyworld's deictic center constructed by the audio recording than does the behavioral context of off-site story reception.

The off-site and on-site behavioral contexts also differ in the temporal information they offer the audience. The visual resources available to an off-site listener enable them to superimpose the story places at the time of narration (cued through the photograph on the web page) and the time of the reported events (cued through the audio track of the recorded voice). The perceived "now" of the narration is duplicated by the photograph, but does not extend the chronological evolution of the storyworld places beyond this point, as the remote time and space of narrative reception are removed exophorically from the deictic center of narrative production. In contrast, the visual resources available to the on-site audience can superimpose the story places at the time of reception (from the viewed location) and the time of narration and reported events (from the audio-recording). This extends the temporal scope of the projected storyworld beyond the time of narration to the present moment of the listener's behavioral context of reception, for as time passes, the landmarks documented on the website from the time of narration may be altered or demolished. Knowledge of the storyworld is not halted retrospectively at the time of narration, but extended to the most recent point in time: the moment at which the listener interacts with the [murmur] story on-site.

The differences in the range of the multimodal ensembles, and their capacity to connect the deictic centers of the imagined storyworld places and experienced behavioral contexts of narrative reception seem to influence the audience's engagement with both the narrated places of the storyworld and the geographical places of the story performance. The [murmur] website points to a heightened engagement made possible by the on-site reception of the stories:

> All our stories are available on the [murmur] website, but their details truly come alive as the listener walks through, around, and into the narrative. By engaging with [murmur], people develop a new intimacy with places, and "history" acquires a multitude of new voices. The physical experience of hearing a story in its actual setting—of hearing the walls talk—brings uncommon knowledge to common space, and brings people closer to the real histories that make up their world.

One reason for this "new intimacy" could include the increased range, dynamism and multisensory nature of the resources that map between the deictic centers of the storyworld and its performance for on-site audiences. Herman points to the increased use of resources from the current environment in his comparison of exophoric and endophoric storytelling. He suggests that storytellers have a preference,

[w]herever possible, [to] recruit elements from the current environment and use them to help interlocutors compute places, thus reducing the amount of simulation that needs to be done and in effect distributing the cognitive burden of place making across as many components of the material setting as possible. (2010, 95)

These preferences also appear to be brought to bear on narrative reception. However, the increased opportunity to ease the "cognitive burden" of modeling place in storyworlds is only half of the story. The behavioral context does not just serve as a source of material from which the storyworld is constructed. In addition, the audience's engagement with the storyworld changes the audience's physical responses to the spaces around them and the conceptual understanding of the places they encounter. Unfortunately, there is little empirical evidence to track exactly what these changes in physical and conceptual engagement might be, at least as far as the [murmur] project is concerned (Orpana 2009). Nonetheless, anecdotal evidence captured in academic accounts of [murmur] and similar projects report that after listening to the stories, listeners approach locations with an altered social perspective. This might take the form of a heightened awareness of community resistance to governmental initiatives to change aspects of the environment or a personalized reflection on the influence of place and space on an individual's life experiences (Ruston 2010). In this way, the audience's narrative interactions make a transition from finding the initial point located as an abstract space on the grid of the [murmur] map, to their own, lived experience of that location as a place made meaningful by the mediation of the story they have listened to. Far from dislocating the listener from their surroundings and creating a chasm of the "absent presence" (Gergen 2002), this use of mobile technology reverses that trend and enables the listener to engage more fully with their surroundings.

SPACE, PLACE, AND IDENTITY IN THE [MURMUR] STORYWORLDS

The ability for a member of the audience to make a deictic shift between his or her location in the behavioral context of the storytelling performance and the referents in the storyworld is enabled to a greater or lesser extent by the linguistic resources used in the [murmur] stories to construct relationships between people and places. The resources for identifying speakers and places include naming. The discourse context of [murmur] does not provide individual profile spaces for the participants to articulate aspects of their persona. In fact, the narrator of the [murmur] stories does not have to identify his- or herself at all: the story can be anonymous. But often narrators do choose to give their name during the course of telling their stories. The generic contexts of [murmur] do not presuppose a format for presenting this information, and in theory the narrator might introduce his- or herself at the start of the story as is typical in conventional oral history interviews. But in the dataset of [murmur] stories selected for this study, narrators only offer their names at the end of stories, in the style of television journalists. Although there are occasions where the speaker gives just their first name alone as a means of identification, "My name is Mike," the speaker may also give information about themselves, including details about where they come from, or their "place-identity" (Proshansky et al. 1983). Examples taken from the [murmur] stories follow.

So I'm Dave Crozier, 41, from Baltic Street, Leith.

I'm Stan Wilson from Edinburgh from the Grantham area, Royston.

My name is Celina Mbwiria, uh originally come from Kenya.

My name is Sandra Shaul, and I live at 6 Kendall, which is just three houses west of Spadina.

That is 666 Spadina, my name is Himy, and I was a resident here from 98 from 99 to 2002 and again for a couple of years after that.

As these examples show, the somewhat routine use of place in establishing speaker identity is flexible and can vary in the scale of the referent (Myers 2006, 322). The scale of the place formulation ranges from the narrower terms of exact addresses, qualified by precise geographical information that provides information for locals and people who do not know the area ("6 Kendall, which is just three houses west of Spadina"), to broader reference to neighborhoods ("Leith" and "the Grantham Area") to towns ("Edinburgh") and even nations ("Kenya"). The place formulations [murmur] narrators use are always geographical, rather than relational (Schegloff 1972), and could be interpreted as objective points of reference that need not be contextualized solely in relation to the speaker and listener's behavioral context of the storytelling performance. However, they are important resources for establishing the speaker's relationship to the extrasituational context by identifying them as residents of a recognized geographical area. The narrator's place identity might then be interpreted as a "territorial warrant" (McCabe and Stokoe 2004), which entitles the speaker to share an anecdote about the location and contribute to the public archive of everyday, lived experience created by the [murmur] recordings.

The relationship between a speaker's identity and the name of places is a recurring theme in the [murmur] stories. The act of naming a place can be used to establish the identity of land ownership for particular individuals or groups (Tuan 1991), with significant political, often contentious outcomes (Alderman 2003). The memorial act of naming streets or landmarks creates a cultural landscape in which links between personal identity, memory, and place are interwoven with everyday life (Hoelscher and Alderman 2004).

The stories that lie behind or emerge from instances of memorial naming are found in several recordings from the Spadina section of the Toronto [murmur] archive. For example, Madeleine Hague recounts a recent visit to a local area where the streets are named after her ancestors:

> I just taught my daughter how to get on the TTC last week and she went straight to Kensington market and uh we turned in on Baldwin Street and you know Augusta, Phoebe those are all names of people I'm related to so it was kind of fun.

In this anecdote, the street names create a familial and historical connection between the identity of the narrator and the places of Spadina, evaluated positively (but trivially) by the narrator. The historic significance of the street names become narrativized by the speaker's journey, where her personal and ongoing life experiences continue to reinvest the memorial naming with contemporary value, transforming spaces into places.

A more extended narrative documenting the transition from space to place through memorial naming occurs in Patsy Aldana's account of the Mark Cohen Park, located on the junction of Spadina and Bloor. In this recording, the relationship between memory, identity, place, and narrative operates on many different levels. The speaker tells stories, first of the decision to create a memorial for her late husband, then of the writer Matt Cohen's life experiences during his time as a resident in the Spadina area. She ends with a specific anecdote recalling the celebrations that took place when the park was opened. These stories detail the human interactions that led to, legitimized and commemorated the naming of the park. The park's status as a place that celebrates and stimulates storytelling is symbolized in the commemorative plaques situated in the park. The narrator explains,

> We thought it would be great to have Matt's own writing here, and that's why there are five plaques, one of which is about Matt himself but the rest of which have writing from his books published, from stories, from novels, from different writing he did, about all of which take place from within a block a block and a half of this corner.

The memorial naming of the park and the embedded narratives within it are intended to inspire future storytelling, especially about the "places that [people] know" in recognition of the significant role played by narrative in constructing identity for people and the places that they inhabit.

IDENTITY AND PERSON DEICTICS

Narrators may choose to identify themselves through individual names, or they can refer to themselves and others through the use of personal pronouns, such as *I, you, he, she, they*, and *we*. These pronouns operate as part of the deictic resources of the English language and form a key intersection between narrative identity and context. Although the distinction between a first-person speaker *I* and a listening *you* might appear straightforward, the referents for the pronouns can shift as the contexts for interaction change. Personal pronouns are ambiguous in scope and need not map on neatly to a contrast between narrator and listener. They are important because they draw attention to the dual nature of indexicality. A key function of person deictics is to establish the speaker in relation to other groups, for example, as a single figure (*I*) or as figure within a group of more than one person (*we*). The speakers can be positioned according to the extent that they share a common experiential ground (Hanks 1992), as well as relative to one another in accordance with parameters of time and space.

The positioning negotiated through person deictics can reflect physical locations in the behavioral context of storytelling, but they might also imply psychological or relational distinctions. Kamio (2001) explains the relative proximal–distal distinctions for the English pronominal system in terms of the speaker's territory, which is conceptualized as a psychological space realized along conversational, natural, or cultural parameters. Within Kamio's framework, the first person speaker's position is assumed as the central point from which all other relations are construed. Pronominal referents are distinguished on the basis of how close or distant they are from the speaker's territory (*I*), with *we* being closest, *you* in an intermediate position, and *they* in the furthest distal range.

In the [murmur] stories selected for discussion, narrators use a range of person deictics to position themselves in relation to a number of different others. As *homodiegetic narrators*, the speakers must identify their position relative to the other storyworld characters. The speakers also position themselves in relation to their audience. The audience is not a single figure, but incorporates the actual audience at the time of narration (a member of the [murmur] production team) and the imagined audience of the individuals who will listen later to the story once published in the [murmur] archive. As we have seen, the [murmur] narrators are not often individuated until they give their names at the end of the story. Instead, they emphasize proximity to and inclusion of others through their use of the generalized pronominal scope of *we* and *you*.

Narrative *We*: Speakers, Addressees, and Characters

The non-individuated pronoun *we* used by the [murmur] narrators can refer to a more or less delimited group of persons of which the narrating *I* is assumed to be a central member.

> Uh this is Doug uh and **we**'re currently at the corner of the south east corner of Cecil and Spadina just in front of the Grossmans Tavern.

> I remember I used to go to Urune Street School and used to walk down town to Major which was uh uh Bloor and kids as kids **we** used to walk past the school.

The flexible scope and potential ambiguity of this group means that the listener has to decide exactly who *we* refers to. As in other cases of *we* narration, this is usually unclear when the story begins, and can shift or oscillate as the story progresses, moving between the use of the generic *we*; *we* to incorporate the narrator and addressee; *we* to incorporate the narrator and other characters in the depicted storyworld. The [murmur] stories are assumed to be nonfictional, and so although they are subjective recollections, they refer to places and people in the actual world. Therefore, the polysemous range and potential ambiguity of *we* narration does not destabilize the boundaries between fictional story participants and actual story audiences in the way that postmodern fiction might (Richardson 2006). That is, a current listener is able to distinguish between their actual experience of the storytelling context and the imagined but separable members of the storyworld. In line with this, the distribution of *we* narration clearly marks a distinction between the participants positioned in the behavioral context of the narration (narrator and addressee) and the participants positioned within the storyworld (narrator and storyworld characters).

We: Narrator and Addressee

In the opening lines of a [murmur] story (though not invariably and not exclusively in that position), *we* narration often includes the speaker and the addressee. The following examples are taken from the opening of stories in the Spadina and Leith archives.

> Here **we** are at the bus stop outside Ladbrokes.

> **We**'re standing in the grounds of South Leith Parish Church.

> Right now **we**'re standing outside the Lighthouse style bar in Leith.

> Here **we** are at the corner of Kendal and Spadina, right in front of the northern exit up to the Spadina Subway Station.

> **We**'re standing here outside 710 Spadina Avenue.

Where *we* refers to the narrator and addressee (both the actual project worker recording the story and imagined, future listeners), the pronoun only ever occurs with verbs in the present tense. This is true even when the use of *we* to represent narrator and addressee is not made in the opening lines of the story. Two examples follow:

And if **we look** across the park, you can see the JCC.

If you look a block to the east of where **we are** you see a transformer uh station.

The use of *we* in these contexts constructs a shared temporal context of narration for speaker and addressee. For the narrator and the project worker, who is present at the time of narrative production, this shared temporal context is characterized by close physical proximity. The use of the present tense locates the conversational space between narrator and imagined audience of future listeners in an illusion of a shared narrational context located in the present moment, "now."

The use of *we* to refer to a group including the speaker and addressee is always accompanied by circumstantial adverbs that describe locations in the behavioral context of the narration. These references are presented as projective locations (Frawley 1992), that is, they give spatial locations relative to the perspective of the constructed *we*, not in abstract terms, such as a map reference. Instead, the places are located in relation to where the speaker and addressee are assumed to be positioned: "across the park," "outside the Lighthouse Bar," or "a block to the East of where we are." Like the use of present tense, the projective locations reflect the behavioral context of the narrator and actual audience at the time of narration. In fact, the [murmur] production team encourages the speakers to give visual cues to direct the listener's gaze (Robin Elliott, personal communication February 21, 2011). But this strategy also takes into account the later experiences of the imagined audience, because the cues are intended to ensure that subsequent listeners can locate the correct landmarks referred to in the storyworld, mapping the story content onto a temporally distant behavioral context of narrative reception. The close proximity between speaker and listener implied by *we*, combined with the use of present tense verbs and projective locations, constructs an imagined behavioral context of co-presence that bridges the asynchronous nature of the narrative production and reception for these [murmur] stories.

We: Narrator and Characters

The use of *we* to refer to the homodiegetic narrator and other characters from the storyworld contrasts with the use of *we* to refer to the narrator and addressee. The two groups who are represented by the pronoun *we* (homodiegetic narrator and storyworld characters, narrator and addressee) are connected insofar as the narrator shares membership of both. However, the two groups are ontologically separate and have different deictic centers, with the storyworld located remotely in time from the present moments of narration and reception. The different deictic centers are related to the use of tense. While *we* for narrator and addressee only ever occurred with present tense verbs, *we* for narrator and storyworld characters occurred with present- and past-tense verb forms. The following examples, the first from the Leith archive and the second from the Spadina archive, illustrate this feature:

Monday night and a Friday night 1958 to 63 the dancing was the assembly rooms Alexander's Rag Time band, **we used to go** there a-jiving, moon dancing, and everything else, it was great, when **we were** in there, **we wore** the drape suits 14 inch bottom trousers the long jackets.

Because writers sometimes have parks named after them but there's never any visible sign of them in the park other than their name **we thought** it would be great to have Matt's own writing here.

The textual context of the [murmur] stories orders the sequence in which the listener encounters the two deictic centers of the present tense narration and past tense storyworld events. The narrators use *we* to refer to narrator and addressee at the opening of each story to construct a narrational frame where the imagined audience can locate his- or herself and the projected storyworld locations relative to their current behavioral context. Once this has been established, the narrator can move on to relate the events of the storyworld *we* and the listener can make the deictic shift from the narrational present to the storyworld past. Hence, the use of *we* for narrator and storyworld characters never happens at the opening of a [murmur] narrative. However, even when the storyworld *we* has shifted to a deictic center in the past, the events are still projected onto the geographical spaces anchored in the listener's current behavioral context. This enables the listener to superimpose the past onto the present, constructing a new connection between their current listening experiences with remotely imagined storyworld others.

The past tense use of *we* for narrator + storyworld characters privileges collective rather than individual identities. These collective identities vary in scale and individuation, ranging from group of friends,

my friend Helen, her dad owned this garage, it was a petrol garage and it also sold old cars and we got kind of pally with the mechanic there, and my friend Helen and I, and he was able to procure for us this old Austin 7 and we had this great idea that we should be Bonny and Clyde in the Leith pageant

to families (even generations of families),

I just taught my daughter how to get on the TTC last week, and she went straight to Kensington market, and uh we turned in on Baldwin street

to passing neighbors,

so now and again I'd bump into Preston Manning in the lobby or in the elevator, and we'd talk shop for a while

to all the residents of a particular location or neighborhood,

It brought together the residents of the building like nothing else had done in my memory. We all complained about it.

The collective identities that emerge as referents for *we* in these contexts often become groups through their shared encounters in particular places. The encounters can range from temporary meetings ("in the lobby or in the elevator") to ongoing residence of the same building. Symbolically, membership within communities or particular communities of practice is marked in the [murmur] stories by entering into buildings. The entry into places marks transition points in the narrators' lived experiences, for example, becoming a member of the church,

> he told me he was a minister for South Leith Parish Church and I eventually found myself **going through their doors** and I've never left ever since

or becoming involved in a civic duty group,

> I guess for me it was an education I'd **go to meetings at their house** and I'd go to meetings in other uh active people's homes and just do whatever I could to stand up and be counted and stop this city dividing neighborhoods really is what it was all about.

The use of geographical entry points to symbolize community membership within the storyworld emphasizes the role of places in [murmur] stories of social connection. The importance of entering into places in order to connect with communities is also important in the behavioral contexts of the narration. While the listener's experiential context is deictically distinct from the storyworlds in temporal context, the principal of using engagement with places, that is, entering in to the locations projected by the storyworld is a way of becoming more closely engaged with the local neighborhoods. Thus the choice of *we* narration to emphasize the social connection embedded in particular communities is not a neutral choice but embodies many of the ideological premises upon which the [murmur] project is founded. This includes the premise that the depersonalizing influence of urban design can and should be resisted by experiencing neighborhoods personally, through the voices of its inhabitants, walking literally in their footsteps and so connecting to local communities.

Narrative *I* and *You*

In contrast to the scope of *we*, the pronominal range of *you* does not project a proximal space shared between the speaking *I* and their audience. Instead, *you* is distinct from but adjacent to the immediate proximal space of the first-person narrator. However, like *we*, the pronoun *you* can embrace a range of reference including the following:

You as addressee:

We're sat outside the Port O' Leith bar, the famous Port O' Leith bar which is run by the legendary landlady Mary Moriarty, I can assure you, she is legendary.

You as character (in reported speech):

We went back to his hotel where his wife slammed the door in face and said no if you go out now you can't come back.

Generic *you*:

But I have friends of my parents who remember on the high holidays you'd have to line up to get in here and you'd have the best cantors.

You synonymous with *we*:

My high school girlfriend and I used to get on our bicycles just north of here, from just north of Bloor Street you could just free wheel down all the way to the waterfront and hardly meet a car.

Despite the distribution of the different uses of *you* in the [murmur] stories, the actual and imagined audiences (*you* as addressee) do not mistake themselves for members of the past tense storyworld (*you* as storyworld character). This suggests that there is no postmodern ontological instability between the imagined storyworld participants and the actual storytelling audience (Herman 2002). Instead, the [murmur] stories clearly demarcate the addressee's position in a framing context of story performance narration from the temporally distant deictic center occupied by the storyworld characters. However, the polysemous scope of *you* means that the relative positioning of individuals as single figures or within wider groups can vary.

You for Addressee

The use of *you* to refer to the addressee shares many of the characteristics of *we* used for the narrator and addressee. *You* as a referent for the addressee typically occurs in conjunction with a present-tense verb. These verbs are often accompanied by adverbials, where projective locations construct a shared behavioral context for the addressee narrator anchored in their current geographical location. The following examples of *you* for addressee are taken from the Spadina and Leith neighborhood [murmur] archives.

And looking straight up Leith walk what you need to do is look um to your right hand side.

Above you, you'll notice the houses that surround you which are artists' studios and a performance rehearsal space.

I had a balcony and if you look up right now they painted it yellow since I lived there.

And when you get to the top, you'll see a big stone wall, beautiful mature trees.

The projective locations in these examples—"to your right hand side," "above you," and "up right now"—accompany present-tense verbs of perception, such as "look," "notice," and "see." The choice of verbs is not coincidental, but is influenced by the generic contexts of [murmur] that encourage narrators to direct the actual and imagined audience's gaze as they listen to the narrative (Robin Elliott, personal communication, February 21, 2011).

Generic *You*

Although there are no occasions where *you* collapses the referents of the audience and the story characters, there are many occasions where the reference to the addressee *you* is blurred with the scope of a generic address which encompasses a group much wider than just the immediate listener. Kamio (2001) points out that the scope of generic pronouns *we* and *you* can vary from including the entire human race to smaller groups constrained by localized contexts of time and space inferred from the discourse context. In its widest scope, the generic pronoun *you* automatically includes the addressee. However, in other contexts, the addressee is excluded from the scope of the pronoun, as when *you* refers to a group separated by a remote temporal and spatial context constructed in the text. The option to exclude or include the addressee within the scope of generic *you* is used in the [murmur] stories to reinforce the deictic separation of a narrational frame (shared by the narrator and actual audience) and a past-tense storyworld (shared by the narrator and storyworld characters).

Generic *You*, Including Addressee

The following examples demonstrate the use of generic *you*. In each case the second person pronoun can be interpreted as referring to the addressee but can also be substituted for the generalized pronoun, *one*.

It is still an open churchyard so if **you** want **you** can still be buried here.

This is 666 Spadina. **You**'d think they could come up with a better number than the devil's number, but no.

As with the other person deictics that represent the addressee (actual and imagined), this pronoun occurs with present-tense verbs, retaining the listener's position within a behavioral context located in the present moment of storytelling performance. But the scope of generic *you* is wider than *you* to refer to the addressee alone. It includes reference to an unlimited number of others, not co-present with the actual listening audience, but who might listen at a later point in time, positioning the individual listener within a wider community of storytelling participants.

Generic *You*, Excluding Addressee / *You* Synonymous with *We*

The following examples indicate some of the constraints on the scope of generic *you* that excludes the addressee.

> When I was young, it was called Laneiths and this was where all the teenagers of Leith congregated. **You** bought a cup of coffee for nine old pennies and that was **you** for four hours on a Sunday.

> I also came here for a bath a soapy bath um because we had no bath in the house and um you came along here and I remember it was 6 pence for a bath **you** went into a little cubicle.

In both cases, *you* is used in a generic form and could be taken as synonymous with the impersonal third-person pronoun, *one*. However, the verbs are in the past tense and anchor the person deictics in a temporal range from which the present day listener is excluded, for example, when the narrator "was young." Instead, these are cases where *you* is synonymous with *we*, where *we* is taken to incorporate narrator and storyworld characters. As Kamio (2001) notes, when *you* and *we* are interchangeable in this way, the separation of first and second person is eroded. The effect is to blur the boundaries between individual and collective identities. For the interchangeable *you/we*, the second person *you* is brought within the proximal range of the speaking *I*, while for the interchangeable addressee/generic *you*, the second person can be both one individual listener or any other listeners who might also listen to the story at a separate point in time. In this sense, the person deictics bridge the ongoing asynchronous nature of the [murmur] storytelling, enabling the narrator to speak to both an individual and general audience simultaneously.

SUMMARY

The analysis of the [murmur] stories emphasizes the importance of behavioral contexts when interpreting storytelling experiences. The possibilities of producing and consuming social media stories via mobile devices extend existing distinctions between endophoric and exophoric storytelling. Two new distinctions arise:

1. Asynchronous exophoric storytelling, where narrator and audience are separate from each other in time and space, and where the

storyworld referents require both to make a deictic shift from the context of narrative production and reception

2. Asynchronous endophoric storytelling, where narrator and audience are separated in time, but share the same geographical setting for the storytelling context. In this case, the storyworld referents may require a deictic shift in time from the present to the past, but can share the same deictic center for person and place.

The [murmur] stories exploit the opportunities for asynchronous endophoric and exophoric storytelling. The use of inclusive person deictics (in particular, the use of *we* and *you*) projects the illusion of a shared narrational context for the narrator and their audiences. However, the extent to which this shared context can be activated depends on whether the behavioral context of narrative reception is endophoric (on the same site as the storyworld events) or exophoric (in a different spatial location). The multimodal resources available in endophoric contexts that might be used to realize the spatial cues projected in the storyworld are greater in range, dynamism, and immediacy than the representation of storyworld places found in the textual contexts of the [murmur] web archive. Even in the computer-mediated genres of social media, it is clear that storytelling is an embodied experience that overlaps with and is not divorced from its offline contexts of production and reception. The importance of offline contexts for interpreting social media stories bears on the topic covered in the next chapter: narratorial authenticity.

8 Fakes, Fictions, and Facebook "Rape"
Narrative Authenticity

THE ETHICS OF AUTHENTICITY
AND ENTITLEMENT CLAIMS

The discursive perspective on identity I have adopted in this book might seem to imply that it does not matter whether or not the identity a narrator constructs through their online storytelling corresponds to the identity they project in offline contexts. If all identities are discursively constructed, they need not be stable or unified, but will always be in flux and susceptible to change. The small stories in Facebook updates are selective versions of the narrator's experience and are often idealized rather than reporting a comprehensive story of all (perhaps less creditable) life events. Similarly, the celebrity stories told in Twitter are carefully crafted performances, rather than a genuine presentation of back stage identity. In this chapter, I examine storytelling situations that draw attention to the gap between the online and offline narratorial identities projected by a storyteller. These are stories where the narrator turns out to be someone other than who they first claimed. In fiction, such a situation is not usually a cause for concern. We do not expect a fictional narrator to mirror the story's actual author.[1] But in the case of first-person narratives of experience, a strong expectation remains that the person uttering the words of the story will turn out to be the same person who experienced the reported events and that the events will be reported as they were experienced. When these expectations are breached, the ethical implications of narratorial authenticity are brought into focus.

The ethical implications of narratorial authenticity are important for a number of reasons that bring together concerns about the narrator's reliability, their perceived communicative intentions, and the right of that speaker to tell a story in the first place. In literary narratology, debates about (un) reliability suggest that the extent to which an audience judges a narrator to be trustworthy can influence the strategies readers adopt when interpreting the text (Olson 2003). But the pragmatic judgments of sincerity, truthfulness, and deception are not matters that are confined to a literary sphere. As Heyd points out, terms like sincerity, truth, and deception "always touch upon a moral dimension that is felt in everyday life" (2008, 145). The moral position implied by equating authenticity with truthfulness is not an absolute measure, but is shaped by the cultural contexts in which the storytelling takes place. Ochs and Capps describe this under the narrative dimension of moral stance, which is "rooted in community and tradition" (2001, 45). As moral stance is transplanted into the different communities and practices of social media, narratorial authenticity is reworked, especially where models of single teller-ship are no longer the norm and where participatory culture enables stories to circulate beyond the hands of their original tellers.

When stories are no longer the work of a single teller who was the eye-witness to or experiential focus for the reported events of the narrative, storytelling is open to misrepresentation and misappropriation. Such mis-appropriation may challenge the legitimacy of the speaker's right to tell a story. Shuman asks, "Who has the right tell a story, who is entitled to it? And we ask, is this representation a sufficient, adequate, accurate, or appropriate rendering of experience?" (2005, 3). Staking a claim to tell or retell a story is a tricky business: it places obligations on both narrator and audience. The narrator must negotiate claims of authenticity and authority in order to tell their own or another's story: a story that must be tellable but also credible. The audience must decide how to interpret the narrative. Should the story be taken at face value? Will the narrative succeed in elicit-ing empathy, "understanding others across time, space, or any difference in experience" (4), or might the narrator risk alienating the audience?

Shuman's eloquent interrogation of entitlement claims includes discussion of work on appropriated stories, that is, first-person accounts that are retold by a third party. Her study of junk-mail narratives used by different political sup-port groups illustrates aptly the risks taken when a new teller claims to speak on behalf of another.[2] In this chapter, I extend Shuman's discussion of the entitlement claims in appropriated stories where narrators speak *for* another teller to instances where a new narrator speaks *as* someone else: appropriating both the former teller's story *and* his or her identity. I examine two cases: the video-blogger Lonelygirl15 who posed as an American teenager, but turned out to be played by an actress, and the phenomenon of Facebook "frapes," whereby a narrator's identity is appropriated without consent by a third party. These acts of ventriloquism are, like the retold junk-mail narratives, examples of multivoiced stories that reconfigure attitudes toward authenticity. Narra-tors who "speak as" another teller draw attention to authenticity as a con-tested attribute of moral stance, and to the uses that contested authenticity might be put in different social media contexts.

AUTHENTICITY AND SOCIOLINGUISTIC APPROACHES TO CMC

Notions of authenticity underpin much of the sociolinguistic work on variation. This is reflected in the use of authenticity as a system that might anchor personal, social, and cultural identities, and in the kind of data that sociolinguistics has prioritized. Bucholz (2003) notes that foundational research in sociolinguistics rejected artificial examples of language in favor of linguistic mundaneness, best realized through apparently natural, everyday language use uncontaminated by the presence of an observer. The stories analyzed in this book have been selected on a similar premise—that is, that the day-to-day stories presented as personal experience by lay writers in blog posts, status updates, and community archives are important resources used to create social meanings such as personal and group identities. However, assumptions of authenticity should not be accepted as a naturalized given.

As Bucholz (2003) and Coupland (2003) point out in the *Special Issue of the Journal of Sociolinguistics* devoted to the concept, authenticity is long overdue for critical attention. The potential for online representation to remain anonymous might make authenticity appear a somewhat misguided focus. But while the radical uncertainty of late modernity might make the quest for authenticity more complex, the qualities of authenticity remain in place as parameters used to monitor life experience (Coupland 2003). In this context, the exploration of authenticity might become more interesting still. In particular, the ambiguities of online representation lead us to a heightened awareness of how authenticity is played out across a spectrum from the apparently genuine to entirely fictional constructions. Examples like Lonelygirl15, who posed as genuine but was exposed as fictional, and "frape" stories, which are deliberately false misrepresentations of a genuine updater, provide opportunities to question the interplay between authenticity, and its less well researched counterpart, inauthenticity.

Inauthenticity might entail a range of related but separable dimensions, including falsity, deception, fictionality, and unreliability, concepts that have been explored in part from literary and pragmatic perspectives. As a superordinate concept, inauthentic identities are a crucial resource for making visible the processes by which authenticity is constructed. The case studies presented in this chapter explore the interactions through which entitlement claims to tell a story of personal experience are challenged, rejected, and affirmed. The stories told that outed the fictional status of Lonelygirl15 make plain the resources used to establish a narrator's authenticity, while the deliberate impersonation of an updater in a "fraped" story presupposes that fake identities can be detected as such. The examples of inauthentic narratorial identities are sometimes surprising, not just because they unsettle assumptions about who the "real" speaker might be but also because of what the stories' reception suggests about how authenticity is understood by the narrative audience.

AUTHENTICITY AND INAUTHENTICITY IN CMC CONTEXTS

Examples of inauthentic identities are by no means limited to CMC. Heyd (2008) notes that hoaxes date back over three hundred years, overlapping with allied genres, such as rumor and gossip. There are many examples of literary hoaxes (Katsoulis 2009 provides a survey) and nonliterary hoaxes, an example of which is the Sokal affair (1996). Within CMC, inauthenticity circulates widely, resulting in the evolution of pre-social media genres such as e-mail hoaxes (Heyd 2008), and "419" or Nigerian scams (Chiluwa 2009). Inauthenticity crosses fictional and nonfictional boundaries. For example, Tim Wright's autofiction, *In Search of Oldton*, is clearly positioned as an artistic, highly constructed narrative but declares itself to be "90% true." There are many examples of hoaxes in forms of social media too. For example, the seventeenth-century diarist Samuel Pepys appears to maintain four Twitter accounts.[3] Debbie Swenson, a healthy adult, was exposed in 2001 as the creator of Kaycee Nicole, who blogged as a college student with leukemia. Inauthenticity can range from playful through to criminal activity, and the threat of inauthenticity in online contexts is illustrated through sites that debunk urban legends (such as www.snopes.com), and cyber-security sites to identify online fraud.

Authenticity and its relationship to inauthenticity has been a critical issue for identity work in CMC since the outset. In the introduction (Chapter 1), I reviewed the early studies that conceptualized identity online as a mask that could be separated from the identities constructed in offline contexts, thereby enabling anonymous or pseudonymous interactions with others (Turkle 1995). This perspective on identity online has been criticized by later ethnographic studies, which draw attention to participants' situated uses of technology, and the potential for online and offline identity work and interactions to overlap, especially with the increased use of mobile technologies. In line with this, it is clear that there is no simple, binary opposition between online (inauthentic) and offline (authentic) identities. Offline identity work can be inauthentic, including the construction of fake and fraudulent personae, and online identities can be constructed in ways that take care to prove their veracity.[4] CMC is not intrinsically inauthentic any more than face-to-face discourse is intrinsically authentic.

Instead, the boundaries between the "fictional" and "real" have been complicated by the contemporary practices of self-representation in digital media. Online identity work is selective and often idealized. Social psychologists have documented the ways in which this idealized self-representation on social media sites in turn influences the less than perfect perception of self in the offline world (Manago et al. 2008; Stefanone et al. 2011). Turkle (2011) argues that humans' emotional engagement with technology (in robotic and virtual forms) is blurring the lines between simulation and human relationships, where the performance of identity mediated through online interactions can become more "real" than offline experiences. But the opportunities to destabilize clear demarcation between the fictional or idealized with actual and offline identities does not mean that conventions of authenticity are abandoned in online contexts, nor are they replaced by a new model of authenticity. Notions persist of authenticity as ontologically grounded in a single self. As Herring and colleagues have pointed out repeatedly, participants do not necessarily "give up" aspects of their transportable identities (like gender) and may well "give off" cues more or less overtly through their talk in CMC that signal authentic membership of particular categories (Herring 2003; Herring and Zelenkauskaite 2009). The ways in which Facebook "frape" operate depend precisely on the ability of the narrative's audience to recognize that the storytelling style is at odds with the idiom expected for the genuine updater.

The searchable nature of the web also enables practices that suggest that authentic identities can be recovered through analyzing online discourse. This is seen in the trend toward digital forensics and a surveillance culture that uses material posted online in processes of what has, somewhat euphemistically, been termed "e-discovery." These practices range from agencies that search social media sites to verify offline claims, for example, in cases of alleged insurance fraud, to companies who will evaluate job applicants on the basis of the applicant's online interactions. This surveillance is predicated on the notion that there is an enduring, authentic self that is displayed in online contexts, and that becomes a source of evidence used by expert authenticators (the searcher) to determine the status of other discourse artifacts in offline contexts (such as an insurance claim). As Marwick (2005) points out, this kind of data mining can also be put to commercial ends, where the demographic information uploaded by participants into social media sites is used to project a target market for advertising companies. Attempts to evaluate whether or not an identity is authentic through investigating wider patterns of online behavior also prove to be important for amateurs too, as for the fans who uncovered the identity of Lonelygirl15's creators and the actress who played her.

DEFINING AUTHENTICITY

Defining authenticity is not straightforward. Authenticity is not an absolute quality that can be positioned relative to a single, polar opposite. Instead, Coupland (2003) sets out a framework of five qualities derived from traditional meanings of authenticity. The five qualities are as follows:

Ontology: whether or not an entity is naturally occurring or artificially constructed. In textual terms, this might also incorporate whether a narrator is considered to belong to the actual world or to be a fictional creation.

Historicity: the longevity of an entity, and its relationship to historical origins.

Systemic Coherence: the place an entity occupies within the context of a wider social system and its values. The specific situational context of an entity governs the values by which authenticity is attributed;

for example, a religious order might attribute different authenticity to scriptures than might a literary class.

Consensus: authenticity depends on an infrastructure of expert authenticators.

Value: authenticity occupies a ratified place in cultural contexts. The ability to recognize authenticity is embedded within social processes, which confer status on the expert authenticators (and, conversely, position those who fail to recognize inauthenticity as losing face).

These five parameters provide a framework that is used to examine the ways in which authenticity is played out in Lonelygirl15 and in cases of "frape." In this discussion, authenticity is not a stable, essentialist attribute that a narrator can attain (or fail to attain), but is better understood as a process of authentication (Bucholz 2003; Bucholz and Hall 2004). The intersubjective nature of authentication practices incorporates at least three perspectives: the audience's recognition of authenticity (their role to generate consensus), the narrator's performance (including the paratextual information that might accompany the stories they tell), and contextually established norms for communication and patterns of language use (as shaped by the values and systemic coherence of a particular context).

EXPOSING INAUTHENTICITY: STORIES OF "BEING OUTED"

The tension between the potential for identity play and the surveillance culture of the web result in heightened anxieties about authenticity, where distrust of pseudo-authenticity and the desire to expose inauthentic representation increases. One symptom of this tension can be traced in the prevalence of outing suspected inauthenticity. In the case of personal storytelling, entitlement claims for narrators rest on their perceived authenticity, framed in ontological terms (narrators and the reported events must exist in the actual world) and the value associated with eyewitness testimony (the narrator must have experienced the events his- or herself). More generally, these entitlement claims rest on the co-operative principles set out by Grice (1975). For communication to be successful, a speaker must comply with the Maxim of Quality:

Do not say what you believe to be false

Do not say that for which you lack adequate evidence. (Grice 1975, 46)

When entitlement claims to tell a narrative of personal experience are challenged, there is a gap between the narrator's performed identity and who they are assumed to "really be" in the actual world. This gap can be interpreted as a moral breach, for example, that the narrator is lying or deceiving their audience.

Donath (1999) points out that many deceptions involve acts of omission, carried out when an individual chooses to hide certain parts of their identity. The decision to remain anonymous or to adopt a pseudonym that obscures some part of an individual's offline identity can be carried out for very good reason. In the early days of the Internet at least, anonymity appeared to ensure freedom of speech in an age when surveillance was (and still is) high. However, choosing to conceal some part of one's identity might also be seen as a failure to comply with another of Grice's maxims for co-operative talk. The Maxim of Quantity demands of a speaker,

Make your contribution as informative as is required

Do not make your contribution more informative than is required. (Grice 1975, 45)

Deception through omission happens when a speaker says too little about who they are. When this occurs, it exposes the moral dimension of authenticity, where the speaker is imagined as "being true to him- or herself" (Coupland 2003, 422). Of course, being truthful in this sense can operate within different systems rather than as an absolute distinction. Nonetheless, anonymity, pseudonyms, and *sockpuppets* tend to prompt suspicion rather than trust, and can conceal a range of activities, from light-hearted pranks to criminal behavior and political manipulation.

Suspicions of a concealed identity can result in storytelling that outs the speaker's "real" identity. The phrase "to be outed" came into common use in the 1990s. I define it as the process by which some private or controversial aspect of a person's identity is publically disclosed without consent. The earlier senses of *outed* recorded in the *Oxford English Dictionary* reflect the combined discursive and social implications of the term, where it was first used in the sense "to speak out" and later to "to drive out." Elsewhere, I have argued that the process of "being outed" is allied to but distinct from narratives of "coming out" (Page 2010c). Existing sociolinguistic research has begun to document the role of coming out stories in authenticating lesbian, gay, and transsexual identities (Liang 1997; Wood 1997). In this work, the speaker's narration of their sexual identity is part of the process of negotiating membership of lesbian, gay, and transsexual communities. In contrast, being outed is a process of de-authenticating an individual's identity, entailing different tellership roles and resulting in complex relational work for the participants.

Coming out is a speech act by an individual who asserts a previously undisclosed element of his or her own identity. Being outed involves at least two participants. The first participant is the individual who conceals some aspect of their identity, but is suspected of inauthenticity. The second participant is the individual who exposes the inauthenticity of the first person's status by asserting the information that has previously been concealed. Usually, assertions that "out" a participant take place in a public context: there is an audience for the speech act. Being outed thus de-authenticates and recontextualizes the first speaker's identity, placing information that was private on a public, front stage platform. The scale of the publication can vary from localized, face-to-face encounters to assertions that are disseminated more widely to unknown audiences through the mainstream media and, of course, the Internet.[5]

The relational work carried out in outing another is complex and influences the face of both participants. Being outed threatens the face of the apparently inauthentic participant, first, because the act violates the individual's wish to remain hidden and, second, because of the pejorative connotations of dishonesty (even if the concealment has been for good reason). The collocational patterns for "being outed" in large datasets like the *British National Corpus* suggest that being outed is usually to the detriment of the person concerned, for "being outed" collocates with "fear of" and "threat of." The act of outing another also influences the face of the participant who reveals the hidden information by positioning him or her as an apparently expert authenticator. As Heyd argues, this can entail positive status for the authenticator on the grounds that being able to recognize an online hoax is a signal of advanced digital literacy (2008, 146).[6]

INAUTHENTICITY AND LONELYGIRL15

Lonelygirl15 began posting video-blog entries on YouTube in the summer of 2006. The narrator of the videos was Bree, a sixteen-year-old, American girl who told short stories of her day-to-day life as a homeschooled teenager living with religious parents. Lonelygirl15 gained a considerable following, with some episodes reaching over half a million views. But by September 2006, Lonelygirl15 was exposed as a fictional creation, where the narrator, Bree, was played by the nineteen-year-old, New Zealand–born actress Jessica Rose. Lonelygirl15 was significant as the first large-scale controversy relating to authenticity in the context of YouTube, and is credited with shifting patterns of self-representation away from the assumed everyday style of webcam documentation, toward the emerging conventions of Internet television (Christian 2009). The controversy surrounding the disclosure of Lonelygirl15 arose because of the values of self-expression in the early days of YouTube where the "vernacular creativity" and assumed authenticity of amateur video-ship was positioned ideologically in opposition to commercial models of mainstream media production (Burgess and Green 2009, 27). When Lonelygirl15 was exposed as a fiction created by aspiring filmmakers Mesh Flinders and Miles Beckett, this was perceived by some as a betrayal of the countercultural, grassroots, participatory ethos of You-Tube. The investigative efforts that revealed Bree's fictional status, and the reactions to this revelation, demonstrate the processes by which entitlement claims can be challenged, processes that are embedded in shifting attitudes toward (in)authenticity in social media contexts.

Within the multimodal world of YouTube, the conventions for self-representation are closely related to how the personality of the narrator is perceived. Christian (2009) explains that there is a binary contrast between sincerity and insincerity, where sincerity is associated with unedited documentation of the self within a community of other, similar video-bloggers. In contrast, fake or insincere video-bloggers self-present in a more constructed manner (e.g., through the use of editing effects, lighting, and soundtrack) and are associated with professional, market-centered uses of YouTube. At the time that Lonelygirl15 first emerged, YouTube was being heralded as "progressive and democratic" (Gehl 2009). To be authentic and sincere was valorized, to be exposed as "fake" smacked of the kind of commercialization that the YouTube community might eschew.

Lonelygirl15's early videos employ the conventions of self-expression associated with sincerity. Although she nowhere makes the claim that she is real (in ontological terms), the entitlement claim to narrate her life experiences on YouTube is implicitly that associated with first-person narration: that she was genuine, existed in the real world, and was an eyewitness to the reported events. The multimodal resources of the first video-blog illustrate this performed authenticity. Bree begins by providing narrative orientation about herself. In the verbal narration, she says, "I guess a video blog is about me, my name is Bree, I'm sixteen." She positions herself as a newcomer within the video-blogging community using similar strategies to those documented in the bodybuilding discussion forums discussed in Chapter 2, including de-lurking ("this is my first video blog, I've been watching for a while"), and showing self-deprecation ("I'm a dork") and deference to more experienced video-bloggers ("I really like Pay to the Order of of of Two, you're really funny and your videos are really interesting").

The visual conventions for self-representation reinforce the performance of authenticity. Bree is positioned close up, looking directly into the camera, film techniques that are said to promote empathy (Christian 2009) and that are common in "real" video-blogging. The blog presents Bree alone in what appears to be her bedroom, again complying with the amateur video-blogging convention of indoor filming. Advice to video-bloggers seems divided on how far a blog entry should be pre-planned, but Bree claims spontaneity, "I didn't really have a plan for this video blog, so I guess I'll just do this." However, the post is also clearly edited, containing cuts and sound effects. Bree's self-description suggests she is not disclosing the full truth at this point. But this concealment is presented as a legitimate strategy to protect privacy. She says, "I don't really want to tell you where I live because you might stalk me." The initial comments on the first post accepted Bree as authentic, but it was not long before the audience began to suspect the videos of inauthenticity.

The process of de-authenticating Lonelygirl15's entitlement to tell stories began when the consensus about her representation as sincere was challenged. Members of the audience adopted the roles of expert authenticators and documented the ways in which her self-presentation failed to sustain the systemic coherence required by the authentic, community-focused style of narration. These challenges took place in the comments appended to the video-blog and in response videos on YouTube, on interactions with the MySpace profile created for Bree, in the forums of the website, Lonelygirl15.com, which was supposedly created for Bree by a fan, throughout the blogosphere, and, on occasion, in the mainstream news media (e.g., the mystery was covered in the *New York Times*). Before Lonelygirl15 was finally exposed as fictional, Brian Flemming (2006) made the most sustained critique of the disparities between the values of "sincere" video-blogs and Lonelygirl15's performance. He pointed to the constructed style of the videos, as indicated by the too-regular posting, the lighting techniques, sophisticated editing, and idealized representation of Bree, who was too attractive and "exactly the kind of girl that the young, male demographic of YouTube would fantasize about."

Flemming also argued that the narrative structure of Lonelygirl15's stories were misaligned with the typical stories told by genuine video-bloggers. Lonelygirl15's posts were too much like canonical narratives. They contained conflict, most notably in the episode, "I probably shouldn't post this . . ." where Bree fought on camera with her not-quite boyfriend and love interest Daniel. The stories also contained narrative suspense, especially in relation to the religious beliefs that Bree alluded to but would not spell out. It seems that the qualities most usually required for a canonical narrative to be a success (i.e., a story should include a conflict to be resolved and a sense of progression toward a climactic high point) were precisely what undermined Lonelygirl15's authenticity: she was too tellable to be true.

The way in which Bree interacted with her audience also undermined her presentation as sincere and authentic. Although Bree (in fact, another member of the production ensemble, Amanda Solomon Goodfried) talked with her audience by e-mail, through her MySpace account, and in the comments on the YouTube site, there were signals that she was not interacting as one peer to another. Instead, from the outset, the audience was positioned as a fan base rather than as fellow video-bloggers. Lonelygirl15's first forays onto YouTube capitalized on the success of a previous, genuine video-blogger, Emily, by intercutting parts of Emily's video with Lonelygirl15's first video "Paytotheorderofof vs. Dinosaur." As Davis (2006) reported, this provided Lonelygirl15 with an established audience and instant credibility within the world of YouTube. It also meant that her audience did not emerge from a set of individual bloggers but was formulated as an aggregated fan base.

While Bree responded to e-mails and MySpace comments from the audience, other bloggers like Nerdkiller suggested that these responses were not always in character, for example, when Bree chose to ignore inappropriately sexual comments but apparently was religious. Finally, although Lonelygirl15 made references to other popular video-bloggers in her first posts, she did not sustain this intertextual referencing for long enough. Instead, she only made generalized references to her audience as "you guys" rather than named bloggers active on YouTube. Like the celebrity practice on Twitter discussed in Chapter 5, Bree's conversations with her audience are best understood as a form of pseudo-interaction, used as a means of gaining and maintaining a following on YouTube.

The paratextual contexts of Bree's interactions with her audience provided the evidence that clinched the question of her ontological inauthenticity. First, the expert authenticators noted that the website made supposedly for her fans, Lonelygirl15.com, was registered in early May 2006, months before Lonelygirl15 gained popularity and actually had any fans. Second, the **IP address** used to respond to Bree's e-mails was traced not to a private home address but to the Creative Artists Agency. Finally, on September 7, 2006, the creators of Lonelygirl15 were left with no choice but to release a statement on Lonelygirl15's website confirming that Bree was a fictional character, not an ontologically authentic figure in the real world.

The stated motivations for outing Bree's false entitlement claim as a video-blogger suggest much about the values that underpinned the systemic coherence of YouTube in its early years. The audience's need to expose inauthenticity appeared less concerned with Bree's ontological status (whether she existed in the actual world or not) and were more strongly associated with the ends to which her performed authenticity were put. Expert authenticators like Brian Flemming suspected the inauthenticity to result from a commercialized strategy, where Lonelygirl15 was the work of a viral-marketing program run by a corporate production team. The distrust of constructedness as representative of commercialization was at odds with the utopian view of YouTube as democratic and community centered. If the creators of Lonelygirl15 were going to avoid losing their audience, they would need to counter the accusations of commercialization and align themselves with the view of YouTube as progressive and participatory. They did this by claiming that Lonelygirl15 was the new form of interactive storytelling (Sternberg 2006).

The creators posted a letter on their website once the fictional status of Bree had been outed that used a careful rhetoric of a community-centered endeavor. The following extract from this letter is full of allusions to the participatory value of the audience.

> To enhance **the community experience** of Lonelygirl15, which you **have already helped to create,** we are in the process of building a website centered around video and interactivity. This website will allow **everyone**

to enjoy the full potential of this new medium [. . .] **You are the only reason for our success,** and we appreciate your devotion. We want you to know that we aren't a big corporation. **We are just like you.** A few people who love good stories. We hope that **you will join us** in the continuing story of Lonelygirl15, and **help us usher in an era of interactive storytelling where the line between "fan" and "star" has been removed,** and dedicated fans like yourselves are paid for their efforts. This is an incredible time for the creator inside **all of us.** ("Letter from the Creators" posted on Lonelygirl15.com; emphasis added)

The creators took pains to stress their similarity with the audience ("we are just like you"), positioned within a "community experience" that recognizes "the creator inside all of us" and the role of the fans ("you are the only reason for our success")—a role that needed to be rewarded as "dedicated fans like yourselves are paid for their efforts." The creators' rhetoric paid off, and predictions that Lonelygirl15 would falter once outed as inauthentic proved unfounded. The Lonelygirl15 universe continued to expand for another five years, with spin-off series created by fans.[7] But the success of Lonelygirl15 was not a straightforward tale of a progressive, participatory art form triumphing over commercialization. In fact, the role of (in)authenticity in promoting a performance culture within YouTube is more complex, and the new art form brought later economic and social gains for its creators.

The reactions to Lonelygirl15's exposure played an authenticating role in establishing social identities for different segments of her audience: those who had been fooled by the deception, those who "got" the joke, and those who would use the joke for their own ends. The first group appeared outraged that they had been duped. On the surface, these video-bloggers were angered that their expectations of authenticity as ontology had been failed. For example, the blogger Renetto (Paul Robinett) posted an emotionally charged video on YouTube, declaiming LonelyGirl15 as fake (2006). He said,

I'm hurt . . . I wanted to get the message out about this, it's a travesty and I can't believe it, I mean Paris Hilton is more real than Lonelygirl. It's time to fight back . . . and kick her off of YouTube. She doesn't belong here.

Jill Walker Rettberg argues that responses like Renetto's emerged because the audience felt they had been "tricked" (2008, 125). Exposing this kind of inauthenticity is deeply face-threatening, for it undermines the solidarity that each member of the audience has projected between his- or herself and the narrator (in this case, Bree). Moreover, it makes the audience appear foolish, for they have not been clever enough to interpret Lonelygirl15's performance within the appropriate frame of reference.

In contrast, the members of the audience who accepted Lonelygirl15 as a fiction did not position themselves as equals who had been deceived by a fellow blogger. The bloggers who "got the joke" described themselves as a viewing audience. For example, the blogger Fathead closed his exposé of Lonelgirl15 saying, "Who cares if it's fake. If you like it, watch it." For this group, authenticity was no longer related to the narrator's ontological status. The entitlement of Lonelygirl15 to tell her story was based on authenticity as a form of emotional resonance, suggesting that perceptual realism had been replaced by social realism (Senft 2008). Christian (2009) argues that, for these participants, the performance is all that matters. Another blogger, Bubbleteamaylee (2006), explains that the interaction with Lonelygirl15 was not perceived as a conversation between peers, but as a strategy that enabled greater emotional engagement with the performance.

> Performance art turns everyone into an artist and that's kind of neat [. . .] sometimes you want to be part of the show and not just watching. You actually start to care and feel like you are in it and that's why [Lonelgirl15]'s going to stay so popular and I don't get why everyone is so upset.

The bloggers who played along with the fiction gained social prestige on the basis that they had seen beyond the surface level realism of Lonelygirl15's performance to the fiction behind.[8] Like readers who are able to detect unreliability, this group of the audience appeared to "share the joke and enjoy having survived the initiation ritual the text appears to require" (Olson 2003, 95). This segment of the audience went on to participate in the construction of Lonelygirl15 as a fiction, much like the members of fandoms and role-playing simulations proliferating elsewhere on the web (Jenkins 1992; Pugh 2005).

The rejection of authenticity as ontology in favor of the claim that performance is all that matters is taken further still by the last group, who responded by using the controversial outing of Lonelygirl15 to promote their own popularity. Members of this group circulated the story of Lonelygirl15 and her (in)authentic entitlement claims in the surge of parodies that appeared on YouTube in the months following September 2006. The parodies of Lonelygirl15 were less like participations that extended Bree's fictional world and more like parasitic narratives that harnessed the opportunities for accruing social capital through the processes of micro-celebrity by treating the fellow video-bloggers as a fan base that could be manipulated and maintained.

The parodies of Lonelygirl15 denaturalized the conventions of authentic self-expression on YouTube by exposing their own constructedness through hyperbole and stylization. Like parody more generally, these texts comment critically on an earlier work (Hutcheon 2006). In particular, the parodies suggest that earlier constructions of any kind of authenticity should not be taken at surface level. The narrators parody the features associated with empathy and intimacy, including Bree's use of close-up shots where she gazes directly into the camera. The voice quality of the narrators shifts at the points where they imitate Bree's voice, by changing pitch (either becoming lower if the narrator is a woman or higher is the narrator is a man), by slowing down and using a more breathy quality. The parodies also expose their own constructedness visually. For example, the blogger TheHill88 mimicked Lonelygirl15's use of a puppet, but replaced the "purple monkey" character with a toy unicorn, an overtly fantastic creature. In another response video, the blogger RoleA40 turned the webcam away from himself to show a constructed camera stand made of a tin can and garlic salt shaker being used to film his entry, adding "the camera stand is original just like me." The parodies of Lonelygirl15 illustrate the possibilities of "inauthentic authenticity" which are now "part of the cultural repertoire of YouTube" (Burgess and Green 2009, 30), a culture where the apparent authenticity of amateur video has been supplanted by the power of performance.

The Lonelygirl15 parodies are implicated in the distribution of power within YouTube. The parodies became successful not because of their own value as an art form, but because they capitalized on the viewer interest in the Lonelygirl15 controversies. Fans can be appropriated, just like stories. Within this economy, the number of views and subscribers to a YouTube channel are all-important. This is one of the outcomes of micro-celebrity, where apparently anyone can achieve fame by manipulating interactions within social media. However, micro-celebrity practices are also shaped by the capitalistic practices of commercialization that underpin the evolution of YouTube (Gillespie 2010). A large number of viewers are not just an indication of a blogger's popularity. The blogger's audience is also a means of generating revenue, for example, from advertising companies who might use a base of subscribers as a potential market for their products.

While the creators of Lonelygirl15 might have claimed they were ushering in "a new era of interactive storytelling," the show was also a landmark in social media's use of product placement to generate revenue. For example, in March 2007, the show's producers signed a deal with Hershey, whose product, Icebreakers Sour Gum Brand, was featured in a one-off episode of Lonelygirl15. Later, in June 2007, Lonelygirl15 introduced a "branded character," Dr Spencer Gilman who worked for Neutrogena, who appeared in episodes for a number of months. The creators' assertion that the fans were "the only reason" for Lonelygirl15's success rings hollow. Financial investors had always been needed to allow the show's production (Davis 2006) and continued to be needed in the years that followed. The commercial success of Lonelygirl15 is symptomatic of wider trends that commodified self-expression as bloggers were encouraged to use their identity online for financial gain (Stelter 2008). The value of authenticity as performance brings home the salutary point that social media interactions are not as neutral or democratic as they might first appear. Instead, they can be used to shore up hierarchies of power.

FACEBOOK "RAPE": INAUTHENTICITY IMPERSONATION

Impersonation is a particularly potent form of inauthencity. Donath writes, "If I can pass as you, I can wreak havoc on your reputation, either online or off" (1999, 51). There are many forms of impersonation, ranging from playful mimicry to mockery and, in its most serious form, criminal acts of identity theft. A recent form of impersonation has been described as Facebook "rape," or "frape."[9] "Frape" occurs when a third party gains access to and then alters the content of another member's account, for example, if the victim leaves their Facebook account logged in but is absent from the device used to access the site. "Frape," like the process of outing, is a multi-voiced speech act that involves at least two participants: the victim (the authentic Facebook member) and the perpetrator, who impersonates the victim by publishing false information on the victim's Facebook profile without their consent or knowledge. At its most basic, this includes posting a status update, but it can also include altering profile information or interacting with other members of the site (adding likes, comments, using online chat).

"Frape" is a complex speech act that misappropriates the entitlement claims for publishing one's life experiences within the systemic coherence of Facebook's context. Facebook requires its members to comply with terms and conditions that state,

> You will not provide any false personal information on Facebook, or create an account for anyone other than yourself without permission.

> You will not share your password, let anyone else access your account, or do anything else that might jeopardize the security of your account.[10]

"Frape" violates both of these conditions, specifically by appearing to allow another person to access the victim's account, and by posting false information. More generally, "frape" rejects eyewitness authenticity as the basis for legitimating narratives of personal experience and flouts Grice's maxims of quality by asserting things that are not true.

The inauthentic updates have two tellers: the victim, whose authentic details (photograph and username) may be retained in the template frame, and the perpetrator, whose inauthentic words are posted in the update slot. The inauthenticity is sometimes, although not always, publically asserted by the victim in their later Facebook interactions, for example, by declaring in a comment or subsequent update that they had been "fraped." Other members of the audience may also participate in reactions to the "frape," for example, by playing along with the impersonation, or by demanding an explanation. In the following example, the victim comments on the impersonated update in order to make the inauthenticity clear.

> Update (by perpetrator): [name] doesn't even like corn on the cob, but it is good for somethings . . . if you know what i mean ;)

> Comment (by victim): [name] frappppeeeeee!!!

The impersonation usually contains false, often humiliating information and on the surface appears to damage the face of the victim. But unlike impersonators who attempt to pass as if they were the victim, "frapes" draw attention to themselves as inauthentic speech acts. The impersonation is a performance that is deemed out of character for the victim. In other words, the "frape" creates a gap between the impersonation and the target reality of the victim's authentic identity.

The scale of the gap and the ability to detect this discrepancy can vary. Some "frapes" play on known information about the victim as an in-joke shared between a small group of friends. Other "frapes" are blatantly false and contradict other information about the victim published on his or her profile (such as changing the victim's gender). Here is an example of a "frape" reported by the victim's teenaged child in their update. The second comment was posted by the victim, and the final comment from the updater's older sibling.

> Update: Hahahahaha my mum actually fraped my dad's Facebook by making him 'like' everything

> Comment 1: I just got about 15 notifications all supposedly from my dad

> Comment 2 (the victim): You know it wasn't really from me as I don't like anything ☺

> Comment 3: I wondered who was doing that

Although this example is a report of a "frape" rather than a "frape" itself, the generic characteristics of a "frape" are still apparent. The victim's account was modified by a third party (in this case, the victim's wife), who impersonated the victim's online behavior in a way that was out of keeping with their usual practice. The inauthenticity was declared by the victim, "You know it wasn't really from me" and suspected by other members of the Friend list, who wrote, "I wondered who was doing that." The potential incongruity generated by a "fraped" update suggests that the audience is not supposed to read such statements as a literal account of first-person experience. Instead, the incongruity suggests that there must be an additional communicative intention beyond and at odds with the surface meaning of the update. The indirectness and inherent ambiguity makes "frape" a risky form of appropriated narrative that may be more or less open to misinterpretation.

Investigating "Frape": Data Sample and Methods

Studying examples of "frape" is problematic. Despite some sites that promote "frape" cases as "hilarious stories" to be shared with others, the potentially offensive nature of "frape" means that inauthentic updates and profile information are often quickly deleted by the victim. From an ethical perspective, it is not clear who the "frape" belongs to in order to seek consent to observe and analyze the phenomenon, for both the victim and a (possibly unidentified) perpetrator are implicated. In addition, the interpretation of "frape" is context sensitive. These are highly embedded stories that cannot be detached from their wider situational context. It is extremely difficult to make sense of the phenomenon by reference to the text alone, and a more ethnographic approach is necessary. The discussion that follows is not a large scale study of "frape." It begins with data collected by my former student, Aaron Bourne, for an assignment on a Language and Gender module in 2010.[11] Aaron collected examples of "frape" that appeared in his Friend feed during the spring months of 2010. His interest was in the gender performativity of the "frapes" and the power that the perpetrator was able to exert in comparison to the victim.

In our discussions about his data, Aaron commented anecdotally that, usually, "frapes" were a source of amusement to his peers. At the time, I was puzzled by how an act that appeared to me so blatantly offensive could be interpreted as funny, but an ethnographic study fell outside the scope of Aaron's term paper, so my curiosity remained unsatisfied. The discussion in this chapter returns to some of the examples of "frape" that Aaron collected, but includes other examples observed from the datasets collected for, but not included in the analysis of Facebook updates in Chapter 4. I also include some participants' perspectives, taken from six e-mail interviews I carried out with members of my current Facebook Friend list who had been victims of "frape." Clearly, the small size and convenience of the data sample will influence the interpretation I present. Nonetheless, the discussion enables us to consider the complex, multiple interpretations of inauthenticity in this context.

Detecting Inauthenticity: Constructing an In-Group

The potential of "frape" to provoke the very different responses of amusement or offence is explained by examining the nature of the inauthentic updates as a *speech act*. The British philosopher J. L. Austin observed that utterances do not just communicate information; they can also be equivalent to actions. According to Austin (1975), there are three components to a speech act, which include

1. The *locutionary act*: the literal meaning of the utterance
2. The *illocutionary act*: the act which is performed by making the utterance (such as welcoming, promising, identifying)
3. The *perlocutionary act*: the effect of the speech act on a listener (being warned, amused, offended).

For inauthentic updates like "frapes," there is a dissonance between the perlocutionary, locutionary, and illocutionary effects of the update. The locutionary content of "fraped" updates usually asserts that the victim has carried out a humiliating action or is displaying an embarrassing state of mind. Here are some examples:

> [name] has found his bright pink tutu surprisingly comfy

> [name] loves skin-tight lycra! ooh. yeah!

> I can't believe I slept with a fat bird last night, never again she was horrid.

Given that updates perform both direct and indirect identity work for the updaters, the illocutionary effect of "fraped" updates might be to project an identity for the victim. As these examples indicate, the identities are usually derogatory, embarrassing, or rude in some way. As a result, the perlocutionary effect of the "frape" might be one of distress, embarrassment, or offense for the victim. The e-mail interviews with "frape" victims confirm this possibility. Here are some excerpts where victims describe their attitude toward the phenomenon of "frape."

> Working within a school environment I have seen the negative effects of 'fraping' which has been used as a bullying mechanism. Pupils are using 'fraping' as a way to offend others thus adding a new stem to cyber-bullying. (Female updater, 25–29 years of age)

> In my own experience of it, it has been embarrassing at most but it seems to have the potential to be very offensive. (Male updater, 30–39 years of age)

But this is not the only perlocutionary effect that results from "frape." Other responses suggest that "frape" is viewed as a harmless and humorous prank.

> It is normally very funny
> (Female updater, 13–18 years of age)

> The 'frape' referred to in this message was funny
> (Female updater, 19–24 years of age)

The possibility for "frapes" to generate humor arises when the audience interprets the update beyond its literal meaning. In Austin's terms, this interpretation is described as an implicature, that is, that the communicative intention of the speaker (here the perpetrator) is taken to extend beyond and be opposite to the locutionary content of the "frape." In "frape," the locutionary content appears intentionally impolite. Therefore, the implicature is that the "frape" is intended as *nonserious* impoliteness, in other words, an example of banter.

Bousfield defines banter as "an insincere form of impoliteness used for the purposes of solidarity or social bonding" (2007a, 213). The interpretation of the perpetrator's insincerity (i.e., their lack of serious intent to harm the face of the victim) and the outcomes of solidarity rest on the contexts in which "frapes" occur. In the examples I observed, the perpetrator of the "frape" was usually (although by no means always) a close friend or family member of the victim. In the interviews, the perpetrators were identified as spouses, siblings, offspring, boy/girlfriends, or best friends. The "frapes" took place in private contexts, such as the victim's home, or in venues where the perpetrator and victim had been in close physical proximity to each other, thereby enabling the perpetrator to access the victim's account.[12] The level of trust that the victims projected onto their relationship with the perpetrator clearly influenced the interpretation of the "frape" as nonserious and without intent to harm, reducing the face-threatening nature of the act.

> I personally have found all frapes to be amusing as they are genuinely only done by people you trust enough to leave your fb account logged in with in the first place.
> (Female updater, 19–24 years of age)

> It doesn't worry or impact me really as i know the only people who know my password is my sisters and my best friend and they are never gonna use it in a spiteful or hurtful way.
> (Female updater, 13–18 years of age)

Of course, there is no guarantee that the perpetrator does not intend harm, or that harm was avoided. The outcomes of a "frape" can be face threatening, with serious social consequences. Nonetheless, if "frapes" are carried out by someone unknown to the victim, the interpretation of speaker's intentions is treated with suspicion. As one "frape" victim put it,

> If I was in a public space such as the uni library for example, if a stranger were to frape me I would be highly offended.
> (Female updater, 19–24 years of age)

The ability to identify narratorial inauthenticity in cases of "frape" serves as an authenticating function for the audience of Facebook Friends, distinguishing between an in-group of Friends who identify inauthenticity and an out-group who do not. This value is shaped by the systemic coherence of Facebook's context. On one level, Facebook's terms and conditions (quoted earlier) construct an environment where the speaker's online identity and offline identity are assumed to be anchored in a single, ontologically verifiable self. In addition, the relationship between a Facebook member and their Friend list is interwoven with an offline context: Facebook Friends usually know each other in the offline world. This means that Facebook members do not rely solely on virtual representation in order to make judgments about the authenticity of a speaker's identity as performed in a status update. They also draw on their knowledge of the Friend's offline identities. But the value of the online and offline representations as evidence against which to judge authenticity is not equal. Offline identity work carries greater weight and changes the perception of inauthentic identity performed online.

In her study of American teens, boyd points out that shared knowledge of the Friends' extrasituational context means that providing inauthentic online identity information (e.g., a false date of birth) was not viewed as deceptive falsehood, "because those for whom they intend their profiles know their real names, ages, locations, and hometowns. They may see their responses as humorous, but they are not trying to create an alternate identity" (2008, 148). The same principle applies when interpreting the social outcomes of "frape." The potentially face damaging nature of "frape" can be dismissed because the audience is supposed to realize that the inauthentic identity is not really the work of the victim. The interviews with victims suggested that they relied on their Friends' shared extrasituational knowledge of them to detect the "frape," although this could not be guaranteed.

> My friends understand how my brother and I interact with one another online.
> (Female updater, 25–29 years of age)

> Many friends instantly knew I had been fraped due to the random out of character update and decided to like it and/or comment with things like haha and even question whether it was a frape.
> (Female updater, 19–24 years of age)

> I suppose there is a risk that some of my friends don't know me so well (like the bishop of [name of city deleted]!!) & might think that I was making the comment.
> (Male updater, 30–39 years of age)

The potential for "frape" to generate face-enhancing solidarity emerges from the offline contextual knowledge shared by the victim and audience that can be used to de-authenticate the entitlement claim of the victim as a first person narrator of a "frape." This enables the in-group of the knowing audience to lessen the face-threatening nature of impersonation by interpreting the "frape" as a joke; a joke that they can participate in by endorsing it through "likes" or by adding comments, as in the following example.

> Update (written by perpetrator): [name deleted] weed the bed :(
>
> Comment (by Friend 1): are you unable to wear your pampers whilst wearing your thong?
>
> Comment (by Friend2): [name deleted] doesn't wee the bed!
>
> Comment (by Friend 3): thong th th thong thong thong

Of course, the collapsed contexts of a Facebook Friend list means that not all members of the audience for a "frape" will share the same extra-situational knowledge of the victim. Reactions to a "frape" may then be one way of temporarily re-segmenting a Friend list into those Friends who know the victim well enough to judge the "frape" to be inauthentic and those who do not. Like insider jokes, reactions to "frapes" can be a way of displaying an exclusive social connection, which heightens the in-group's perception of intimacy.

"Frapes" That Go Wrong: A Cautionary Tale

"Frapes" can breach the norms of tellability in update stories by projecting identities that, if deemed authentic, might be taken as extremely offensive. When the impersonation extends beyond altering representational details (photographs, birthdates, status updates) to interfering in the victim's interactions with others (e.g., by posting comments or engaging in online chat), the face-threatening potential of "frape" can erode, rather than foster, solidarity between participants. Assumptions that the perpetrator's intentions are harmless and that the audience will detect and therefore dismiss the inauthentic offense do not always hold true. "Frape" as banter can go wrong. I close the discussion of "frape" by recounting the story told to me by one interviewee. I include her story here as an important reminder that my discussion of the apparent playfulness of inauthenticity as banter should not detract from the serious, real world, relational consequences that inauthenticity can entail.

In this case, the perpetrator posted what the victim described as "sexually suggestive" status updates, engaged in online chat with the victim's Friends to talk about "dirty things" and impersonated the victim, offering to take part in sex acts. The victim did not find the impersonation amusing at all but was "angry and upset." The experience undermined her sense of identity online and inhibited her relationship with others. She explained to me that she apologized individually to every member of her Friend list, and then left Facebook for a year, having de-activated her account. The possibility that the audience would detect inauthenticity in the "fraped" behavior was not enough to remedy the damage to the victim's self esteem and her interactions with others.

> I felt as though even if people knew it wasn't me, just the horrible things that were said were now associated with me . . . It became awkward to chat to people online because I didn't know what previous conversations with them entailed . . . It's definitely made me more wary of friendship and trust.

Quite clearly, the effects of inauthenticity are not limited to the online world, but cross over into offline social contexts. Inauthenticity is not a neutral matter of harmless identity play, but a potent resource to enact power over others that can impact negatively on their identity and interactions with others.

SUMMARY

This chapter has examined two ways in which inauthentic entitlement claims to tell personal narratives operate in social media. First, I discussed the controversy surrounding the video-blogger Lonelygirl15, who concealed her fictional status. In the last part of the chapter, I analyzed impersonation in relation to the phenomenon of Facebook "rape." Although the values associated with inauthenticity in social media are more varied than I can take account of in this chapter, it does seem that the meaning of authenticity associated with ontology has been supplanted by the equation of authenticity with emotional resonance or credibility, as assessed by the narrative's audience. This has freed inauthenticity from pejorative connotations of lying or deception and enabled the audience to co-construct inauthenticity as a participatory fiction or an insider joke.

The ability to detect (in)authenticity serves an authenticating function for the members of the audience. This includes establishing their identities as expert authenticators, where the ability to distinguish between fake and "real" narrators positions the audience as a member of a knowing in-group or a duped out-group. These groups do not map neatly on to an in-group that prizes a belief in authentication as ontologically grounded. Rather, the in-groups who recognize inauthenticity appear to use the performances of inauthenticity to enhance their own status. The video-bloggers who parodied Lonelygirl15 used the controversy surrounding her authenticity to boost their own viewing figures, and the Facebook Friends who played along with Frapes displayed their membership of an exclusive group who shared an insider joke. That said, these examples of inauthenticity in social media should not be interpreted superficially as a harmless form of fictional creativity. The ends to which inauthenticity are put can mask ulterior motives. Nor should the value of inauthenticity as participatory fiction be taken to imply that the outcomes of such representation are inconsequential fictions. The sometimes negative effects of inauthenticity do not stay on the screen but have consequences on the identities and interactions that people engage in their offline contexts.

9 Familiar, Reconfigured, and Emergent Dimensions of Narrative

NEW NARRATIVES?

The aim of this book was to establish the distinctive features of the narrative genres developed in social media, identifying points of commonality and contrast across a range of storytelling types. The storytelling examples span from early to more recent applications of social media (discussion forums to social network sites), across topics (serious and lightweight; authentic and fake; public and private), storytelling purposes (to share experience or for self promotion), and different groups of participants (bodybuilders, cancer survivors, celebrities, creative writers, and local residents). My analysis of these examples has identified the ways in which social media storytelling has given rise to new narrative genres (like Reflective Anecdotes), new categories of narrative production and reception (such as asynchronous, on-site storytelling via mobile devices), and previously unrecognized narrative identities (including the Conveners and Collaborators who emerge in collaborative storytelling endeavors). However, the trends across these storytelling examples suggest that there is rarely a unified, dichotomous contrast between the stories told in old and new forms of technology. Instead, the new forms of storytelling found in social media contexts have points of connection with earlier narrative genres, transforming these practices in more or less innovative ways.

Herring (2011) describes the multilayered process of change in CMC as *familiar, reconfigured,* and *emergent.* Familiar aspects of social media are those that are more or less reproduced from earlier formats without any change, like printed stories that are uploaded to the web as electronic files (such as the books stored in archives like *Project Gutenberg*), or narrative interviews recorded and published online as podcasts (like the excerpts published in the *StoryCorps* project). Reconfigured genres have antecedents in earlier formats but have been adapted to operate within a new technological environment. Examples of reconfigured stories include blogs as new forms of diary writing, or conversational storytelling distributed in the asynchronous threads of discussion forums. Emergent forms of CMC are entirely innovative and are qualitatively distinct from their predecessors, like the use of wiki software to construct a single story told by multiple authors. Across this spectrum of familiar, reconfigured, and emergent narrative genres, the narrative dimensions of linearity, tellership, tellability, and embeddedness are also transformed. The concluding chapter reviews each narrative dimension in the light of the analysis presented in earlier chapters, identifying the key trends in social media storytelling as it has evolved in the last decade.

LINEARITY REVISITED

The narrative dimension of linearity includes two separable but interrelated facets: the temporal organization of events and the macro-level structural coherence found in storytelling. Both elements are present in social media stories, but they are influenced by the formats and values of social media in different ways.

Narrative Time

Social media stories reaffirm temporality as the core property required to identify narrative. Temporal sequences underpin the stories told by bodybuilders in discussion forums, bloggers recounting their diagnosis of cancer, Facebook updaters reporting day-to-day activities, tweets told about celebrity activities, Lonelygirl15's video-blog entries, and podcasts of oral histories in the [murmur] project. But unlike conversational or print narratives, the resources used to construct a chronological frame of reference for these social media stories are not drawn solely from the story content created by the narrators. Temporality is also inferred from the discourse and behavioral contexts in which the process of storytelling is embedded. The extent to which the chronological framework that enables narrative production and reception is reconfigured in social media contexts depends on three elements:

1. Whether or not the discourse template uses a time stamp
2. Whether or not the generic context uses chronological principles to sequence the archive of material, and whether that sequence is in standard time order or is reverse chronological
3. How the production and reception of social media stories are embedded in the lived experience of time (e.g., is posting once off, or continuously updated?).

These options for representing time reconfigure the extent to which narrative linearity is contextualized (i.e., how far the interpretation of time can be detached from the story's discourse, generic, and behavioral contexts), and the extent to which the events of the narrative are represented as taking place in the past, present, or future.

With the exception of the oral history podcasts, all of the discourse contexts of social media stories discussed in earlier chapters included a timestamp in the template used to frame the story content. These timestamps document the point at which the narrative discourse has been published online, and are then used by sites to position individual entries within their archives of published material. The design of the timestamp reflects the importance of recency in the linearity of social media stories. When a timestamp appears in a Facebook or Twitter update template, it will initially describe the time of publication relative to the present moment at which the audience is viewing the update. For example, the most recent updates posted on my Friend list or Twitter Follower list note that the updates appeared, "32 seconds ago," "7 minutes ago," and then "1 hour ago." It is only when posts have been published a day previously that the update uses a calendar date and time in the timestamp instead.

The importance of recency is also felt in the use of reverse chronological order to sequence the archives of material posted on social media sites. Reverse chronological order is used in blogs, Facebook, and Twitter, and governed the arrangement of page histories of the wiki software used to create *A Million Penguins*. But not all social media sites use reverse chronological ordering to structure their archives. The posts in the discussion forum threads in Bodybuilding.com and the episodes of the addventure story created by the Protagonize members present the posts in the order in which they were published (with the most recent last). YouTube does not use chronology to order its archive (using popularity rankings instead), and [murmur] avoids rankings but uses spatial metaphors of the town landscape to organize the stories available on its web archive.

The production and reception of social media stories are also embedded in the distinct behavioral contexts of the narrator and audiences' life experiences. As the creation and consumption of social media in online and offline contexts become increasingly interwoven, the lived experience of time is a further contextual resource used to reconstruct narrative temporality for a sequence of story fragments. Some social media stories are posted as one-off artifacts, like the podcasts of the oral history project [murmur]. Other stories are produced and received episodically over time, like the blog posts that were updated somewhat intermittently (in the data samples used in this study, usually no more frequently than weekly).

In more recent social media genres, updating is both more fragmentary (the posts are shorter) and more frequent. The behavior of the Facebook updaters studied in Chapter 4 suggests that the frequency of posting to social network sites is increasing over time. In 2008, 30 percent of the participants were updating their status at least twice a week, and a further 7 percent updated their status at least once a day. In 2010, 35 percent of the updaters were posting updates at least twice a week, and a further 18 percent were updating at least once a day—an increase of 16 percent overall. The contextualized experience of producing and receiving story episodes in the lived time of the narrator and their audience means that narrativity can be interpreted even when time is not mentioned in the content of a story at all. For example, a series of Facebook updates, like the following example taken from the data sample used in Chapter 4, may not include any explicit references to time in the update content.

> May 21
> <F06–08> is going to throw the printer out of the window.
> 12:00pm
> <F06–08> is smiling at [name deleted].
> 1:53pm
> <F06–08> is facebooked out.
> 4:29pm
> <F06–08> has just won a delicious new lense for her camera.
> 10:00pm
> <F06–08> is actually happy for man utd!
> 10:34pm

There are no causal connections between individual updates, and the topic shifts from one subject (like technology) to another (like football). However, the consistent reference to a named participant's life experience (here the updater <F06–08>) functions as a unifying frame across individual episodes—episodes that are marked by Facebook's timestamp and thereby imbued with chronological order.

The contextual resources used to reconfigure temporal dimensions of narrative linearity combine to form a spectrum of possibilities that place more or less emphasis on recency as a governing characteristic of stories told in social media. The examples discussed in earlier chapters of this book are plotted within this spectrum in Figure 9.1.

Level of Innovation	Example	Post Template Uses a Timestamp	Reverse Chronological Order in Archive	Frequency of Posting
Familiar ↓	[murmur] podcasts	No	No	One-off
Reconfigured	Discussion forum posts	Yes	No	Variable
	Lonelygirl15	Yes	No	Weekly
	Blogs	Yes	Yes	Weekly or less
Emergent	Facebook, Twitter	Yes	Yes	At least daily

Figure 9.1 Options for temporal linearity in social media.

The options in this spectrum include stories with familiar narrative linearity, which do not rely so heavily on their discourse context for cues of temporal sequence, like the oral history podcasts produced by [murmur]. Other genres are more or less reconfigured, like discussion forum posts that are time-stamped but still use conventional chronology in their archive, and blog posts that use reverse chronological sequencing but are updated relatively infrequently. The influence of recency as a contextual constraint on narrative temporality is most evident in the more recent social media sites, Facebook and Twitter.

The increasing importance of recency in the temporal linearity of social media stories does not just bear on the contexts of narration and reception; it also influences the language used to represent temporal sequence in the stories found in podcasts, posts, and updates. It is possible for narrators of social media stories to make reference to time spans that are located in the distant past (such as the memories recounted in the oral history project [murmur]). In this respect, the temporal aspect of these social media stories is similar to the canonical examples of stories found in narrative interviews or life history. However, more often, the temporal emphasis of the stories discussed in earlier chapters concerned the period in close proximity to the present moment of narration. The story told by the new bodybuilder when seeking advice from others on a bodybuilding forum (Chapter 2) concerned her experiences that had taken place the same night that she published the post:

> I went to the gym **tonight,** walked in and saw there wasn't ONE girl in the whole gym . . . I LEFT. . . . that's right, didn't even complete a workout.

Similarly, the Recounts and Anecdotes of cancer bloggers in Chapter 3 were updates anchored in the near present. For example, this blogger reports on the events of "today" from the point at which she is "now [. . .] home."

> The chemo is done for **today.** I've had fluids, anti-nausea medication and the chemo drugs and **now I'm home.** The whole process took about 4.5 hours, and the worst part was the needle stick into my port.

The influence of presentism is emphasized further still in more recent social media genres like microblogging and social network sites. Breaking news stories continued to dominate small story genres found in the 2010 data sample of Facebook updates analyzed in Chapter 4, accounting for 59 percent of all the small stories like the following examples, which report what has "just" happened,

> <F21–08> **just** shut her finger in the car door :(.
>
> (Female updater, age 19–24, April 15, 2008 at 19:13)

<F80–10> Our next door neighbour's cat **just** tried to eat a squirrel, **now** it's half dead in our back garden! I haven't got a clue what to do with it! :(

(Female updater, age 13–18 2010, July 29, 2010 at 15:45)

The stories told by celebrity figures in Twitter similarly foreground the present moment through their preference for temporal references like *today*, *tonight*, and *tomorrow*, as we saw in the examples discussed earlier in Chapter 5.

> Roasting in paris **today**. Hitting with pablo cuevas at 2pm . . .
> Andy_Murray: Sun, 23 May 2010 10:34:56.

> Nighty nighty! Just arrived in Manchester ready for my very early performance on the Andrew Marr show **tomorrow**. Up in less than 5 hours! Xxx
> (KJofficial: Sat, 03 Oct 2009 23:44).

The emphasis on temporal recency as a form of narrative linearity is well suited to the moment-by-moment updating that has become increasingly characteristic of social media practices, and is familiar from the open-ended linearity of conversational narrative (Ochs and Capps 2001). But prioritizing recency is also an apt strategy for constructing a sense of co-presence and social connection between the narrator and audience as if they were co-spectating on the same life events—a strategy required by the asynchronous nature of social media formats. Although broadly speaking, the stories told in social media are anchored in the present moment; the extent to which this sense of immediacy is enacted by the narrators' linguistic choices varies from one social media genre to another. A comparison of the temporal adverbs associated with the near present (*today, tomorrow*, and *tonight*) with adverbs associated with the past (*yesterday* and *then*) for each of the datasets used in this study suggests that an emphasis on the present increases sharply for the most recent genres: Facebook and Twitter. The results of this comparison are summarized in Figure 9.2.

The relative frequency of the temporal adverbs found in the social media genres in this study as compared with their occurrences in the two reference corpora used in Chapter 5, the *British National Corpus* (BNC) and the *Concordance of Contemporary American English* (COCA), suggests that earlier social media genres (discussion forums, podcasts, and blogs) use temporal references with similar frequency to that found in offline spoken and written language. The familiar representation of time does not emphasize the present moment (through adverbs like *today* and *tonight*),

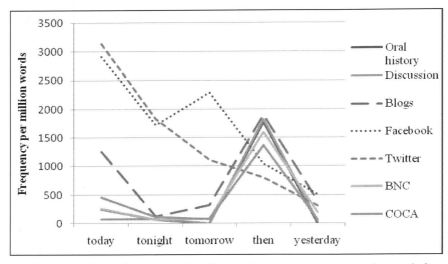

Figure 9.2   Relative frequency of *today, tonight, tomorrow, yesterday,* and *then* across social media genres (per million words).

but more often uses the adverb conventionally associated with chronological sequence, *then*. For example, *today* occurs 254 times per million words in the oral history dataset and 263 times per million words in the BNC, while *then* occurs 1,775 times per million words in the oral histories, 1,824 times per million words in the discussion forums, and 1,595 times per million words in the BNC. Blogs begin to move away from this trend, over-using *today* and *tomorrow* in comparison with offline language. But the updates in Facebook and Twitter are distinctive, in that they overuse the adverbs associated with the time of narration (*today, tonight,* and *tomorrow*) more than do the other social media genres and offline corpora, and underuse conventional narrative adverbs like *then*. In fact, the Facebook dataset showed *today* occurring nearly three times more frequently than *then* did, similarly to Twitter, where *today* occurred nearly four times more frequently than did *then*. In line with their emergent contextual frames of temporality, the language of Facebook and Twitter updates strongly foregrounds recency as a constraining feature on narrative linearity in these contexts—contexts that also foreground networks of connection between narrators and their audience and so increase the requirement that stories create an illusion of co-presence.

Narrative Sequences

Ochs and Capps (2001) contrast the closed structures of retrospective narration with open-ended narrative linearity. Although social media stories seem to favor recent time spans rather than distant retrospection, the temporal aspect of linearity does not automatically mean that all narrative sequences are necessarily open-ended, or open-ended in the same way. The extent to which a story is open-ended also depends on the episodic nature of social media formats. Narrative sequencing can vary according to whether a narrative is told in its entirety within a single textual unit or as episodes across multiple units, and whether the multiple episodes are contained in the same archive or are dispersed across sites beyond their originating generic context. The stories discussed in earlier chapters exploit these sequencing opportunities in different ways.

1. *Stories can be contained within a single unit*: examples include the Recounts and Anecdotes told by bloggers (Chapter 3), the small stories told in Facebook status updates (Chapter 4), and the oral history podcasts of the [murmur] project (Chapter 7).
2. *Stories are told episodically, across units within a single archive*: examples include the Second Stories narrated across multiple posts in discussion forum threads (Chapter 2), the episodes added to the story stem in the addventure genre used in the Protagonize collaborative storytelling community (Chapter 6), and the episodes of the YouTube blogger Lonelygirl15 (Chapter 8).
3. *Stories told across units that link to sites beyond their generic context*: examples include the tweets that amplify narrative content by linking to additional photos, videos, blog posts, or news reports about the tweeter (Chapter 5).

The open-ended linearity enabled by social media formats is not necessarily reconfigured or emergent. Instead, the possibility of telling stories episodically across multiple units is in many respects familiar from the turn-by-turn recounting of conversational stories, and the serial narration found in literary genres (like the epistolary novel, diary writing, or magazines) or mainstream media formats (like daily news reports or soap operas). Moreover, familiar patterns of closed-sequence linearity associated with canonical narratives are also retained even in emergent social media formats. It is remarkable that when innovative wiki software was used for the collaborative project *A Million Penguins*, the participants still expressed an ongoing desire for canonical narrative coherence (Chapter 6). Without a structure like a plot arc, the project disintegrated into what one participant called an "apparent orgy in hyperactive vandalism." Instead, closed and open-ended options for linearity are reconfigured as they take on particular ideological meanings in social media contexts. In the case of the YouTube blogger Lonelygirl15, the use of conventional narrative trajectories of plot-like conflict in need of resolution was associated with constructed, commercial marketing. This canonical narrative linearity contributed to the unveiling of Lonelygirl15 as a commercial product, because it was felt to be at odds with the open-ended stories of self-expression associated with an authentic, more democratic use of YouTube for content creation. Closed narrative sequences are thus associated with a particular constructed, literary, and artificial narrative genre, while open-ended narrative sequences are considered closer to day-to-day lived experiences, and so more authentic.

The innovations of episodic social media formats that enable open-ended linearity do not automatically entail an atomistic or fragmentary mode of interpretation. Although the stories (or story episodes) told in single textual units *can* be read in isolation from each other, this does not mean that they are interpreted without reference to the discourse and behavioral contexts in which they are embedded. Readers are remarkably adept at creating larger narrative contexts, even when individual items of narrative material are dispersed across multiple, often nonadjacent, textual units. Similarly, narrators can create intertextual association between stories and story episodes. For example, the Second Stories created in forum threads did not require that stories be textually adjacent in order to be interconnected: narrators could signal pragmatic and intertextual interdependence through quotation or politeness devices. The use of narrative captions and links in narrative tweets illustrates another kind of intertextual embeddedness, where the linked material can extend or enhance the meaning given in the caption.

More generally, the episodic linearity of social media is embedded within larger generic contexts that enable members of the audience to make connections between individual narrative items. In this respect, social media stories are like examples of pointillist art that are created over time. Individual stories (or story episodes) are brush strokes that are separate from each other but co-occur as part of a greater whole (such as the narrator's ongoing life story). The viewer of a pointillist portrait, who focused on a single brush stroke, would miss the effect of the larger picture. Similarly, reading one tweet, update, or blog post alone cannot capture the ongoing, digital self-portrait that emerges as the archives found in those social media forms accrue over time. Instead, the narrative units of social media stories together contribute to a greater whole, where the narrative coherence of these episodic, open-ended sequences can be derived from the units' positioning within their generic, behavioral, and discourse contexts.

The closed, linear sequences of canonical narrativity mean that teleology has been prioritized as a master trope for coherence in discussions of narrative theory. The opportunity for open-ended, non-chronological associations between the parts of a social media story unsettles this dominant framework. As Mischler points out, despite the established traditions that treat teleology as a norm for narrativity, this linearity does not account well for "the trajectories of our lives nor the stories we construct to understand ourselves and others" (2008, 43). The kinds of connections entailed between the episodic units of social media stories are not necessarily constrained to operate within a single, closed linear sequence based on chronological connections. Members of the audience can also navigate reading paths through social media sites based on topical connections via hyperlinks or tags. Readership patterns offer another mode of navigation through YouTube and the storytelling community Protagonize, which both use the popularity of videos or stories as a search parameter. There is no single metaphor that will replace teleology as an explanatory frame for narrative linearity, but the interconnected, multiple, and contextualized character of social media stories suggests an alternative concept: the network.

The networked nature of hypertextual narrative was documented by the early critics of digital fiction (Aarseth 1997; Landow 1997). But it is not only technological networks of hypertextuality that are important for shaping the linearity of social media. The linearity of social media stories is reconfigured by the interpersonal networks projected and realized by the interactions between narrators and the members of their audiences. The interpersonal demands that social media contexts place on narrators and their audiences mean that the linguistic resources used to signal social connection come to the fore. As existing narrative genres familiar from research on conversational narrative like Second Stories (Sacks 1995), Anecdotes and Recounts (Martin and Plum 1997), small stories (Georgakopoulou 2007), and chronicles (Ryan 2006) are transplanted into social media contexts like forum threads, blog posts, updates, and podcasts, these familiar narrative genres are not simply reproduced but are reconfigured by the relational ends to which they are put.

This book has identified many kinds of interactive and linguistic strategies that are used to accomplish relational work for storytellers in social media contexts. My analysis has drawn attention to the influence that this relational work bears on narrative structure and styles, leading me to identify new genres and categories of storytelling. For example, the analysis of the evaluation used by women bloggers in Chapter 3 brought to light a new subgenre: the Reflective Anecdote. In recognizing that relational work is not always face-enhancing but may be face-threatening, I refined the criteria used to classify Second Stories and described the features of a new type of Second Story: face-threatening stories of dissociation. Earlier work on small stories has emphasized their social nature in terms of discourse function: in Chapter 4, I trace the stylistic resources that are used when telling small stories to perform sociality, and how these performances vary for different participant groups and evolve over time.

In each storytelling instance, the range and frequency of the resources used to project connection between narrator and audience (politeness devices, comparators, intensifiers, present-tense forms, and inclusive person deictics) subtly altered the balance between the structural elements found in each narrative genre where events are subordinated to the relational work accomplished by the storytelling. Above all, it is the *social* nature of storytelling that is amplified in these stories, reconfiguring the style and sometimes the structure of the narrative genres that develop as a result.

This is true for genres that are reconfigured from conversational types of story (like Anecdotes, Second Stories, and small stories) and for attempts to rework literary narratives in social media contexts (like the addventure genres reworked by Protagonize). Storytelling has always been an interpersonal activity, but in the absence of paralinguistic cues of sociality used in face-to-face contexts, the verbal resources used to create interpersonal connection in the asynchronous, dialogic contexts of social media are all the more significant.

In summary, the linearity typical of social media stories includes retrospective, completed accounts of past-tense events but more often favors recency over retrospection. While the emergent nature of social media promotes episodic narrative sequences, the individual units of social media stories (posts, updates, or tweets) do not have to be interpreted atomistically, but are positioned within broader generic, discourse, and behavioral contexts that are underpinned by networked connections between narrators and their audiences. The emphasis on social interaction promoted by social media prioritizes the interpersonal connection between storytellers and their audiences, especially as signaled by linguistic resources that reshape existing story genres into new configurations. This suggests that while temporal sequence remains a core property of narrative as a macro-level text type, the qualities associated with canonical narrativity are by no means universal but result from the focus of particular research traditions, especially the focus on literary texts in classical narratology and narrative interviews in sociolinguistics. As the corpus of stories continues to grow beyond literary and conversational contexts, the primacy of completed, teleologically focused narrative progression appears less like a norm from which all other narratives can be compared and more like a subtype of narrative associated with assumptions of artifice and artistic control.

TELLERSHIP REVISITED

The stories told in social media formats make use of a range of tellership options, which range from single teller narratives with apparently low involvement (like the oral history podcasts of the [murmur] project) to stories with multiple tellers who compete in making their contribution to the narrative (like the collaborative storytelling project *A Million Penguins*). However, single tellership is relatively rare in the examples discussed in this book. Instead, the dialogic possibilities of social media enabled through commenting, liking, and contributing to discussion pages or forums tend to promote options for multiple tellership. The practices of multiple tellership in social media stories rely on turn-taking structures that are familiar from conversational narratives. For example, the narrator may tell their story, and members of the audience then respond by adding an evaluative assessment or asking for more information. This sequential report of events (by the narrator) and follow up evaluation (from the audience) is found in sequences of forum posts (Chapter 2), blog posts and comments (Chapter 3), and status updates and comments (Chapter 4). But these familiar turn taking patterns are reconfigured to greater and lesser extents by the different interactive formats used in social media.

The options for multiple tellership in social media formats can be contrasted in two ways. First, multiple tellership can be distributed across turns published in a series of individual textual units (e.g., a story episode can be made in a blog post and the audience's response written in a comment) or multiple turns can be compressed into the same textual unit (like the modified retweets discussed in Chapter 5 or the wikinovel discussed in Chapter 6).

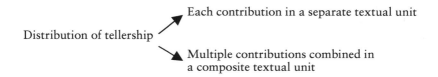

Distribution of tellership → Each contribution in a separate textual unit

→ Multiple contributions combined in a composite textual unit

Second, multiple tellership varies according to whether or not control of the text is equally distributed between co-tellers. For example, all contributors to a discussion forum can author posts, but moderation is retained by a third party who does not tell stories at all: the site administrator. In contrast, the blogger retains the right to moderate the comments that are posted on their webpage: the commenter cannot control whether or not their contribution is published. In a modified retweet, the original teller no longer has control of their narrative: it is the second co-teller, the retweeter, who can alter and publish the text. However, in wiki software, all tellers have equal control of the text, and can add, change or delete the narrative material added by another author.

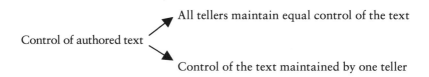

Control of authored text → All tellers maintain equal control of the text

→ Control of the text maintained by one teller

The textual distribution and control of tellership combine to allow more or less involvement between the multiple tellers, which can be expressed as a continuum that moves from more familiar to emergent co-tellership practices (Figure 9.3).

Level of Innovation	Distribution and Control of Tellership	Examples
Familiar	Multiple tellership distributed across multiple units, where all co-tellers have equal control of the text	Discussion forum posts
Reconfigured	Multiple tellership distributed across multiple units, but control of the text is asymmetrically distributed	Blog posts and comments; Facebook updates and comments
	Multiple tellership compressed into a single textual unit, where control of the text resides with one author	Modified retweets
Emergent	Multiple tellership compressed into a single textual unit, where control of the text is equally available to all co-tellers.	Wiki software

Figure 9.3   Options for co-tellership in social media.

At one end of the continuum, the posts made to discussion forums like those used to tell Second Stories (Chapter 2) appear closest to the familiar co-tellership of face-to-face narration, in that turns are equally distributed and controlled by the co-tellers. However, co-tellership is reconfigured by interactive formats that allow one teller to withhold the contribution of another. For example, templates that allow comments to be appended (blog posts and Facebook updates) have antecedents in conversational turn-taking structures (where a narrative report is followed by an evaluative assessment made by the audience), but contrast in the asymmetrical relationship they construct between teller and audience. While conversational narrators can use various tactics to hold the floor, they cannot literally delete words that have been uttered by another contributor.[1] However, the asynchronous, verbal modes of some computer-mediated discourse mean that a participant like a blogger can withhold or delete a comment from the audience on their blog.

A more dramatic example of reconfigured tellership is found in modified retweets. Retweeting reconfigures the process of e-mail forwarding and, more generally, the process of quoting another's story. When an e-mail is forwarded, the additional comment by a second author is conventionally added at the top of the trail of correspondence and the authorship of each contribution is indicated by the e-mail signatures. In a retweet, the additional comment and original retweet are compressed into the same textual segment. As discussed in Chapter 5, the added assessment is often placed immediately before the forwarded message is reproduced. In the following example, Demi Moore's evaluation, "Amazing," appears to the left of the original tweet posted by the Twitter member, @rowdeezy227:

> Amazing! RT @rowdeezy227: in 1992 the NY State Appeals Court ruled that women have the right to go topless, just like men
>
> (MrsKutcher: Wed, 14 Apr 2010 22:26)

Because Western patterns of reading more from left to right, the later recipients of the retweet might have to reverse the textual order of the assessment and original message to restore chronological structure of the original turn-taking sequence.

The reconfigured format for multiple tellership in a retweet suggests that the importance of recency as an ordering principle can be applied to horizontal as well as textual sequences. More generally, it points to the flexibility of positioning an evaluative assessment in relation to narrative content. In conversational storytelling, evaluations made by the audience cannot be made before the story has been told: there is nothing for them to make an assessment of. The asynchronous nature of computer-mediated discourse, combined with possibility of cutting and pasting digital text, means that in a retweet, additional material can be later inserted at any textual point in the sequence of the original text. Audience assessment can be placed as a text-initial, anticipatory evaluation of the material that will follow, not textually constrained to a retrospective position, as a comment on what has already been told.

At the most innovative point in the spectrum of tellership, emergent forms of co-tellership appear in the wikinovel *A Million Penguins*. There is no offline antecedent for multiple narrators creating a story within the same textual space while geographically separate from each other, and where control of the text enables authors to add and edit the contribution made by others. The capabilities of wiki software expand the range of interactions between the tellers, audiences and text in new directions. But the principles of wiki creation are at odds with single-teller processes of narration associated with canonical narrative and the turn-by-turn structures of conversational storytelling. The analysis of the commentary to *A Million Penguins* presented in Chapter 6 showed participants expressing a desire for controls on co-tellership in the form of some kind of "umpire"—a figure that emerged as a discourse identity of the Convener in other collaborative storytelling projects like Protagonize.

In summary, the dialogic capabilities of social media stories enable a range of co-tellership practices to emerge. This is not a binary opposition of single versus multiple tellership, but rather a spectrum of possibilities that move from single tellership of print narrative and familiar patterns of co-tellership derived from conversational narration to reconfigured and emergent options that compress the contribution from multiple narrators into single textual units. The co-tellership in social media is not freely democratic but operates within textual and social constraints including who has control of the text and agreements for co-tellers to communicate co-operatively. Based on the examples considered in this book, it would appear that opportunities for uncontrolled co-tellership in social media formats do not enable narrative production. When technological and social constraints on tellership were removed in the innovative, apparently democratic context for *A Million Penguins*, the participants still expressed a desire that multiple tellership should be controlled. How far this trend might continue will remain to be seen. It may be that over time, recognized practices for co-tellership will emerge for narrative wikis in the same way that they have for non-narrative projects like Wikipedia. As new forms of multimodal collaboration become possible (e.g., through voice threading in YouTube videos) further dimensions of co-tellership will also emerge.

REVISITING TELLABILITY

The narrative dimension of tellability entails two dimensions: subjective judgments about the relevance of a story's subject matter and the rhetorical resources used to create involvement between narrator and audience. The tellability found in the social media stories discussed in this book confirms the conclusions drawn in recent, discourse-analytic narrative research. Tellability is not a stable narrative attribute realized by a single factor such as "conflict." Instead, the norms for tellability are context sensitive, shaped by the generic contexts of social media sites and expectations derived from offline extrasituational contexts. The inherently interpersonal requirement for narrative tellability is related to the face needs of narrators and their audiences. In social media contexts that promote connection with others, the familiar narrative maxim for narrators to make their narratives tellable (Labov 1972) incorporates two dimensions: to tell stories in such a way to enable face-enhancing involvement between narrator and audience, and to avoid telling stories which damage the face of the narrative participants.

These maxims influence the kinds of stories that are told in many social media contexts. The desire for social alignment through projecting similarity between narrators was seen in the familiar, face-enhancing Second Stories told in forum threads (Chapter 2). The Reflective Anecdotes (a genre that promoted solidarity and self-reflection) occurred in blog writing where the authors encouraged connection with others through links and comments (Chapter 3). Similarly, the celebrity figures used modified retweets to construct their image as involved with their fans (Chapter 5) and the success of Protagonize's collaborative endeavors was due in part to the efforts of the narrative Convener, who created face-enhancing social connection within the community of tellers (Chapter 6).

But the maxim to foster face-enhancing connection and avoid damage to face of self and other was placed under particular pressure by the collapsed contexts that characterize social media genres. There are three types of collapsed contexts that constrain the narrative dimension of tellability:

1. Aggregated audiences that bring together groups usually segmented in offline interactions between narrator and audience (such as Friend lists on Facebook, Twitter Follower lists, blog audiences)
2. Erosion of public and private boundaries (exemplified by the controversies relating to the status of information posted in Twitter)
3. Increasing crossover between online and offline performances (particularly relevant to judgments made about authenticity in Chapter 8).

The collapsed contexts of social media do not influence tellability in a uniform fashion. Instead, the subject matter and rhetorical styles used in social media stories vary across a wide spectrum from what might be considered "low" (everyday and unpolished) and "high" (landmark and rhetorically accomplished) tellability. In Facebook, narrators negotiated the risks of an aggregated Friend list by telling stories about deliberately inoffensive, everyday topics, while simultaneously using a rhetorical style that projected high involvement between participants. In Twitter, celebrities emphasized their mainstream, professional activities in the front stage stories they tell, but also created an illusion of back-stage intimacy by incorporating stories from their private lives. As social media interactions become increasingly interwoven with offline activities (especially through the use of wi-fi–enabled mobile devices), judgments about tellability are based on both online norms and knowledge of a narrator in the offline world. The role of offline situational knowledge was most relevant to the explanation of "fraped" stories (Chapter 8), where the inauthentic impersonation of another speaker could be detected by close acquaintances with knowledge of the authentic speaker from the offline world.

Narrators do not always comply with the requirement that their stories should enable face-enhancing involvement and avoid damage to face. When the expected norms for tellability are breached, storytelling can become a socially divisive act. A clear example is the "fraped" updates, in which the narrative subject matter ranged from apparently light-hearted falsehoods to inappropriately and offensively sexually explicit content. In order to avoid damage to face in that context, the members of the audience interpreted the atypical tellability as an impersonation rather than an authentic update, and nonserious banter rather than face threatening. When members of an audience display their knowledge of the narrative norms (by assessing what is appropriate and what is not), this positions them within an in-group of experts. Different kinds of in-groups emerge within the collapsed contexts of social media, such as the YouTube viewers who spotted that Lonelygirl15 was a fake; the members of a Friend list who detected that "frapes" were inauthentic impersonations; and expert members of discussion forums like Bodybuilding.

com. Other stories are used for clearly face-threatening purposes. The Second Stories found in forum threads (Chapter 2) included examples where the subsequent narrators chose to dissociate from earlier tellers in order to assert the boundaries of their social identity as serious bodybuilders. Storytelling was used to exclude others, not to create involvement. In each case, membership of the insider group is desirable, implying superior status within the wider, collapsed audiences of social media forms like Facebook and YouTube.

In summary, the analysis of tellability in social media stories confirms the subjective and context-sensitive nature of this narrative dimension. In these social media contexts, tellability is constrained by the face needs of the narrator and the audience, promoting face-enhancing involvement and avoiding damage to face. These face needs are relevant in other offline storytelling contexts, but are particularly shaped by the collapsed contexts of social media, including aggregated audiences, the erosion of a boundary between the public and private, and the blurring of offline and online interactions. Although the face needs of narrators and audiences lie at the heart of demands for narrative tellability, social media stories do not always promote face-enhancing involvement. It would also be foolish to assume that constraining tellability according to the face needs of the narrative participants maps on to the actual qualities of social relationships between tellers and their audiences. Tellability is part of a narrative performance, not a transparent reflection of reality. The involvement that is projected through the rhetorical resources of tellability does not mean that an audience will necessarily engage with the story or the storyteller. Instead, tellability is constrained by the need for narrators to present themselves as attentive to their audience, even if their audience chooses not to listen.

EMBEDDEDNESS REVISITED: STORYTELLING IN CONTEXT

The linearity, tellability, and tellership of social media stories are inextricably shaped by the contexts in which they are embedded. Ochs and Capps (2001) suggest that canonical narratives can apparently be detached in some measure from their surrounding context. As they point out, that appearance is illusory: all narratives are produced and received in particular contexts. The analysis of the social media stories in this book has identified a range of contextual elements that influence the generic forms and linguistic features used by narrators: textual, generic, behavioral, and extrasituational contexts. These contextual elements provide the resources that shape the narrative interactions and identities that emerge from storytelling in the digital environments of social media.

Textual Contexts: Identities and Interaction

Textual contexts include the surrounding discourse in which a story is positioned and include the thread in which a Facebook post might be published, the template in which an update is written, and the interactive resources of a story, such as links or comments. Each of these discourse contexts is dynamic, changing in response to factors in the wider extrasituational context (like the gender of the participants) or to factors in the generic context (such as the changes to the Facebook status update template after July 2008). In turn, these textual contexts influence the way in which stories are told and the identities that the narrators construct for themselves and others.

The discursive elements of the textual context like comments and "likes" allow narrators to display their engagement with others and their position within a wider social group. The analysis of commenting was particularly relevant to blogs (Chapter 3), Facebook updates (Chapter 4), and the collaborative storytelling project Protagonize (Chapter 6). In each case, the quantity of the comments was interpreted as a measure of the narrator's interactive involvement with their audience: the higher the number of comments, the greater the assumed interaction with the group. For the Protagonize members, further discourse identities emerged, based on the variation in the types of comments that were made. This expanded the functions relevant to the process of narrative production and reception to include Reviewers, Editors, Creators, Conveners, and Collaborators. These roles are also relevant to the production and reception of print narrative, but not as well recognized because of the textual focus of literary narratology and the more dispersed nature of creating and consuming print narratives, which is not always documented publically in the same way that online interactions can be.

The frequency of commenting on blogs and Facebook updates also showed variation. The distribution of comments in the datasets of blog posts (Chapter 3) and Facebook updates (Chapter 4) uncovered interactive patterns that indicated gender difference, where women tended to comment more on posts or updates written by women and men commented more on posts or updates written by men. These patterns echo findings of gender difference in other studies of CMC (Herring and Zelenkauskaite 2009), but are not interpreted as resulting from a universal, essentialist model of gender. Instead, the interactions between commenters and the narrators of cancer blogs are shaped by offline patterns relating to the particular demands of the illnesses in question (breast and prostate cancer); and in the case of Facebook updates, the differences contributed to the construction of Facebook as a linguistic market place whose dominant user group was young women.

Hyperlinks are another interactive element of the textual context that enabled narrators to situate their storytelling within the wider intertextual resources of the Internet. A quantitative analysis of linking practices was included in the stories told in blogs (Chapter 3) and the narrative tweets (Chapter 5). In both cases, the analysis suggested that linking was not just intertextual but had a social dimension: narrators used links to indicate their interests or areas of expertise, with some narrators using more links than others. However, there is no isomorphic mapping between the frequency of linking and a particular type of identity. The celebrity figures in Twitter used a higher frequency of links in their tweets than did "ordinary" tweeters. In this case, linking was a strategy used by celebrities to amplify their offline status as elite persons. Cancer blogs written by women contained more links to personal blogs (and were more linked to by others) than cancer blogs written by men. But rather than amplifying the women blogger's status as elite persons, the increased linking to personal blogs suggests that these writers were strengthening their connections to other bloggers who were writing about similar experiences. Linking may be based on a principle of information sharing, but it can be used to construct different kinds of identity.

Generic Contexts

The characteristics of particular generic contexts shape the tellability and choice of linguistic features used to signal interpersonal connection between narrator and audience. For example, Twitter's public, fast-paced environment for sharing news emphasizes immediacy in its preference for temporal adverbs like *today*, *tonight*, *tomorrow*, and *now*, and foregrounds professional activity in the tweeters' story content. Facebook's emphasis on social connection between networks of peers similarly foregrounds temporal adverbs that construct immediacy, but also makes the use of an affective discourse style an apt strategy for performing sociality. A blog's dual capacity to share information and connect with others makes it well suited as an alternative avenue for those seeking advice and support in relation to critical illness like cancer, while its textual expansiveness provides scope for writers like the women bloggers to create genres like the Reflective Anecdote. But generic contexts also change their characteristics over time. The debates concerning the authenticity of Lonelygirl15 arose at the point at which the ethos of YouTube as an apparently democratic, participatory environment began to shift toward a more performance-oriented culture where viewers came to be considered as fans rather than peers.

The influence of generic and textual contexts overlaps with offline contextual factors such as behavioral and extrasituational contexts in complex ways. The importance of the physical setting in which a social media story is produced and received is often neglected in text-immanent analysis of narratives and of CMC more generally. But the discussion of the podcasts used to reconfigure oral history narratives in the innovative project [murmur] suggests that physical space can be exploited as a narrative resource, especially in the new category of asynchronous-endophoric storytelling of which [murmur] is an example. As social media are accessed increasingly through mobile devices, sites like Foursquare and Gowalla, along with the location-based updates of Twitter and opportunities for geo-tagging will no doubt exploit the importance of physical places and spaces in future social media storytelling too.

Extrasituational Context: Transportable Identities

It is clear from the analysis of social media stories in this book that online storytelling is not divorced from its offline contexts. Although narrators and their audiences can recreate their identities in online discourse, the transportable identities that are performed in offline contexts are not abandoned but carried over into social media contexts. Although by no means the only aspect of transportable identity, the discussions in earlier chapters have pointed to the ongoing salience of gender as a participant category. However, "feminine" discourse styles are not monolithic constructs, and are not used by all women in the same way. The narrator of the story "Guys Staring at the Gym" told in the bodybuilding forums discussed in Chapter 2 expressed an expectation that the Female Subforum would be a place to find "a sympathetic ear." But her expectations of sociality and support were disappointed, and many of the women dissociated from her stance by telling face-threatening Second Stories that criticized and insulted her.

The narrators of the cancer blogs also drew attention to the importance of gender, as their biological and social resources for performing gender were disrupted by the treatments for critical illness. Even while their gendered identities were challenged by their offline experiences, the narrative genres used by women and men bloggers emphasized discourse styles associated with hegemonic femininity and masculinity. Women used comparators to emphasize emotion, creating Reflective Anecdotes, while men avoided this kind of personal disclosure, concentrating on factual information instead. The tendency for women's personal storytelling to emphasize emotion was repeated in the small stories told in Facebook updates, where female updaters used more APPRAISAL, nonverbal displays of affection, and intensification devices than did male updaters. An affective discourse style including these features has been interpreted in other Western contexts as signaling sociality. This interpretation holds true for the results found here, but the women's use of affective discourse to this end also varied according to the age of the updater and over time. This suggests that the interpretation of storytelling styles as an index of gender is not static or universal. Other styles may well be used in different social media contexts, by participants from different cultural backgrounds and for different purposes. As social media continues to expand, future research needs to explore the complex relationships between online and offline performances of transportable identity in a wider range of contexts.

In summary, the stories told in social media are highly embedded in their textual, generic, and extrasituational contexts. Storytelling may take place via screens, but is produced, received, and interpreted in contexts that bridge online and offline environments. The interactions that take place in the process of storytelling are many and various: formatted in textual contexts (templates, comments, and threads), but shaped by extrasituational practices and values. New discourse identities emerge from these interactions, like the Convener required for collaborative storytelling, but the patterns of interaction are often shaped by familiar indexes of transportable identity, like gender. It would seem that even while technological features found in the textual and generic contexts of social media change, some contextual factors, like the construction of social identity, have stayed convincingly familiar.

NARRATIVE DIMENSIONS AND THE STORY OF SOCIAL MEDIA

The familiar, reconfigured, and emergent narrative dimensions of linearity, tellability, tellership, and embeddedness are positioned within a broader trajectory of changes in social media. The early stories told about the advent of social media presented the phenomena as a decisive break from the past, narrated with a rhetoric that coupled emergent technological formats with revolutionary social value. The developments of open source software, content development by nonspecialists, and increased interaction between users were mapped onto "new" social values of democracy, participation, collaboration, and dynamic change. This story of social media is not neutral and is strongly influenced by the commercial contexts in which it was situated. Marwick (2010) points out that the rhetoric of Web 2.0 was strategically positioned to re-energize the e-commerce sector following the collapse of the dot-com industries in the early years of the twenty-first century. There are clear advantages to telling this kind of story that, on the surface, suggests the possibility of social change and relocates power to create and manipulate computer-mediated discourse in the hands of the everyday Internet user. Within this schema, engagement with social media in the guise of countercultural, community co-operation is the solution to the problem of commercial failure. But social media formats are more reconfigured than emergent, and have always had their roots in earlier web genres and practices. There is no simple, unified transition from old commercial to new community-centered models of technology. As social media have evolved, it is clear that a utopian, democratic, and participatory outcome was not the end of the story.

Instead, social media have developed in line with the capitalist ideologies that promote networks dominated by commercial interest and rewards competition with increased social and economic gains.[2] Later social media genres have evolved as "walled gardens," that is, as sites with firmly delineated boundaries which do not release their content or code for free development (e.g., Facebook). Many of the largest social media sites are now owned by large commercial investors, while Facebook generates revenue through advertisement placement.[3] These large-scale trends are reflected in micro-level design choices found in social media formats. It is not accidental that the linearity of social media stories should be dominated by recency and enable frequent, episodic interactions over time. If the most recent story is ascribed with the greatest value (e.g., through its most visible position in an archive), the need for a participant to post new content on a regular basis increases, thereby increasing the time spent on a site and its market value for advertisers. Similarly, narrative maxims to create face-enhancing involvement with others, particularly in sites like Facebook, YouTube, and Twitter could be interpreted as a strategy designed to boost the narrator's popularity, where popularity is measured by the scale and engagement of an audience made visible through comments, "likes," and ratings. The options for co-tellership are not evenly distributed between participants but operate within textual and social controls that construct interactive hierarchies between participants. Far from a utopian, collaborative environment where all tellers and their stories are valued equally, the narrative dimensions of social media suggest a hierarchical system based in a linguistic market where visibility and interaction are the prized values.

As interaction becomes increasingly valuable, the scale and scope of the audience changes, and narrators must adapt their communicative practices accordingly to reap the rewards and mitigate the risks of storytelling in collapsed contexts that require performances of sociality. Interaction between an updater and a Facebook Friend list or Twitter follower list that runs into thousands cannot sustain dyadic, peer-to-peer communicative practices with all members of the audience. Instead, the stories of personal experience become published as one-to-many broadcasts like Twitter or Facebook updates, where an audience of peers becomes increasingly similar to a fan base like the viewers of the most popular YouTube bloggers. Ironically, the dialogues that social media appeared to enable as an alternative to corporate, mass-media communication seem to be shifting toward a model pseudo-interaction where direct interaction between participants is an illusion. As processes of micro-celebrity increase, the higher the popularity of the narrator (tweeter, updater, blogger), the greater the need for broadcast communication like status updates and modified retweets, and lower the likelihood for dyadic, addressed messages to occur.

The benefits to be gained from social media interaction include social capital (increased status and enhanced social relationship), as evidenced from the interviews with Facebook updaters (Chapter 4) and the comments expressing mutual support found on cancer blogs. Economic benefit is also gained through social media interaction, as in the commercial success of Lonelygirl15 and the practice of celebrity Tweeters. In order to gain these benefits, narrators must make use of appropriate narrative dimensions, that is, they must negotiate the requirements that the story be recent, ongoing, and perform sociality in order to maintain audience interest, while avoiding face damage to self or others. In their development of new narrative genres like the Reflective Anecdote (Chapter 3) and in setting the trends for discourse styles in updates (Chapter 4), women appear to be leading the way in shaping communicative patterns that are associated with preferred styles of performed sociality. Nonetheless, their interactions are often trivialized as forms of "small talk" or gossip and where personal disclosure is interpreted negatively and may result in loss of status (Marwick 2010, 36). Young women's role in creating discourse norms in social media contexts (Herring, Kouper et al. 2004) is at odds with the minimal representation of women entrepreneurs in the creation of new social media technology. Marwick (2010) documents ongoing sexism that systematically devalues the contributions women make to the development of social media. Although women might gain social capital within semi-private networks that consist of their known peers, this does not translate into social or political power in wider contexts. Far from a democratic and participatory endpoint, the story of social media suggests that there will be ongoing divides in online and offline influence for different social groups, such as those distinguished on the basis of gender.

FUTURE DIRECTIONS

This book has examined a range of stories told in different social media contexts, but it is by no means the last word on the subject. There are other social media sites, communities of storytellers, and narrative genres that I did not have space to include in this project. The analysis in this book is also limited by its chronological focus. Computer-mediated discourse is fast changing, and new sites and formats continue to emerge that will enable and constrain the future narrative dimensions of storytelling in as yet unforeseen ways. The increased diversity and scale of adoption of Internet use means that future narrative research in CMC will need to extend the corpus of its sample texts in further directions. Future research should attend to the multimodal, multilingual, multi-platformed, mobile, and localized uses of the Internet by participants who identify as belonging to different cultures, age groups, sexual orientations, nationalities, and ethnic groupings. To close, I set out a list of future research questions, grouped under each of these headings.

Multimodality

- What are the narrative enabling and constraining features of the increasingly multimodal resources used in emergent forms of social media?
- How are modalities (words, image, sound, audiovisual resources) distributed between narrative participants (tellers and audience)?
- How might multimodality rework narrative dimensions of tellability (e.g., which modes signal involvement and relevance)?

- How are judgments about narrative authenticity reconfigured in different modalities (visual shifts from the graphic to photographic; audio resources like accent, voice quality, prosody)?

Multilingualism

- What are the discourse features of social media stories told in languages other than English?
- What identity work is accomplished through code switching by multilingual storytellers?
- What is the story of endangered languages in social media contexts?

Multi-Platform Use of Social Media

- How do participants modify their storytelling behavior across different social media sites to accomplish different kinds of identities?
- What might an ethnographically grounded study of a single person's social media storytelling as performed across multiple platforms tell us?
- How does the use of RSS feed aggregators (such as Google Reader and Social Scope) to recontextualize story episodes from multiple sites influence processes of narrative production and reception?

Mobile Use of Social Media

- How is the possibility for on-site storytelling via mobile devices exploited in new social media genres (e.g., FourSquare, Gowalla and Twitter)?
- What is the narrative role of place and space for stories told "on the move"?
- What are the ideological implications for documenting space and place in social media stories (e.g., in promoting activism or capitalism)?

More Varied Participant Groups

- How is the story of the digital divide told, and how does this reflect actual use of social media?
- What contexts for and values of storytelling are created in social network sites targeted at preteen populations?
- How is narrative inauthenticity understood by preteens who use sites like Facebook?
- How are coming-out stories reconfigured in social media formats?
- How is hetero-normativity constructed and contested in social media stories?
- What is the relationship between the storytelling styles of late adopters and early innovators for different social media genres?

- How might narrators signal their ethnic orientation in sites like Facebook and Twitter, which do not categorize participants according to race or ethnicity?

As narrative researchers attempt to address these (and other) questions we will need to move further toward interdisciplinary and multifaceted modes of analysis. Focusing on the text alone will not suffice, and the contextualized approach I have gestured toward in this book is but the first step toward more nuanced forms of analysis that can take into account the multiple modes and contextual elements that are interwoven in our day-to-day storytelling in social media. Nor are these the only questions that might be asked about the stories that continue to proliferate on the social media sites that have developed in the last decade. The conclusion of this book is necessarily as open-ended and dialogic as many of the social media stories that have been analyzed in its pages. My hope is that this book has also prompted you to ask questions of your own, and that those questions will help chart future research that uncovers the work that stories accomplish for their tellers as they make sense of themselves, one another, and their worlds.

Notes

CHAPTER 1

1. Hoffman's (2010) edited collection includes several chapters that deal with personal narrative in CMC, namely, message boards (Arendholz 2010) and weblogs (Eisenlauer and Hoffman 2010). However, the focus of his collection is not on social media and is more concerned with a broader approach to multimodal narratives.
2. For further and much fuller discussions of narrativity, see Herman (1997), Fludernik (1996), and Ryan (2004, 2006, 2007).
3. Of course, present-tense verbs do occur along with past-tense forms in personal narratives. This has been documented in Wolfson (1978) and Schiffrin (1981) who describe the Conversational Historical Present as a resource for narrative immediacy.
4. There are postmodern novels that play with reverse-order sequencing, like Martin Amis's *Time's Arrow*. However, in social media, it is the design of the software that prompts the anachronistic presentation of the posts. The reverse order relates primarily to the archiving of the discourse creation, not necessarily to the content of the posts themselves.
5. The sociologist and social media researcher, danah boyd, chooses to present her name without conventional capitalization.

CHAPTER 2

1. Arendholz (2010) distinguishes between forums and message boards. I use the terms interchangeably.
2. In some forums, posts from new members are pre-moderated before they are published. This is the practice on the BBC's 606 sports forum.
3. It is possible that bodybuilders might become involved in the sport through physiotherapy prescribed in order to recover from ill health, but no examples of this kind were found in the data sample used in this chapter.
4. The competitive behavior within Bodybuilding.com also extends to members who compete with themselves by attempting to outdo previous records for strength, weight, and timing in lifting records or training.
5. The threads are archived according to recency, where the more recent the activity, the higher up the list the thread appears in the subforum archive. The archive also lists the number of posts that have been made to each thread.

CHAPTER 3

1. As stated in the introduction (Chapter 1), the quotations from the cancer blogs in this chapter were from blogs that were publically available. Where it was possible to contact the blogger to gain consent to quote from their writing, I did so. The blogger's names have been retained in recognition of their authorship. URLs to the blogs are provided in the list immediately preceding the References.

CHAPTER 4

1. It is also possible to add privacy settings to blogs (e.g., Wordpress, Blogger, and MySpace all provide settings that can restrict the visibility of a blog), and discussion forums can be hosted in semi-private environments. However, the data considered in this chapter contrast with the forums, blogs, podcasts, and tweets analyzed in the other parts of this book in that the Facebook updates were not publically available. Participant consent was sought, and all the updates have been anonymized.
2. See Page (2010b) for a full discussion of the narrative potential of updating in Facebook.
3. All names of participants have been removed from the updates and replaced by a code. The code was generated on the basis of the declared gender of the participant, the frequency of their updating behavior, and the year in which the dataset was collected. Hence <F01–08> indicates a female updater, who was the first most frequent updater in the 2008 dataset, <M50–10> indicates a male updater, who was the fiftieth most frequent updater in the 2010 dataset, and so on.
4. This was also true to the datasets analyzed by Lee (2011), which she describes under the category of updates concerned with "everyday life."
5. The references to the Spending Review relate to the Comprehensive Spending Review published by the British government in October 2010. Nick Clegg was the leader of the Liberal Democrat Party and Deputy Prime Minister at that point. The reference to Mahmut's match was to the tennis match between John Isner and Nicolas Mahmut in the Wimbledon Tennis Tournament in 2010. The match was the longest in tennis history, lasting over eight hours in total.
6. The references to the Chilean miners relates to their rescue after sixty-nine days trapped underground. The rescue of the thirty-three miners was broadcast internationally on the mainstream news (see http://www.bbc.co.uk/news/world-latin-america-11518015, accessed March 1, 2011). The reference to "Anne Widicombe dancing the salsa" reports on the retired British politician, Anne Widdicombe, who took part somewhat notoriously in the British television talent show *Strictly Come Dancing* (http://www.bbc.co.uk/strictlycomedancing/2010/dancers/celebrity/ann_widdecombe.shtml, accessed March 1, 2011). Again, this event was given national news coverage in the mainstream media during the time that the program was aired.
7. Discussions of APPRAISAL conventionally use block capitals to differentiate the technical use of the terms used to categorize the evaluative and interpersonal resources identified in this framework.
8. Further levels of delicacy are usually applied within APPRAISAL analysis, indicating the subtypes of AFFECT, JUDGMENT, and APPRECIATION (Martin 2000). However, the distinction between the subcategories is somewhat controversial and not used here for the top-level analysis carried out

for the status updates. In this case, all updates were coded using the three main attitudinal categories of APPRAISAL and for their negative or positive polarity.

9. It is possible that updaters can use their Friend list in order to gain economic benefits too, for example, by promoting products or services. Marwick (2005) documents the use of Facebook data by advertisers in order to market products. Nonetheless, this commoditization of the Friend network is overlaid by metaphors of sociality, where social status and capital are gained by interacting with Friends.

10. It was not possible to carry out a parallel analysis of "liking" according to the gender of the person who had added the "like" as Facebook did not itemize this information for updates with likes added by more than three people.

CHAPTER 5

1. Ostrow (2009) reports that the number of unique visitors to Twitter increased 1,382 percent from 475,000 in February 2008 to 7,038,000 in February 2009.

2. A writer can extend the length of a tweet by using a service like tweetlonger. com, or by using Twitter to direct their followers to a blog post.

3. Private communication between Twitter members is possible through Direct Messages (DMs). No Direct Messages were included in this study.

4. O'Reilly (2009) describes this as the "asymmetric follow," which is advantageous for handling the scale of the audience garnered in social networks and for promoting the growth of social media sites.

5. Recent examples include Liverpool footballer Ryan Babel (Markham 2011) and Arsenal footballer Jack Wilshire (*Mirror Newspaper*, February 7, 2011) who were fined or censured for using Twitter to criticize officials or other players.

6. On May 23, 2011, the limitations of super-injunctions to protect individual privacy were called into question when the British MP John Hemming named the footballer Ryan Giggs as the sports figure previously protected by injunctions against media reports of an alleged affair. The MP used both the protection of parliament and the existing disclosure of Giggs' name on Twitter in order to expose the limitations of the current judicial system's ability to deal with privacy rights in the age of social media. See http://www. bbc.co.uk/news/uk-13507031 (accessed May 24, 2011) for an example of the national news coverage on this topic.

7. Marwick (2010, 203–206) documents the rise of celebrity figures as the top users of Twitter as the site evolved from early adoption to mainstream use, noting that a significant change occurred between 2008 and 2009.

8. Sarah Brown is notable for having achieved her Twitter prominence through her husband's achievements rather than her own.

9. In some profiles, tweeters provide links to external sites like their personal homepage in order to provide more information about their online identity. Others use verification systems in order to claim authenticity, or create usernames to distinguish themselves from imposters. Examples include "THEREAL-MISCHA" (for Mischa Barton), "THEREALSHAQ" (for Shaquille O'Neale).

10. The British National Corpus is a 100 million–word collection of samples of written and spoken language from a wide range of sources, designed to represent a wide cross-section of current British English, both spoken and written (http://www.natcorp.ox.ac.uk/, accessed June 1, 2011). The Corpus of Contemporary American English is a 425 million–word collection of written and spoken language, again from a wide range of offline sources designed to reflect current American English (http://www.americancorpus.org/, accessed June 1, 2011).

11. Celebrity figures, like "ordinary" tweeters, also commented on national events like political elections or events of international significance. Events like the Japanese tsunami (March 2011) or, in the United Kingdom, the wedding of HRH the Prince of Wales to Catherine Middleton (April 2011) also attracted widespread commentary on Twitter.
12. Because the length of a tweet is constrained to 140 characters, tweeters often use a URL-shortening service like TinyURL to provide an abbreviated link to a longer URL address.

CHAPTER 6

1. There are many other examples of collaborative writing practices that have been used in offline contexts. For example, oral storytelling traditions from which *Morte D'Arthur* and other Middle English romance narratives emerged were cumulatively developed by multiple tellers. The siblings Charlotte, Emily, Anne, and Bramwell Brontë created a series of tales about fantasy worlds, Angria and Grondol, but each miniature book was individually authored. More recently, chapters in television series that combine into an overarching narrative sequence are often authored by different contributors, such as the US show "Desperate Housewives" or the UK series "Dr Who."
2. There are many possibilities for multiple authorship that predate the conventions of authorship associated with print literature. For example, there are debates about the agency and number of scribes involved in producing narratives from the early and later medieval periods (*Beowulf*, *The Book of Margery Kempe*, and so on).
3. All references from the text of *A Million Penguins* are taken from archived screen shots available at http://replay.web.archive.org/20100827183401/ http://www.amillionpenguins.com/wiki/index.php?title=Main_Page. Unfortunately, it is no longer possible to explore the full site of *A Million Penguins* as it is no longer hosted by Penguin.
4. The community's web pages are available at http://www.protagonize.com/ (accessed May 13, 2011).
5. The name "Addventure" is a pun that blends *add* and *adventure*, highlighting the two main characteristics of the genre: that participants add new episodes to an event-driven adventure story.
6. The gender of the participants is one aspect of their identity that cannot be verified in offline contexts. In this chapter, the gender of the story contributors is inferred from information in their profile pages (such as names, use of personal pronouns, and photographs).
7. I am grateful to Nick Bouton, who supplied me with this information.

CHAPTER 7

1. I follow the convention set out by the international project to employ square brackets and lower case for references to the project name, [murmur].

CHAPTER 8

1. The contested nature of autobiography is a good example that illustrates the assumption that a fictional narrator is separable from an "actual" author.

2 Shuman's (2005) discussion of junk-mail narratives examines examples of stories used in unsolicited e-mail campaigns by groups like Planned Parenthood, Rights to Life, and Amnesty International. Shuman examines the multiple voices invoked through the retellings of stories, and the political ends to which personal narratives are put.

3. Twitter is a particular rich environment for creating hoaxes, where the rapid recirculation of information can accrue "factual" status once it passes on from the hands of the story's original narrators. Recent examples include "The IT Crowd" creator Graham Linehan's account of how rumors of Bin Laden watching his show circulated on Twitter: http://www.bbc.co.uk/news/magazine-13467407 (accessed May 23, 2011).

4. The technological use of "authentication" refers to the use of strategies (such as username and password) that verify a person's identity when they log on to a site. In 2009, Twitter launched verified accounts to distinguish between imposter and genuine members of the site.

5. Examples of individuals who were outed because of their social media interactions include the sex blogger Zoe Margolis (Girl with a One-Track Mind) in 2006, and the police officer Richard Horton, who blogged under the name "Night Jack" and was refused anonymity by the High Court in the United Kingdom (June 2009). Twitter has also been used as a site to out the identity of celebrity figures who had used legal injunctions to prevent disclosure of their alleged misdemeanors by reporters in the British mainstream media (May 2011), leading to a critique of the legal rulings on privacy rights (see BBC news reports at http://www.bbc.co.uk/news/uk-13330409, accessed May 29, 2011).

6. Of course, the authenticator could also be attributed with negative characteristics, like a muckraker or blackmailer.

7. This included the British series "KateModern," which was integrated into the social networking site Bebo, the Polish series, "N1ckola," and the alternative reality game "LG15: Outbreak."

8. Of course, these responses need not be taken at value and could be face-saving fictions used to present the bloggers as well versed in the knowledge of YouTube culture and conventions.

9. The use of the term "rape" to describe the unwanted impersonation of a Facebook updater by a third party is contentious and cannot be taken as equivalent to the violations associated with the use of "rape" to refer to a sexual act. However, because it is used by Facebook members as a means of describing the impersonation under scrutiny here, I will retain it in the following discussion.

10. The terms and conditions for Facebook membership can be found at http://www.facebook.com/terms.php?ref=pf (accessed May 4, 2011).

11. I am grateful to Aaron for allowing me to reproduce his data here. I received the data in anonymous form. All names and references to places were removed in Aaron's original study and were not reinstated here.

12. When "frapes" entail making changes to an existing Facebook profile, they are often carried out by a person known to the victim. This is because of practical factors, as the perpetrator needs to be in close proximity to an account that has been left logged on (e.g., on a laptop left in a shared living space). Other kinds of "frape," where impersonated accounts are created, do not entail a perpetrator to have access to the victim's account. These kinds of "frapes" are carried out by perpetrators are socially distant from, if not unknown to the victim.

CHAPTER 9

1. Judges can place jurisdiction over whether existing words can be published or not, as when literary works are censored or when the media

cannot name individuals protected by high court injunctions in the United Kingdom.

2   Marwick (2010) traces the evolution of neoliberal individualism in relation to the Silicon Valley capitalism in a detailed ethnographic study of social media entrepreneurs.

3. For example, Google bought YouTube in 2006, and also owns Blogger. Yahoo! bought Delicious in 2005 and sold it to AVOS (owned by the founders of YouTube) in 2011.

Glossary

@mentions folder is the area of a Twitter account where any publically posted tweet using the tweeter's username will be filed.

Addventure stories are a collaborative storytelling genre, in which multiple tellers can add later episodes to an existing narrative stem.

Adjacency pairs are the dyadic structures that occur in conversational turn-taking, where the first turn generates the expectation of a second part. Examples include question–answer, greeting–greeting, and request–acceptance/refusal.

API is an abbreviation of Application Program Interface. The API is the tools and protocols used for building software applications. They allow programmers to put together software that will operate within a given environment.

Boosters are devices used to scale up the intensity of an utterance, for example, *really* in "that's really awful."

Cataphoric references are cohesive devices that refer back to an earlier point in the text.

Choose your own adventure is a series of children's game books in which the reader assumes the same role as the protagonist. At the end of each chapter, the reader/protagonist makes choices to determine the protagonist's actions and the plot outcome.

A **conditional** clause is used to express the conditions under which the main clause can be fulfilled. For example, "If the price for the car is reduced (conditional) the buyer will purchase it (main clause)."

A **declarative** clause in English uses a Subject-Verb-Object- (Adverbial) or Subject-Verb-Complement construction, such as "The author (Subject) wrote (Verb) the book (Object)" or "The book (Subject) was (Verb) heavy

(Complement)." The communicative function of a declarative clause is usually to make a statement.

Deictics. In linguistics, deictics are the resources that are used to indicate the relative position of a person or object within their environment. These are sometimes glossed as "pointing words" and includes person deictics (the personal pronoun system), place deictics (adverbs such as *here* and *there*), and temporal deictics (adverbs such as *now* and *then*).

Genre refers to a standardized form of text that is used regularly for the same standard function. In literary criticism, this applies to macro-level categories such as poetry, prose, or drama. From a linguistic perspective, genres can include any text type established through repeated pattern and social purpose (such as letter writing, adverts, lessons, etc.). In this book, genre is used to refer both to narrative forms (like Anecdotes) and to social media forms (like blogs and social network sites).

GPS stands for Global Positioning System, a radio navigation system that enables users to determine their exact location at any point in the world.

Hedges are mitigating devices used to soften the impact of an utterance, for example, "I *sort of* lost your phone."

Homodiegetic narrator. In literary narratology, the theorist Genette (1980) distinguished between narrators who were also characters in the stories that they told (homodiegetic narrators) and narrators who did not appear as characters in the stories that they tell (heterodiegetic narrators). An example of a homodiegetic narrator would be Marlow in *Heart of Darkness* who both narrates the story and takes part in the storyworld events. An example of a heterodiegetic narrator would be the Pardoner in Chaucer's "Pardoner's Tale." Although the Pardoner tells the story of the three thieves, he does not appear in that tale as a character.

An **imperative** clause in English uses a Verb-Object construction, such as "Clear (Verb) the table (Object)." The communicative function of an imperative clause is usually to make a request or demand.

Interrogative clauses usually ask a question (as opposed to making a statement or giving an instruction).

IP address (Internet Protocol Address) is the exclusive number assigned to all technology devices that can send or receive information within a computer network, and that can be used to identify the position of that device within a known network.

Modality refers to the resources that a speaker uses to signal their relative commitment to a proposition. In linguistics, modality is separated into further categories: **epistemic modality**, which relates to how certain a proposition is (*shall*, *might*, *may*); **deontic modality**, which includes verbs used to mark necessity or obligation (*must*, *should*, *ought to*); and **dynamic modality**, which indicates permission (*can*, *able to*, *may*).

MP3 file formats are a popular form of digital audio files that compress a sound sequence into a very small file size. MP3 files revolutionized music-sharing practices in the late 1990s.

Narratee is the (usually fictional) character to whom the narrator addresses the story that is told. In the *Heart of Darkness*, the sailors who listen to Marlow's story are the narratees.

Netiquette is the blend formed from "Net" and "etiquette" used to refer to the conventions that govern socially acceptable discourse used in online contexts.

A **nonfinite** verb does not carry tense agreement. The infinitive, past participle (-*ed* form of the verb), and present continuous participle (-*ing* form of the verb) are all nonfinite verb forms.

Politeness. In linguistics, politeness refers to the linguistic resources that a person will use in order to ease interpersonal interactions and to avoid conflict. It is conventionally separated into the behaviors that attend to the self-esteem of the conversational participants and behaviors that negotiate the demands placed on another's resources.

RSS feeds. Really Simple Syndication or Rich Site Summary is the name given to a family of applications that aggregate items from recently updated sites (like blogs, news sites, social networks) and displays them in a single channel on a web page.

Semiotics refers to the sign systems used to convey meanings. Semiotic systems include language, music, sound, color, dress codes, and any recognized set of conventions that is used to convey communicative meaning.

Smart phones are cell phones that offer advanced computing and connectivity options. For example, they may enable connection to the Internet or include a camera and audiovisual facilities, or both.

SMS stands for Short Message Service, which is the text component of communication between mobile or web-based devices. Examples include text messages used on cell phones.

A **Sockpuppet** is an online identity created for deceptive purposes. The term is currently used when a person creates more than one identity for his or herself within the same community (such as a forum or wiki).

Speech act. The British philosopher J. R. Searle argued that words did not just convey information; they also performed acts. Recognized speech acts include apologies, refusals, complaints, warnings, greetings, invitations, and compliments.

Turn-taking. In Conversation Analysis, conversation is said to be organized in "turns" where each person taking part in the conversation will speak in turn. The rules that govern the organization of the turns were developed by the sociologist Harvey Sacks (1995).

Wi-fi is short for "wireless fidelity" and refers to the wireless networking technology that allows computers and other devices to communicate over a wireless signal.

References

WEBSITES

These are the URLs for the websites used to provide the storytelling examples in this book, should readers wish to visit the sites themselves.

A Million Penguins archived edition (text only, no talk pages). Available at https://docs.google.com/document/pub?id=14GxyTg2ePTJRe2boZIFbhnmMlNsavWALspx59PiSJlY. Accessed May 24, 2011.

Bodybuilding.com: The World's #1 Bodybuilding Website and Store. Available at http://www.bodybuilding.com/. Accessed May 24, 2011.

Facebook Homepage. Available at http://www.facebook.com/. Accessed May 24, 2011.

Lonelygirl15 Homepage. Available at http://www.lg15.com/. Accessed May 24, 2011.

[murmur] Homepage. Available at http://murmurtoronto.ca/about.php. Accessed May 24, 2011.

Protagonize: Collaborative Storywriting and Fiction Community. Available at http://www.protagonize.com/. Accessed May 24, 2011.

Twitter Homepage. Available at http://twitter.com/. Accessed May 24, 2011.

Blogs Used in the Analysis Presented in Chapter 3

Blogs Authored by Women

Beth Brophy: My Breast Cancer Network.com
http://www.healthcentral.com/breast-cancer/c/11/. Accessed May 24, 2011.

Dana: Journey Through Breast Cancer
http://fightingbreastcancer.blogspot.com/. Accessed May 24, 2011.

Jackie: My Breast Cancer Blog
http://cancerspot.org/?p=3. Accessed May 24, 2011.

Jeanette: Two Hands
http://2hands.blogspot.com/2004/07/about-this-blog.html. Accessed May 24, 2011.

Lori Miller: Too Sexy for my Hair
(since removed from the web)

Jenny: Jenny's Belly
http://jennys-belly.blogspot.com/. Accessed May 24, 2011.

Karen Weber: My Breast Cancer Journal
(since removed from the web)

Kelly's Blog
    http://www.breastcancercare.org.uk/content.php?page_id=4818. Accessed
    May 24, 2011.
Lorraine Chandler: Battling Breast Cancer
    http://www.bbc.co.uk/herefordandworcester/content/articles/2006/12/04/
    lorraine_chandler_blog_feature.shtml. Accessed May 24, 2011.
Mary Blocksma
    http://www.beaverislandarts.com/. Accessed May 24, 2011.
Minerva: A Woman of Many Parts
    http://womanlyparts.blogspot.com/. Accessed May 24, 2011.
P J Hamel
    http://www.healthcentral.com/breast-cancer/c/78/. Accessed May 24, 2011.
Sunnyside (now opened to invited readers only)
    http://sunnyside2day.blogspot.com/. Accessed May 24, 2011.
Sylvie Fortin: Sylvie Fortin's Breast Cancer Victory
    http://www.breastcancervictory.com/. Accessed May 24, 2011.

Blogs Authored by Men

Ben B's Hodgkin's Blog
    http://bb.redtoenail.org/. Accessed May 24, 2011.
Daniel Rahenkamp
    http://roontoon.com.blog/
    (since removed from the web)
David
    http://cancerblog.blogspot.com. Accessed May 24, 2011.
David E. The Big 'C'
    http://prostatecancer42.blogspot.com/. Accessed May 24, 2011.
David Hahn: Chronicles of a Cancer Patient
    http://www.preservationrecords.com/. Accessed May 24, 2011.
Diehl Martin
    http://diehlmartin.com/index.html. Accessed May 24, 2011.
Hugh Cook Cancer Patient
    http://hughcook.blogspot.com/. Accessed May 24, 2011.
Jim H.: Prostate Cancer Survivor
    http://www.healthdiaries.com/cancer/prostate-cancer-survivor/. Accessed May
    24, 2011.
John Slatin: The Leukemia Letters
    http://leukemialetters.blogspot.com/. Accessed May 24, 2011.
Leroy Sievers
    http://www.npr.org/blogs/mycancer/. Accessed May 24, 2011.
Manuel: Living with Prostate Cancer
    http://spainprostatehelp.blogspot.com/. Accessed May 24, 2011.
Mike Meets World
    http://mikecousins.blogspot.com/. Accessed May 24, 2011.
Owen: PTLD
    http://ptld.blogspot.com/. Accessed May 24, 2011.
Rlowe: Proton Experience
    http://loweproton.blogspot.com/. Accessed May 24, 2011.
Robert: Llama Farming with Colon Cancer
    http://www.healthdiaries.com/coloncancer/llama/. Accessed May 24, 2011.

REFERENCES

140 Novel. Available at http://twitter.com/140novel. Accessed August 8, 2011.

Aarseth, Espen J. 1997. *Cybertext: Perspectives on Ergodic Literature.* Baltimore, MD: John Hopkins University Press.

Abdul-Mageed, M., A. AlAhmed, and M. Korayem. 2011. "Linguistic Features, Language Variety, and Sentiment in Arabic Comments on Aljazeera and Alarabiya YouTube Videos." Paper presented at Georgetown University Round Table on Languages and Linguistics (2011), "Language and New Media: Discourse 2.0." Washington, DC, March 10–13.

Alderman, Derek H. 2003. "Street Names and the Scaling of Memory: The Politics of Commemorating Martin Luther King, Jr Within the African American Community." *Area* 35 (2): 163–173.

Andrews, Gavin J., Mark I. Sudwell, and Andrew C. Sparkes. 2005. "Towards a Geography of Fitness: An Ethnographic Case Study of the Gym in British Body-Building Culture." *Social Science and Medicine* 60: 877–891.

Androutsopoulos, Jannis. 2006. "Introduction: Sociolinguistics and Computer-Mediated Communication." *Journal of Sociolinguistics* 10 (4): 419–438.

———. 2008. "Discourse-Centred Online Ethnography." In Data and Methods in Computer-Mediated Discourse Analysis, edited by Jannis Androutsopoulos and Michael Beißwenger. Special Issue, *Language@Internet* 5. Available at http://www.languageatinternet.de/articles/2008. Accessed April 5, 2011.

———. 2010. "Multilingualism, Ethnicity, and Genre: The Case of German Hip-Hop." In *The Languages of Global Hip Hop*, edited by Marina Terkourafi, 19–43. London: Continuum.

———. 2011 (in press). "From Variation to Heteroglossia in the Study of Computer-Mediated Discourse." In *Digital Discourse: Language in the New Media*, edited by Crispin Thurlow and Kristine Mroczek. Oxford: Oxford University Press.

Antaki, Charles, and Sue Widdicombe. 1998. "Identity as an Achievement and as a Tool." In *Identities in Talk*, edited by Charles Antaki and Sue Widdicombe, 1–14. London: Sage.

Anstead, Nick, and Ben O'Loughlin. 2010. *The Emerging Viewertariat: Explaining Twitter Responses to Nick Griffin's Appearance on BBC Question Time* (UEA School of Political, Social and International Studies Working Paper Series 1). Available at http://newpolcom.rhul.ac.uk/storage/Anstead_OLoughlin_BBCQT_Twitter_Final.pdf. Accessed February 23, 2011.

Anthony, Laurence. 2011. "The Antconc Homepage." Available at http://www.antlab.sci.waseda.ac.jp/software.html. Accessed May 11, 2011.

Arendholz, Jenny. 2010. "'Neeed to put this out there (My Story)'—Narratives in Message Boards." In *Narrative Revisited*, edited by Christian R. Hoffman, 109–142. Amsterdam: John Benjamins.

Arminen, Ilkka. 2004. "Second Stories: The Salience of Interpersonal Communication for Mutual Help in Alcoholics Anonymous." *Journal of Pragmatics* 36: 319–347.

Arminen, Ilkka, and Alexandra Weilenmann. 2009. "Mobile Presence and Intimacy: Reshaping Social Actions in Mobile Contextual Configuration." *Journal of Pragmatics* 41: 1905–1923.

Asur, Sitaram, and Bernardo A. Huberman. 2010. "Predicting the Future with Social Media." In *2010 IEEE/WIC/ACM International Conference on Web Intelligence, WI 2010, Toronto, Canada, August 31–September 3, 2010, Main Conference Proceedings*, edited by Jimmy Xiangji Huang, Irwin King, Vijay V. Raghavan, and Stefan Rueger, 492–499. Toronto: WI2010.

Austin, John L. 1975. *How to Do Things with Words*. Oxford: Clarendon.

Balka, Ellen, Guenther Krueger, Bev J. Holmes, and Joanne E. Stephen. 2010. "Situating Internet Use: Information-Seeking Among Young Women with Breast Cancer." *Journal of Computer-Mediated Communication* 15 (3): 389–411.

Bamberg, Michael, Deborah Schiffrin, and Anna De Fina. 2007. *Selves and Identities in Narrative and Discourse*. Amsterdam: John Benjamins.

Baym, Nancy K. 1995. "The Emergence of Community in Computer-Mediated Communication." In *Cybersociety: Computer-Mediated Communication and Community*, edited by Steven G. Jones, 138–163. London: Sage.

Baynham, Mike. 2004. "Narrative in Time and Space: Beyond 'Backdrop' Accounts of Narrative Orientation." *Narrative Inquiry* 13 (2): 347–366.

Bazzanella, Carla. 2010. "Contextual Constraints in CMC Narrative." In *Narrative Revisited*, edited by Christian R. Hoffmann, 19–37. Amsterdam: John Benjamins.

Beaulieu, Anne. 2005. "Sociable Hyperlinks: An Ethnographic Approach to Connectivity." In *Virtual Methods: Issues in Social Research on the Internet*, edited by Christine Hine, 183–198. Oxford: Berg Publishers.

Bell, Alice. 2010. *The Possible Worlds of Hypertext Fiction*. Basingstoke, UK: Palgrave Macmillan.

Bell, Alice, Astrid Ensslin, Dave Ciccoricco, Hans Rustad, Jess Laccetti, and Jessica Pressman. 2010. "A (S)creed for Digital Fiction." *Electronic Book Review*. Last modified July 3, 2010. Available at http://www.electronicbookreview.com/thread/electropoetics/DFINative. Accessed January 13, 2011.

Bell, Allan. 1991. *The Language of News Media*. Oxford: Blackwell.

Bennett, Joel B. 2000. *Time and Intimacy: A New Science of Personal Relationships*. Mahwah, NJ: Lawrence Erlbaum.

Benwell, Bethan, and Elizabeth Stokoe. 2006. *Discourse and Identity*. Edinburgh: Edinburgh University Press.

Biber, Douglas, and Edward Finegan. 1989. "Styles of Stance in English: Lexical and Grammatical Marking of Evidentiality and Affect." *TEXT* 9 (1): 93–124.

Bingley, A. F., E. McDermott, C. Thomas, S. Payne, J. E. Seymour, and D. Clark. 2006. "Making Sense of Dying: A Review of Narratives Written Since 1950 by People Facing Death from Cancer and Other Diseases." *Palliative Medicine* 20: 183–195.

Boland Abraham, Linda, Marie Pauline Mörn, and Andrea Vollman. 2010. "Women on the Web: How Women are Shaping the Internet." *ComScore Inc.* Available at http://www.comscore.com/Press_Events/Presentations_Whitepapers/2010/Women_on_the_Web_How_Women_are_Shaping_the_Internet. Accessed February 10, 2011.

Bolander, Brook, and Miriam Locher. 2010. "Constructing Identity on Facebook: Report on a Pilot Study." In *SPELL: Swiss Papers in English Language and Literature 24: Performing the Self*, edited by Karen Julod and Didier Maillat, 65–188. Tübingen: Narr.

———. 2011. "'(Name) is a dumb nut': Status Updates and Reactions to Them as 'Acts of Positioning' in Facebook." Paper presented at the Georgetown University Round Table on Languages and Linguistics, March 10–13.

Bourdieu, Pierre. 1977. "The Economics of Linguistic Exchanges." *Social Science Information,* 16 (6): 645–668.

Bourne, Craig. 2006. *Future for Presentism*. Oxford: Oxford University Press.

Bousfield, Derek. 2007a. "'Never a Truer Word Said in Jest': A Pragmastylistic Analysis of Impoliteness as Banter in Henry IV, Part I." In *Contemporary Stylistics*, edited by Marina Lambrou and Peter Stockwell, 209–220. Continuum: London.

———. 2007b. *Impoliteness in Interaction*. Amsterdam: John Benjamins.

Bousfield, Derek, and Miriam Locher. 2008. *Impoliteness in Language Studies: On Its Interplay with Power in Theory and Practice.* Berlin: Mouton de Gruyter.

boyd, danah. 2008. *Taken out of Context: American Teen Sociality in Networked Publics.* PhD diss., University of California, Berkeley.

boyd, danah, and Nicole Ellison. 2007. "Social Network Sites: Definition, History, and Scholarship". *Journal of Computer Mediated Communication* 13 (1). Available at http://jcmc.indiana.edu/vol13/ issue1/ boyd.ellison.html. Accessed April 26, 2010.

boyd, danah, Scott Golder and Gilad Lotan. 2010. "Tweet, Tweet, Retweet: Conversational Aspects of Retweeting on Twitter." Paper presented at *HICSS-43. IEEE*: Kauai, HI, January 6.

boyd, danah, and Eszter Hargittai. 2010. "Facebook Privacy Settings: Who Cares?" *First Monday* 15 (8). Available at http://webuse.org/p/a32/. Accessed February 9, 2011.

Boyle, Lex. 2005. "Flexing the Tensions of Female Muscularity: How Female Bodybuilders Negotiate Normative Femininity in Competitive Bodybuilding." *Women's Studies Quarterly* 33 (1–2): 134–149.

Brockmeier, Jens, and Donal A. Carbaugh. 2001. *Narrative and Identity: Studies in Autobiography, Self and Culture.* Amsterdam: John Benjamins.

Brown, Penelope, and Steven Levinson. 1987. *Politeness: Some Universals in Language Usage.* Cambridge: Cambridge University Press.

Bubbleteamaylee. 2006. "Re: LonelyGirl15 is a FAKE . . . PLEASE WATCH!!!" *YouTube.* Available at http://www.youtube.com/watch?v=yQhT9VqTolg. Accessed March 28, 2011.

Bucholz, Mary. 2003. "Sociolinguistic Authenticity and the Authentication of Identity." *Journal of Sociolinguistics* 7 (3): 398–416.

Bucholz, Mary, and Kira Hall. 2004. "Language and Identity." In *A Companion to Linguistic Anthropology*, edited by Alessandro Duranti, 268–294. Oxford: Basil Blackwell.

Burgess, Jean, and Joshua Green. 2009. *YouTube: Online Video and Participatory Culture.* Cambridge: Polity.

Burns, Shaun Michael, and James R. Mahalik. 2008. "Treatment Type and Emotional Control as Predictors of Men's Self-Assessed Physical Well-Being Following Treatment for Prostate Cancer." *Psychology of Men & Masculinity* 9 (2): 55–56.

Butler, Judith. 1990. *Gender Trouble: Feminism and the Subversion of Identity.* New York and London: Routledge.

Butler, Toby. 2006. "A Walk of Art: The Potential of the Sound Walk as Practice in Cultural Geography." *Social & Cultural Geography* 7 (6): 889–908.

Cha, Meeyoung, Hamed Haddadi, Fabricio Benevenuto, and Krishna P. Gummadi. 2010. "Measuring User Influence in Twitter: The Million Follower Fallacy." In *Proceedings of the Fourth International Association for the Advancement of Artificial Intelligence Conference on Weblogs and Social Media, Washington, DC, May 23–26, 2010.* Menlo Park, CA: The AAAI Press. Available at http://www.aaai.org/Library/ICWSM/icwsm10contents.php. Accessed May 21, 2011.

Chacksfield, Marc. 2010. "Twitter Boasts of 105 Million Registered Users." Available at http://www.techradar.com/news/internet/twitter-boasts-of-105-million-registered-users. Accessed February 23, 2011.

Chatman, Seymour. 1978. *Story and Discourse: Narrative Structure in Fiction and Film.* Ithaca, NY: Cornell University Press.

Charteris-Black, Jonathan, Clive Seale, and Susan Ziebland. 2006. "Gender, Cancer Experience and Internet Use: a Comparative Keyword Analysis of Interviews and Online Cancer Support Groups." *Social Science & Medicine* 62: 2577–2590.

Cheshire, Jenny, and Sue Ziebland. 2005. "Narrative as a Resource in Accounts of the Experience of Illness." In *Sociolinguistics of Narrative*, edited by Jennifer Coates and Joanna Thornborrow, 17–40. Amsterdam: John Benjamins.

Chiluwa, Innocent. 2009. "The Discourse of Digital Deceptions and 419 Emails." *Discourse Studies* 11 (6): 635–660.

Christian, Aymar Jean. 2009. "Real Vlogs: The Rules and Meanings of Online Personal Videos. *First Monday* 14 (1–2). Available at http://firstmonday.org/htbin/cgiwrap/bin/ojs/index.php/fm/article/viewArticle/2699/2353. Accessed March 23, 2011.

Ciccoricco, David. 2007. *Reading Network Fiction*. Tuscaloosa: University of Alabama Press.

Clary-Lemon, Jennifer. 2010. "'We're not Ethnic, We're Irish!' Oral History and the Discursive Construction of Oral History." *Discourse Society* 21 (1): 5–25.

ClickyMedia. 2011. "UK Facebook Statistics for March 2011." Available at http://www.clickymedia.co.uk/2011/03/uk-facebook-statistics-for-march-2011/. Accessed May 31, 2011.

Coates, Jennifer. 2003. *Men Talk*. Oxford: Blackwell.

Cormode, Graham, and Balachander Krishnamurthy. 2008. "Key Differences Between Web 1.0 and Web 2.0." *First Monday* 13 (6). Available at http://firstmonday.org/htbin/cgiwrap/bin/ojs/index.php/fm/article/viewArticle/2125/1972. Accessed April 5, 2011.

Couldry, Nick. 2002. "Playing for Celebrity: Big Brother as Ritual Event." *Television and New Media* 3 (3): 283–293.

Coupland, Nikolas. 2003. "Sociolinguistic Authenticities." *Journal of Sociolinguistics* 7 (3): 417–431.

Culpeper, Jonathan. 1996. "An Anatomy of Impoliteness." *Journal of Pragmatics* 25: 349–367.

Culpeper, Jonathan, Derek Bousfield, and Anne Wichmann. 2003. "Impoliteness Revisited: With Special Reference to Dynamic and Prosodic Aspects." *Journal of Pragmatics* 35: 1545–1579.

Currie, Mark. 2006. *About Time: Narrative, Fiction and the Philosophy of Time*. Edinburgh: Edinburgh University Press.

Dargonzine. Available at http://www.dargonzine.org/. Accessed April 1, 2010.

Davies, Mark. 2011. "Word Frequency Data from the Corpus of Contemporary American English (COCA)." Downloaded from http://www.wordfrequency.info on May 10, 2011.

Davis, Joshua. 2006. "The Secret World of Lonelygirl15." *Wired*, December 14, 2006. Available at http://www.wired.com/wired/archive/14.12/lonelygirl.html?pg=2. Accessed March 24, 2011.

De Fina, Anna, Deborah Schiffrin, and Michael Bamberg. 2006. *Discourse and Identity*. Cambridge: Cambridge University Press.

Derks, Daantje, Agneta H. Fischer, and Arjan E. R. Bos. 2007. "The Role of Emotion in Computer-Mediated Communication: A Review." *Computers in Human Behaviour* 23 (1): 11–31.

Derks, Daantje, Arjan E. R. Bos, and Jasper von Krumbkow. 2008. "Emoticons in Computer-Mediated Communication: Social Motives and Social Context." *CyberPsychology* 11 (1): 99–101.

Derrida, Jacques. 1976. *Of Grammatology*. Translated by Gayatri Chakravorty Spivak. Baltimore, MD: Johns Hopkins University Press.

Donath, Judith S. 1999. "Identity and Deception in the Virtual Community." In *Communities in Cyberspace*, edited by Marc A Smith and Peter Kollack, 29–59. London: Routledge.

Dubriwny, Tasha N. 2009. "Constructing Breast Cancer in the News: Betty Ford and the Evolution of the Breast Cancer Patient." *Journal of Communication Inquiry* 33 (2): 104–125.

Duranti, Alessandro, and Charles Goodwin. 1992. *Rethinking Context: Language as an Interactive Phenomenon*. Cambridge: Cambridge University Press.

Eggins, Suzanne, and Diana Slade. 1997. *Analysing Casual Conversation*. London: Cassell.

Eisenlauer, Volker, and Christian R. Hoffmann. 2010. "Once Upon a Blog . . . Storytelling in Weblogs." In *Narrative Revisited*, edited by Christian R. Hoffmann, 79–108, Amsterdam: John Benjamins.

Ellison, Nicole B., Charles Steinfield, and Cliff Lampe. 2007. "The Benefits of Facebook 'Friends': Social Capital and College Students' Use of Online Social Network Sites." *Journal of Computer-Mediated Communication* 12 (4), article 1. Available at http://jcmc.indiana.edu/vol12/issue4/ellison.html. Accessed February 9, 2011.

Ensslin, Astrid. 2007. *Canonizing Hypertext: Explorations and Constructions*. London: Continuum.

Ess, Charles, and the AoIR Ethics Working Committee. 2002. "Ethical Decision-Making and Internet research: Recommendations from the AOIR Ethics Working Committee." Approved by AoIR, November 27, 2002. Available at http://www.aoir.org/reports/ethics.pdf. Accessed March 27, 2009.

Featherstone, Mike. 1982. "The Body in Consumer Culture." *Theory, Culture and Society* 1 (2): 18–33.

Ficlets. Available at http://ficly.com/. Accessed April 4, 2010.

Fiske, John. 1987. *Television Culture*. London: Methuen.

Flemming, Brian. 2006. "Lonelygirl15 Jumps the Shark." Available at http://www.brianflemming.org/archives/002277.html. Accessed March 24, 2011.

Fludernik, Monika. 1996. *Towards a "Natural" Narratology*. London: Routledge.

Frank, Arthur W. 1994. "Reclaiming an Orphan Genre: The First-Person Narrative of Illness." *Literature and Medicine* 13 (1): 1–21.

———. 1995. *The Wounded Storyteller: The Body, Illness, Ethics*. Chicago: University of Chicago Press.

Frawley, William. 1992. *Linguistic Semantics*. Hillside, NJ: Lawrence Erlbaum.

Galegher, Jolene, Lee Sproull, and Sara Kiesler. 1998. "Legitimacy, Authority and Community in Electronic Support Groups." *Written Communication* 15 (4): 493–530.

Gadsby, Sam. 2010. "UK Facebook User Statistics April 2010." Available at http://www.clickymedia.co.uk/2010/04/uk-facebook-user-statistics-april-2010/. Accessed June 2, 2011.

Gehl, Robert. 2009. "YouTube as Archive: Who Will Curate This Digital Wunderkammer?" *International Journal of Cultural Studies* 12 (1): 43–60.

Genette, Gerard. 1980. *Narrative Discourse: An Essay in Method*. Translated by Jane E. Lewin. Ithaca, NY: Cornell University Press.

Georgakopoulou, Alexandra. 2003. "Plotting the 'Right Place' and the 'Right Time': Place and Time as Interactional Resources in Narratives." *Narrative Inquiry* 13: 413–432.

———. 2004. "To Tell or Not to Tell? Email Stories Between On- and Offline Interactions." *Language@Internet* 1. Available at http://www.languageatinternet.de/articles/2004/36/?searchterm=None. Accessed March 15, 2010.

———. 2007. *Small Stories, Interaction and Identities*. Amsterdam: John Benjamins.

Gergen, Kenneth G. 2002. "The Challenge of the Absent Presence." In *Perpetual Contact: Mobile Communication, Private Talk, Public Performance*, edited by James E. Katz and Mark Aakhus, 227–241. Cambridge: Cambridge University Press.

Gillespie, Tarleton. 2010. "The Politics of Platforms." *New Media and Society* 12 (3): 347–364.

Goffman, Erving. 1959. *The Presentation of the Self in Everyday Life*. New York: Anchor Books.

Graham, Sage. 2007. "Disagreeing to Agree: Conflict, (Im)politeness and Identity in a Computer-Mediated Community." *Journal of Pragmatics* 39: 742–759.

Granovetter, Mark. 1973. "The Strength of Weak Ties." *American Journal of Sociology* 78 (6): 1360–1380.

Gray, Ross E., Margaret Fitch, Catherine Phillips, Manon LaBrecque, and Karen Fergus. 2000. "To Tell or Not to Tell: Patterns of Disclosure Among Men with Prostate Cancer." *Psycho-Oncology* 9: 273–282.

Greenspan, Brian. 2011. "Songlines in the Streets: Story Mapping with Itinerant Hypernarrative." In *New Narratives: Stories and Storytelling in the Digital Age*, edited by Ruth Page and Bronwen Thomas, 153–169. Lincoln: University of Nebraska Press.

Grice, H. Paul. 1975. "Logic and Conversation." In *Syntax and Semantics III*, edited by Peter Cole and Jerry Morgan, 41–58. New York: Academic Press.

Grisakova, Marina, and Marie-Laure Ryan. 2010. *Intermedial Storytelling*. Amsterdam: John Benjamins.

Hanks, William F. 1992. "The Indexical Ground of Deictic Reference." In *Rethinking Context: Language as an Interactive Phenomenon*, edited by Alessandro Duranti and Charles Goodwin, 43–76. Cambridge: Cambridge University Press.

Harpold, Terry. 2005. "Digital Narrative." In *Routledge Encyclopedia of Narrative Theory*, edited by David Herman, Manfred Jahn, and Marie-Laure Ryan, 108–112. New York: Routledge.

Harrison, Sandra. 1998. "E-mail Discussions as Conversation: Moves and Acts in a Sample from a Listserv Discussion." *Linguistik Online* 1. Available at http://www.linguistik-online.de/harrison.htm. Accessed May 14, 2011.

Harrison, Sandra, and Julie Barlow. 2009. "Politeness Strategies and Advice-Giving in an Online Arthritis Workshop." *Journal of Politeness Research* 5: 93–111.

Hatton, Sarah, Melissa McGurgan, and Xiang-Jun Wang. 2010. "Keg Party Extreme and Conversation Party: Two Multimodal Interactive Narratives Developed for the SMALLLab." In *New Perspectives on Narrative and Multimodality*, edited by Ruth Page, 202–218. London: Routledge.

Haviland, John B. 2000. "Pointing, Gesture Spaces, and Mental Maps." In *Language and Gesture: Window into Thought and Action*, edited by David McNeill, 13–46. Cambridge: Cambridge University Press.

Hayles, N. Katherine. 2001. "The Transformation of Narrative and the Materiality of Hypertext." *Narrative* 9 (1): 21–39.

Herman, David. 1997. "Scripts, Sequences, and Stories: Elements of a Postclassical Narratology." *Publications of the Modern Language Association* 112 (5): 1046–1059.

———. 2002. *Story Logic: Problems and Possibilities of Narrative*. Lincoln: University of Nebraska Press.

———. 2010. "Word-Image/Utterance-Gesture: Case Studies in Multimodal Storytelling." In *New Perspectives on Narrative and Multimodality*, edited by Ruth Page, 78–98. London: Routledge.

Herring, Susan C. 2003. "Gender and Power in Online Communication." In *The Handbook of Language and Gender*, edited by Janet Holmes and Miriam Meyerhoff, 202–228. Oxford: Blackwell.

———. 2004. "Computer-Mediated Discourse Analysis: An Approach to Researching Online Behavior." In *Designing for Virtual Communities in the Service of Learning*, edited by Sasha A. Barab, Rob Kling, and James H. Gray, 338–376. New York: Cambridge University Press.

———. 2010. "Computer-Mediated Conversation: Introduction and Overview." *Language@Internet,* 7, article 2. Available at http://www.languageatinternet.de/articles/2010/2801/index_html/. Accessed January 23, 2011.

————. 2011. "Discourse in Web 2.0: Familiar, Reconfigured, and Emergent." Paper presented at Georgetown University Round Table on Languages and Linguistics (2011), "Language and New Media: Discourse 2.0." Washington, DC, March 10–13.

Herring, Susan C., Inna Kouper, Lois Ann Scheidt, and Elijah L. Wright. 2004. "Women and Children Last: The Discursive Construction of Weblogs." In *Into the Blogosphere: Rhetoric, Community, and Culture of Weblogs*, edited by Laura J. Gurak, Smiljana Antonijevic, Laurie Johnson, Clancy Ratliff, and Jessica Reyman. Available at http://blog.lib.umn.edu/blogosphere/women_and_children.html. Accessed September 24, 2007.

Herring, Susan, and John C. Paolillo. 2006. "Gender and Genre Variation in Weblogs." *Journal of Sociolinguistics* 10 (4): 439–459.

Herring, Susan C., Lois Ann Scheidt, Sabrina Bonus, and Elijah Wright. 2004. "Bridging the Gap: A Genre Analysis of Weblogs." *Proceedings of the 37th Hawai'i International Conference on System Sciences (HICSS-37)*. Los Alamitos, CA: IEEE Computer Society Press.

Herring, Susan C., and Asta Zelenkauskaite. 2009. "Symbolic Capital in a Virtual Heterosexual Market." *Written Communication* 26 (1): 5–31.

Herrmann, Andrew F. 2007. "People Get Emotional About Their Money: Performing Masculinity in a Financial Discussion Board." *Journal of Computer-Mediated Communication* 12 (2), article 12. Available at http://jcmc.indiana.edu/vol12/issue2/herrmann.html. Accessed May 15, 2011.

Heyd, Theresa. 2008. *Email Hoaxes*. Amsterdam: John Benjamins:

Hine, Christine. 2000. *Virtual Ethnography*. London: Sage.

Hoelscher, Steven and Derek H. Alderman. 2004. "Memory and Place: Geographies of a Critical Relationship." *Social and Cultural Geography* 5 (3): 347–356.

Hoey, Michael. 1995. *Patterns of Lexis in Text*. Oxford: Oxford University Press.

————. 2001. *Textual Interaction: An Introduction to Written Discourse*. London: Routledge.

Hoffmann, Christian R. 2010. *Narrative Revisited*. Amsterdam: John Benjamins.

Holmes, Janet. 1995. *Women, Men and Politeness*. London: Longman.

Honeycutt, Courtenay, and Susan C. Herring. 2009. "Beyond Microblogging: Conversation and Collaboration via Twitter." *Proceedings of the Forty-Second Hawai'i International Conference on System Sciences* (HICSS-42). Los Alamitos, CA: IEEE Press.

Huberman, Bernardo A., Daniel M. Romero, and Fang Wu. 2009. "Social Networks That Matter: Twitter Under the Microscope." *First Monday* 14 (1). Available at http://firstmonday.org/htbin/cgiwrap/bin/ojs/index.php/fm/article/view/2317/2063. Accessed February 23, 2011.

Hutcheon, Linda. 2006. *A Theory of Adaptation*. London: Routledge.

Hyden, Lars-Christer, and Jens Brockmeier. 2008. *Health, Illness and Culture: Broken Narratives*. London and New York: Routledge.

Ito, Mimi. 2005. "Intimate Visual Co-Presence, in Workshop on Pervasive Image Capture and Sharing." Paper presented at the 7th International Conference on Ubiquitous Computing (Ubicomp 05), Tokyo, September 11–14.

Ito, Rika, and Sali Tagliamonte. 2003. "*Well* Weird, *Right* Dodgy, *Very* Strange, *Really* Cool: Layering and Recycling in English Intensifiers." *Language in Society* 32: 257–279.

Jansen, Bernard J., Mimi Zhang, Kate Sobel, and Abdur Chowdury. 2009. "Twitter Power: Tweets as Electronic Word of Mouth." *Journal of the American Society for Information Science and Technology* 60 (11): 2169–2188.

Jenkins, Henry. 1992 *Textual Poachers: Television Fans and Participatory Culture*. London: Routledge.

———. 2006. *Convergence Culture: Where Old and New Media Collide*. New York: New York University Press.

Johnson, Steven. 2009. "How Twitter Will Change the Way We Live." *Time*, June 04, 2009. Available at http://www.time.com/time/business/article/0,8599,1902604,00. html. Accessed February 23, 2011.

Jones, Rodney H. 2005. "Sites of Engagement as Sites of Attention: Time, Space and Culture in Electronic Discourse." In *Discourse in Action: Mediated Discourse Analysis*, edited by Sigfrid Norris and Rodney H. Jones, 141–154. New York: Routledge.

Jones, Rodney H., and Sigfrid Norris. 2005. *Discourse in Action: Introducing Mediated Discourse Analysis*. New York: Routledge.

Kamio, Akio. 2001. "English Generic *We, You* and *They*: An Analysis in Terms of Territory of Information." *Journal of Pragmatics* 33: 1111–1124.

Katsoulis, Melissa. 2009. *Telling Tales: A History of Literary Hoaxes*. London: Constable.

Kiss, Alexander, and Siegfried Meryn. 2001. "Effect of Sex and Gender on Psychosocial Aspects of Prostate and Breast Cancer." *British Medical Journal* 323 (7320). Available at http://www.bmj.com/content/323/7320/1055.extract. Accessed April 5, 2011.

Klaiber, Isabell. 2010. "Implied Author(s) in Collaborative Fiction." Paper presented at the 25th Annual Conference of the International Society for the Study of Narrative, Cleveland, April 8–11.

Klemm, Paula, Melanie Hurst, Sandra L. Dearholt, and Susan R. Trone. 1999. "Cyber Solace: Gender Differences on Internet Cancer Support Groups." *Computers in Nursing* 17 (2): 65–72.

Kopytoff, Verne G. 2011. "Blogs Wane as the Young Drift to Sites Like Twitter." *The New York Times*, February 20, 2011. Available at http://www.pewinternet. org/Media-Mentions/2011/Blogs-Wane-as-the-Young-Drift-to-Sites-Like-Twitter.aspx. Accessed April 11, 2011.

Kress, Gunther, and Theo Van Leeuwen. 1996. *Reading Images: The Grammar of Visual Design*. 2nd edition. London: Routledge.

———. 2001. *Multimodal Discourse*. London: Hodder Arnold.

Kwak, Haewoon, Changhydun Lee, Hosung Park, and Sue Moon. 2010. "What Is Twitter, a Social Network or a News Media?" Paper presented at the World Wide Web Conference 2010, April 26–30, Raleigh, NC.

Labov, William. 1972. *Language in the Inner City*. Philadelphia: University of Pennsylvania Press.

———. 1984. "Intensity." In *Meaning, Form and Use in Context: Linguistic Applications*, edited by Deborah Schiffrin, 43–70. Washington, DC: Georgetown University Press.

Landow, George P. 1997. *Hypertext 2.0: The Convergence of Contemporary Critical Theory and Technology*. Baltimore, MD: Johns Hopkins University Press.

Lanser, Susan. 2003. "The Author's Queer Clothes: Anonymity, Sex(uality) and *The Travels and Adventures of Mademoiselle de Richelieu*." In *The Faces of Anonymity and Psyeudonymous Publication*, edited by Robert John Griffith, 81–102. Basingstoke, UK: Palgrave Macmillan.

Lee, Carmen. 2011 (in press). "Micro-Blogging and Status Updates on *Facebook*: Texts and Practices." In *Digital Discourse: Language in the New Media*, edited by Crispin Thurlow and Kristine Mroczek. New York: Oxford University Press.

Leech, Geoffrey N. 1983. *Principles of Pragmatics*. London: Longman.

Leeds-Hurwitz, Wendy. 2005. "Making Marriage Visible: Wedding Anniversaries as the Public Component of Private Relationships." *TEXT* 25 (5): 595–631.

Lemke, Jay. 2005. "Place, Pace and Meaning: Multimedia Chronotopes." In *Discourse in Action: Mediated Discourse Analysis*, edited by Sigfrid Norris and Rodney H. Jones, 110–122. New York: Routledge.

Lenhardt, Amanda, Kristen Purcell, Aaron Smith, and Kathryn Zickuhr. 2010. *Social Media and Young Adults* (Pew Internet and American Life Project). Available at http://pewinternet.org/Reports/2010/Social-Media-and-Young-Adults/Summary-of-Findings.aspx. Accessed June 2, 2011.

Lepore, Stephen J., Vicki S. Helgeson, David T. Eton, and Richard Schulz. 2003. "Improving Quality of Life in Men with Prostate Cancer: A Randomized Controlled Trial of Group Education Interventions." *Health Psychology* 22 (5): 443–452.

Liang, A. C. 1997. "The Creation of Coherence in Coming Out Stories." In *Queerly Phrased: Language, Gender and Sexuality*, edited by Anna Livia and Kira Hall, 287–309. Oxford: Blackwell.

Linde, Charlotte. 1993. *Life Stories: The Creation of Coherence*. Oxford: Oxford University Press.

Locher, Miriam. 2004. *Power and Politeness in Action: Disagreements in Oral Communication*, Berlin: Mouton de Gruyter.

———. 2006. "Polite Behavior within Relational Work: The Discursive Approach to Politeness." *Multilingua* 25: 249–267.

Locher, Miriam, and Richard J. Watts. 2005. "Politeness Theory and Relational Work." *Journal of Politeness Research* 1: 9–33.

Lonelygirl15.com. "A letter from the creators." Available at http://old.lg15.com/lonelygirl15/forum/viewtopic.php?t=36. Accessed March 31, 2011.

———. "First Post/Dorkiness Prevails." *YouTube*. Available at http://www.youtube.com/watch?v=-goXKtd6cPo. Accessed March 28, 2011.

Lunenfeld, Peter. 2000. *Snap to Grid: A User's Guide to Digital Arts, Media and Cultures*. Cambridge, MA: MIT Press.

Manago, Adrianna M., Michael B Graham, Patricia M. Greenfield, and Goldie Salimkhan. 2008. "Self-Presentation and Gender on MySpace." *Journal of Applied Developmental Psychology* 29: 446–458.

Markham, Annette N., and Nancy K. Baym. 2009. *Internet Inquiry: Conversations About Method*. Los Angeles, CA: Sage.

Markham, Carl. 2011. "Ryan Babel Accepts Charges over Twitter Remarks." *Independent Newspaper*, January 13, 2011. Available at http://www.independent.co.uk/sport/football/premier-league/ryan-babel-accepts-charges-over-twitter-remarks-2183943.html. Accessed April 28, 2011.

Martin, James R. 2000. "Beyond Exchange: APPRAISAL Systems in English." In *Evaluation in Text*, edited by Susan Hunston and Geoff Thompson, 142–175. Oxford: Oxford University Press.

———. 2003. "Introduction." *TEXT* 23 (2): 171–181.

Martin, James R., and Gunther A. Plum. 1997. "Construing Experience: Some Story Genres." *Journal of Narrative and Life History* 7 (1–4): 299–308.

Martin, James R., and Peter R. R. White. 2005. *The Language of Evaluation: Appraisal in English*. London: Palgrave.

Marwick, Alice. 2005. "Selling Yourself: Online Identity in the Age of the Commodified Internet." MA diss., University of Washington, Seattle, WA.

———. 2010. "Status Update: Celebrity, Publicity, and Self-Branding in Web 2.0." PhD diss., New York University, New York, NY.

Marwick, Alice, and danah boyd. 2011. "To See and Be Seen: Celebrity Practice on Twitter." *Convergence* 17 (2): 139–158.

Mason, Bruce, and Sue Thomas. 2008. "A Million Penguins Research Report." Available at http://www.ioct.dmu.ac.uk/projects/millionpenguinsanalysis.html. Accessed April 1, 2010.

McCabe, Scott, and Elizabeth Stokoe. 2004. "Place and Identity in 'Day Visitor' Narratives." *Annals of Tourism Research* 31 (3): 601–622.

McIlvenny, Paul, Mathias Broth, and Pentti Haddington. 2009. "Editorial: Communicating Place, Space and Mobility." *Journal of Pragmatics* 41 (10): 1879–1886.

McLellan, Faith. 1997. "'A Whole Other Story': The Electronic Narrative of Illness." *Literature and Medicine* 16 (1): 88–107.

McLuhan, Marshall. 1964. *Understanding Media*. New York: Mentor.

Miall, David S. 1999. "Trivializing or Liberating? The Limitations of Hypertext Theorizing." *Mosaic* 32 (2): 157–171.

Mirror Newspaper. 2011. "Wilshire Escapes Rap over Twitter Comments." Available at http://www.mirrorfootball.co.uk/news/Jack-Wilshere-escapes-FA-rap-over-Twitter-comments-in-the-aftermath-of-Arsenal-s-4–4-draw-at-Newcastle-article693079.html. Accessed April 28, 2011.

Mishler, Elliot. 2006. "Narrative and Identity: The Double Arrow of Time." In *Discourse and Identity*, edited by Anna De Fina, Deborah Schiffrin, and Michael Bamberg, 30–47. Cambridge: Cambridge University Press.

Montfort, Nick. 2003. *Twisty Little Passages: An Approach to Interactive Fiction*. Cambridge, MA: MIT Press.

Morrow, Phillip R. 2006. "Telling About Problems and Giving Advice in an Internet Discussion Forum: Some Discourse Features." *Discourse Studies* 8 (4): 531–548.

Mr. Beller's Neighborhood. Available at http://www.mrbellersneighborhood.com/. Accessed April 1, 2010.

Myers, Greg. 2006. "Where Are You from? Identifying Place in Talk." *Journal of Sociolinguistics* 10 (3): 320–343.

———. 2010. *The Discourse of Blogs and Wikis*. London: Continuum.

Nilsson, Stephanie. 2007. "The Function of Language to Facilitate and Maintain Social Networks in Research Weblogs." D-essay, Umeå University, Engelsk sprakvetenskap. Available at htttp://www.eng.umu.se/stephanie/web/Language-Blogs.pdf. Accessed January 7, 2011.

Norrick, Neal R. 2005. "Interaction in the Telling and Retelling of Interlaced Stories: The Co-Construction of Humorous Narratives." In *Narrative Interaction*, edited by Uta M. Quasthoff and Tabea Becker, 263–283. Amsterdam: John Benjamins.

———. 2007. "Conversational Narrative." In *The Cambridge Companion to Narrative*, edited by David Herman, 127–141. Cambridge: Cambridge University Press.

———. 2008. "Negotiating the Reception of Stories in Conversation: Teller Strategies for Modulating Response." *Narrative Inquiry* 18: 131–151.

Nunning, Ansgar. 2005. "Implied Author." In *Routledge Encyclopedia of Narrative*, edited by David Herman, Manfred Jahn, and Marie-Laure Ryan, 239–240. London: Routledge.

O'Reilly, Tim. 2005. "What Is Web 2.0." Available at http://oreilly.com/web2/archive/what-is-web-20.html. Accessed April 5, 2011.

———. 2009. "Goodreads vs Twitter: The Benefits of Asymmetric Follow." *O'Reilly Radar*, May 10, 2009. Available at http://radar.oreilly.com/2009/05/goodreads-vs-twitter-asymmetric-follow.html. Accessed April 28, 2011.

Obel, Camilla. 1996. "Collapsing Gender in Competitive Bodybuilding: Researching Contradictions and Ambiguity in Sport." *International Review for the Sociology of Sport* 31 (2): 185–203.

Ochs, Elinor, and Bambi Schieffelin. 1989. "Language has a Heart." *TEXT* 9 (1): 7–25.

Ochs, Elinor, and Lisa Capps. 2001. *Living Narrative: Creating Lives in Everyday Storytelling*. Cambridge, MA: Harvard University Press.

Olson, Greta. 2003. "Reconsidering Unreliability: Fallible and Untrustworthy Narrators." *Narrative* 11 (1): 93–109.

One Million Monkeys Typing. Available at http://www.1000000monkeys.com/. Accessed April 1, 2010.

Orgad, Shani. 2005. "The Transformative Potential of Online Communication." *Feminist Media Studies* 5 (2): 141–161.

———. 2006. "The Cultural Dimensions of Online Communication: A Study of Breast Cancer Patients' Internet Spaces." *New Media and Society* 8 (6): 877–899.

Orpana, Jennifer. 2009. "Signs of Life: Relational Aesthetics and the [Murmur] Project." *SHIFT: Queen's Journal of Visual and Material Culture* 2: 1–20.

Ostrow, Adam. 2009. "Twitter Now Growing at a Staggering 1,382 Percent." *Nielsen online*, February 18, 2009. Available at http://blog.nielsen.com/nielsen-wire/online_mobile/twitters-tweet-smell-of-success/. Accessed May 10, 2011.

Owen, Jason E., Joshua C. Klapow, David L. Roth, and Diane C. Tucker. 2004. "Use of the Internet for Information and Support: Disclosure among Persons with Breast and Prostate Cancer." *Journal of Behavioral Medicine* 27 (5): 491–505.

Owyang, Jeremiah. 2010. "A Collection of Social Media Stats for 2010." Available at http://www.web-strategist.com/blog/2010/01/19/a-collection-of-social-network-stats-for-2010/. Accessed May 10, 2011.

Page, Ruth. 2003. "An Analysis of APPRAISAL in Childbirth Narratives with Special Consideration of Gender and Storytelling Style." *TEXT* 23 (2): 211–237.

———. 2010a. *New Perspectives on Narrative and Multimodality*. London: Routledge.

———. 2010b. "Revisiting Narrativity: Small Stories in Status Updates." *Text and Talk* 30 (4): 423–444.

———. 2010c. "New Challenges for Feminist Stylistics. The Case of *Girl with a One Track Mind*." *Journal of Literary Theory* 4 (1): 81–98.

Page, Ruth, and Bronwen Thomas. 2011. *New Narratives: Stories and Storytelling in the Digital Age*. Lincoln: University of Nebraska Press.

Papacharissi, Zizi. 2004. "Democracy Online: Civility, Politeness, and the Democratic Potential of Online Political Discussion Groups." *New Media and Society* 6: 259–283.

Pennebaker, James W. 2000. "Telling Stories: The Health Benefits of Narrative." *Literature and Medicine* 19 (1): 3–18.

Perks, Robert, and Al Thomson. 2006. "Critical Developments." In *The Oral History Reader*, 2nd ed., edited by Robert Perks and Al Thomson, 1–14. London: Routledge.

Peuronen, Saija. 2011 (in press). "Using Finnish and English for Identity Construction in a Subcultural Internet Discussion Forum." In *Digital Discourse: Language in the New Media*, edited by Crispin Thurlow and Kristine Mroczek. New York: Oxford University Press.

Project Gutenberg. Available at http://www.gutenberg.org/wiki/Main_Page. Accessed May 24, 2011.

Proshansky, Harold M., Abbe K. Fabian, and Robert Kaminoff. 1983. "Place-Identity: Physical World Socialization of the Self." *Journal of Environmental Psychology* 3: 57–83.

Pugh, Sheenagh. 2005. *The Democratic Genre: Fan Fiction in a Literary Context*. Seren, Wales: Bridgend.

Purdy, James P. 2009. "When the Tenets of Composition go Public: A Study of Writing in Wikipedia." *College Composition and Communication* 61 (2): 351–373.

Quasthoff, Uta M., and Tabea Becker. 2005. *Narrative Interaction*. Amsterdam: John Benjamins.

Rettberg, Scott. 2011. "All Together Now: Hypertext, Collective Narratives, and Online Collective Knowledge Communities." In *New Narratives: Stories and Storytelling in the Digital Age*, edited by Ruth Page and Bronwen Thomas, 187–204. Lincoln: University of Nebraska Press.

Rettberg, Scott, with William Gillespie, Frank Marquardt, and Dirk Stratton. 1998–2002. *The Unknown: A Hypertext Novel*. Available at http://unknown-hypertext.com/. Accessed March 15, 2010.

Richardson, Brian. 2006. *Unnatural Voices: Extreme Narration in Modern and Contemporary Fiction*. Columbus: Ohio State University Press.

Riley, Mark, and David Harvey. 2007. "Talking Geography: On Oral History and the Practice of Geography." *Social and Cultural Geography* 8 (3): 345–351.

Rimmon-Kenan, Shlomith. 2002. "The Story of 'I': Illness and Narrative Identity." *Narrative* 10 (1): 9–27.

Rivera-Ramos, Zully A., and Lydia P. Buki. 2011. "I Will No Longer Be a Man! Manliness and Prostate Cancer Screenings among Latino Men." *Psychology of Men & Masculinity* 12 (1): 13–25.

Roberts, Lynne D., and Malcolm Parks. 1999. "The Social Geography of Gender Switching in Virtual Environments on the Internet." *Information, Communication & Society* 2 (4): 521–540.

Robinett, Paul (a.k.a Renetto). 2006. "Lonelygirl15 is a FAKE...PLEASE WATCH!!!" *YouTube*. Available at http://www.youtube.com/watch?v=rLI2vFFE1FQ. Accessed May 20, 2011.

Robinson, Ian. 1990. "Personal Narratives, Social Careers and Medical Courses: Analysing Life Trajectories in Autobiographies of People with Multiple Sclerosis." *Social Sciences and Medicine* 30 (2): 1173–1186.

Ruston, Scott. 2010. "Storyworlds on the Move: Mobile Media and their Implications for Narrative." *Storyworlds: A Journal of Narrative Studies* 2: 101–120.

Ryan, Cynthia. 2004. "Am I Not a Woman?" The Rhetoric of Breast Cancer Stories in African American Women's Popular Periodicals." *Journal of Medical Humanities* 25 (2): 129–150.

Ryan, Marie-Laure. 1991. *Possible Worlds, Artificial Intelligence and Narrative Theory*. Bloomington: Indiana University Press.

———. 2004. *Narrative Across Media: The Languages of Storytelling*. Lincoln: University of Nebraska Press.

———. 2005. "Tellability." In *The Routledge Encyclopedia of Narrative Theory*, edited by David Herman, Manfred Jahn, and Marie-Laure Ryan, 589–591. New York: Routledge.

———. 2006. *Avatars of Story*. Minneapolis: University of Minnesota Press.

———. 2007. "Toward a Definition of Narrative." In *The Cambridge Companion to Narrative*, edited by David Herman, 22–35. Cambridge: Cambridge University Press.

———. 2009. "From Playfields to Fictional Worlds: Ariosto Revisited." *New Literary History* 40 (1): 159–176

Sacks, Harvey. 1995. *Lectures on Conversation*. Vols. 1–2. Edited by Gail Jefferson, with an introduction by Emanuel A. Schegloff. Oxford: Blackwell.

Schegloff, Emanuel. 1972. "Notes on a Conversational Practice: Formulating Place." In *Studies in Social Interaction*, edited by David Sudnow, 75–119. New York: Free Press.

Schiffrin, Deborah. 1981. "Tense Variation in Narrative." *Language* 5 (1): 45–62.

———. 2009. "Crossing Boundaries: The Nexus of Time, Space, Person and Place in Narrative." *Language in Society* 38: 421–445.

Seale, Clive, and Jonathan Charteris-Black. 2008. "The Interaction of Class and Gender in Illness Narratives." *Sociology* 42 (3): 453–469.

Seale, Clive, Sue Ziebland, and Jonathan Charteris-Black. 2006. "Gender, Cancer Experience and Internet Use: A Comparative Keyword Analysis of Interviews and Online Cancer Support Groups." *Social Science and Medicine* 62 (10): 2577–2590.

Sebba, Mark, S. Mahootian, and C. Jonsson. (forthcoming). *Language Mixing and Code-Switching in Writing: Approaches to Mixed-language Written Discourse*. London: Routledge.

Senft, Theresa M. 2008. *Camgirls, Community and Celebrity in the Age of Social Networks*. New York: Peter Lang.

Seng, Loh Kah. 2009. "History, Memory and Identity in Modern Singapore: Testimonies from the Urban Margins." *Oral History Review* 36 (1): 1–24.

Shickel, Richard. 2000. *Intimate Strangers: The Culture of Celebrity in America.* Chicago: Ivan R. Dee.

Shuman, Amy. 2005. *Other People's Stories: Entitlement Claims and the Critique of Empathy.* Urbana: University of Illinois Press.

Sokal, Alan D. 1996. "Transgressing the Boundaries: Towards a Transformative Hermeneutics of Quantum Gravity." *Social Text* 46–47: 217–252

Sorapure, Madeleine. 2003. "Screening Moments, Scrolling Lives: Diary Writing on the Web." *Biography* 26 (1): 1–23.

Spencer-Oatey, Helen. 2002. "Managing Rapport in Talk: Using Rapport Sensitive Incidents to Explore the Motivational Concerns Underlying the Management of Relations." *Journal of Pragmatics* 34: 529–545.

Stanton, Annette L., Sharon Danoff-Burg, Lisa A. Sworowski, Charlotte A. Collins, Ann D. Branstetter, Alicia Rodriguez-Hanley, Sarah B. Kirk, and Jennifer L. Austenfeld. 2002. "Randomized, Controlled Trial of Written Emotional Expression and Benefit Finding in Breast Cancer Patients." *Journal of Clinical Oncology* 20 (20): 4160–4168.

Stefanone, Michael, and Derek Lackaff. 2009. "Reality Television as a Model for Online Behavior: Blogging, Photo and Video Sharing." *Journal of Computer-Mediated Communication* 14: 964–987.

Stefanone, Michael, Derek Lackaff, and Devan Rosen. 2011. "Contingencies of Self-Worth and Social-Networking-Site Behavior." *Cyberpsychology, Behavior and Social Networking* 14 (1–2): 41–49.

Steinkuehler, Constance, and Sean Duncan. 2008. "Scientific Habits of Mind in Virtual Worlds." *Journal of Science, Education and Technology* 17 (6): 530–543.

Stelter, Brian. 2008. "YouTube Videos Pull in Real Money." *New York Times*, December 10, 2008. Available at http://www.nytimes.com/2008/12/11/business/media/11youtube.html?_r=1. Accessed March 28, 2011.

Sternberg, Adam. 2006. "Hey There Lonelygirl." *New York Times*, August 20, 2006. Available at http://nymag.com/arts/tv/features/19376/. Accessed March 28, 2011.

StoryCorps: Available at http://storycorps.org/. Accessed May 24, 2011.

Suler, John. 2008. "Image, Action, Word: Interpersonal Dynamics in a Photo-Sharing Community." *CyberPsychology and Behavior* 11: 555–560.

Tagliamonte, Sali, and Chris Roberts. 2005. "So Weird; So Cool; So Innovative: The Use of Intensifiers in the Television Series *FRIENDS*." *American Speech* 80 (3): 280–300.

Tannen, Deborah. 2011. "How Social Media Make Cross-Generational Discourse Like Cross-Cultural Communication." Paper presented at the Georgetown University Round Table on Languages and Linguistics (2011), "Language and New Media: Discourse 2.0." Washington, DC, March 10–13.

Thurlow, Crispin, Laura Lengel, and Alice Tomic. 2004. *Computer-Mediated Communication: Social Interaction and the Internet.* London: Sage.

Toolan, Michael. 2001. *Narrative: A Critical Linguistic Introduction.* 2nd ed. London: Routledge.

Tuan, Yi-Fu. 1977. *Space and Place: The Perspective of Experience.* Minneapolis: University of Minnesota Press.

———. 1991. "Language and the Making of Place: A Narrative-Descriptive Approach" *Annals of the Association of American Geographers* 81 (4): 684–696.

Tumasjin, Andranik, Timm O. Sprenger, Philipp G. Sadner, and Isabell M. Welpe. 2010. "Election Forecasts With Twitter: How 140 Characters Reflect the

Political Landscape." *Social Science Computer Review* 28. First published on December 12, 2010.

Turkle, Sherry. 1995. *Life on the Screen: Identity in the Age of the Internet*. New York: Simon Schuster.

———. 2011. *Alone Together. Why We Expect More From Technology and Less from Each Other*. New York: Basic Books.

Turner, Graeme. 2004. *Understanding Celebrity*. London: Sage.

Vasquez, Camilla. 2007. "Moral Stance in the Workplace Narratives of Novices." *Discourse Studies* 9 (5): 653–675.

Veen, Mario, Hedwig te Molder, Bart Gremmen, and Cees van Woerkum. 2010. "Quitting Is Not an Option: An Analysis of Online Diet Talk Between Celiac Disease Patients." *Health* 14 (1): 23–40.

Walker Rettberg, Jill. 2008. *Blogging*. Cambridge: Polity Press.

Wen, Kuang-Yi, Fiona McTavish, Gary Kreps, Meg Wise, and David Gustafson. 2011. "From Diagnosis to Death: A Case Study of Coping With Breast Cancer as Seen Through Online Discussion Group Messages." *Journal of Computer-Mediated Communication* 16: 331–361.

White, Peter. 1997. "Death, Disruption and the Moral Order: The Narrative Impulse in Mass-Media Hard News Reporting." In *Genres and Institutions: Social Processes in the Workplace and School*, edited by Frances Christie and James R. Martin, 101–133. London: Cassell.

Wiegers, Yvonne. 1998. "Male BodyBuilding: The Social Construction of a Masculine Identity." *Journal of Popular Culture* 32 (2): 147–161.

Wilhelm, Alex. 2010. "Twitter Statistics: The Full Picture." Available at http://thenextweb.com/socialmedia/2010/02/22/twitter-statistics-full-picture/. Accessed May 20, 2011.

Wolf, Alecia. 2000. "Emotional Expression Online: Gender Differences in Emoticon Use." *CyberPsychology and Behavior* 3 (5): 827–834.

Wolfson, Nessa. 1978. "A Feature of Performed Narrative: The Conversational Historical Present." *Language in Society* 7: 215–237.

Wood, Kathleen M. 1997. "Narrative Iconicity in Electronic-Mail Lesbian Coming Out Stories." In *Queerly Phrased: Language, Gender and Sexuality*, edited by Anna Livia and Kira Hall, 257–275. Oxford: Oxford University Press.

Wright, Tim. 2004–Present. *In Search of Oldton*. Available at http://www.oldton.com/. Accessed March 22, 2011.

Zhang, Weiyu, and Rong Wang. 2010. "Interest-Oriented versus Relationship-Oriented Social Network Sites in China." *First Monday* 15 (8). Available at http://firstmonday.org/htbin/cgiwrap/bin/ojs/index.php/fm/article/view/2836/2582. Accessed February 9, 2011.

Zimmerman, Don H. 1998. "Identity, Context and Interaction. Identities in Talk." In *Identities in Talk*, edited by Charles Antaki and Sue Widdicombe, 87–106. London: Sage.

Index

Printed in Great Britain
by Amazon.co.uk, Ltd.,
Marston Gate.